Linux® System Commands

Linux® System Commands

Patrick Volkerding
Kevin Reichard

M&T Books
An imprint of IDG Books Worldwide, Inc.

Foster City, CA • Chicago, IL • Indianapolis, IN • New York, NY

Linux® System Commands

Published by
M&T Books
An imprint of IDG Books Worldwide, Inc.
919 E. Hillsdale Blvd., Suite 400
Foster City, CA 94404
www.idgbooks.com (IDG Books Worldwide Web site)

Library of Congress Cataloging-in-Publication Number: 00-100826

ISBN: 0-7645-4669-4

Printed in the United States of America

10 9 8 7 6 5 4 3 2 1

1B/QR/QT/QQ/FC

Distributed in the United States by IDG Books Worldwide, Inc.

Distributed by CDG Books Canada Inc. for Canada; by Transworld Publishers Limited in the United Kingdom; by IDG Norge Books for Norway; by IDG Sweden Books for Sweden; by IDG Books Australia Publishing Corporation Pty. Ltd. for Australia and New Zealand; by TransQuest Publishers Pte Ltd. for Singapore, Malaysia, Thailand, Indonesia, and Hong Kong; by Gotop Information Inc. for Taiwan; by ICG Muse, Inc. for Japan; by Intersoft for South Africa; by Eyrolles for France; by International Thomson Publishing for Germany, Austria and Switzerland; by Distribuidora Cuspide for Argentina; by LR International for Brazil; by Galileo Libros for Chile; by Ediciones ZETA S.C.R. Ltda. for Peru; by WS Computer Publishing Corporation, Inc., for the Philippines; by Contemporanea de Ediciones for Venezuela; by Express Computer Distributors for the Caribbean and West Indies; by Micronesia Media Distributor, Inc. for Micronesia; by Chips Computadoras S.A. de C.V. for Mexico; by Editorial Norma de Panama S.A. for Panama; by American Bookshops for Finland.

For general information on IDG Books Worldwide's books in the U.S., please call our Consumer Customer Service department at 800-762-2974. For reseller information, including discounts and premium sales, please call our Reseller Customer Service department at 800-434-3422.

For information on where to purchase IDG Books Worldwide's books outside the U.S., please contact our International Sales department at 317-572-3337 or fax 317-572-4002.

For consumer information on foreign language translations, please contact our Customer Service department at 800-434-3422, fax 317-572-4002, or e-mail rights@idgbooks.com.

For information on licensing foreign or domestic rights, please phone + 1-650-653-7098.

For sales inquiries and special prices for bulk quantities, please contact our Sales department at 800-434-3422 or write to the address above.

For information on using IDG Books Worldwide's books in the classroom or for ordering examination copies, please contact our Educational Sales department at 800-434-2086 or fax 317-572-4055.

For press review copies, author interviews, or other publicity information, please contact our Public Relations department at 650-653-7000 or fax 650-653-7500.

For authorization to photocopy items for corporate, personal, or educational use, please contact Copyright Clearance Center, 222 Rosewood Drive, Danvers, MA 01923, or fax 978-750-4470.

ABOUT IDG BOOKS WORLDWIDE

Welcome to the world of IDG Books Worldwide.

IDG Books Worldwide, Inc., is a subsidiary of International Data Group, the world's largest publisher of computer-related information and the leading global provider of information services on information technology. IDG was founded more than 30 years ago by Patrick J. McGovern and now employs more than 9,000 people worldwide. IDG publishes more than 290 computer publications in over 75 countries. More than 90 million people read one or more IDG publications each month.

Launched in 1990, IDG Books Worldwide is today the #1 publisher of best-selling computer books in the United States. We are proud to have received eight awards from the Computer Press Association in recognition of editorial excellence and three from Computer Currents' First Annual Readers' Choice Awards. Our best-selling ...For Dummies® series has more than 50 million copies in print with translations in 31 languages. IDG Books Worldwide, through a joint venture with IDG's Hi-Tech Beijing, became the first U.S. publisher to publish a computer book in the People's Republic of China. In record time, IDG Books Worldwide has become the first choice for millions of readers around the world who want to learn how to better manage their businesses.

Our mission is simple: Every one of our books is designed to bring extra value and skill-building instructions to the reader. Our books are written by experts who understand and care about our readers. The knowledge base of our editorial staff comes from years of experience in publishing, education, and journalism — experience we use to produce books to carry us into the new millennium. In short, we care about books, so we attract the best people. We devote special attention to details such as audience, interior design, use of icons, and illustrations. And because we use an efficient process of authoring, editing, and desktop publishing our books electronically, we can spend more time ensuring superior content and less time on the technicalities of making books.

You can count on our commitment to deliver high-quality books at competitive prices on topics you want to read about. At IDG Books Worldwide, we continue in the IDG tradition of delivering quality for more than 30 years. You'll find no better book on a subject than one from IDG Books Worldwide.

John J. Kilcullen

John Kilcullen
Chairman and CEO
IDG Books Worldwide, Inc.

Eighth Annual Computer Press Awards ≥1992

Ninth Annual Computer Press Awards ≥1993

Tenth Annual Computer Press Awards ≥1994

Eleventh Annual Computer Press Awards ≥1995

IDG is the world's leading IT media, research and exposition company. Founded in 1964, IDG had 1997 revenues of $2.05 billion and has more than 9,000 employees worldwide. IDG offers the widest range of media options that reach IT buyers in 75 countries representing 95% of worldwide IT spending. IDG's diverse product and services portfolio spans six key areas including print publishing, online publishing, expositions and conferences, market research, education and training, and global marketing services. More than 90 million people read one or more of IDG's 290 magazines and newspapers, including IDG's leading global brands — Computerworld, PC World, Network World, Macworld and the Channel World family of publications. IDG Books Worldwide is one of the fastest-growing computer book publishers in the world, with more than 700 titles in 36 languages. The "...For Dummies®" series alone has more than 50 million copies in print. IDG offers online users the largest network of technology-specific Web sites around the world through IDG.net (http://www.idg.net), which comprises more than 225 targeted Web sites in 35 countries worldwide. International Data Corporation (IDC) is the world's largest provider of information technology data, analysis and consulting, with research centers in over 41 countries and more than 400 research analysts worldwide. IDG World Expo is a leading producer of more than 168 globally branded conferences and expositions in 35 countries including E3 (Electronic Entertainment Expo), Macworld Expo, ComNet, Windows World Expo, ICE (Internet Commerce Expo), Agenda, DEMO, and Spotlight. IDG's training subsidiary, ExecuTrain, is the world's largest computer training company, with more than 230 locations worldwide and 785 training courses. IDG Marketing Services helps industry-leading IT companies build international brand recognition by developing global integrated marketing programs via IDG's print, online and exposition products worldwide. Further information about the company can be found at www.idg.com.   1/26/00

Credits

Acquisitions Editor
Laura Lewin

Project Editor
Terri Varveris

Technical Editors
David Cantrell
Christopher Negus
Joseph Traub

Copy Editors
Amy Eoff
Bill McManus

Project Coordinators
Linda Marousek
Louigene A. Santos

Quality Control Specialists
Laura Taflinger
Chris Weisbart

Graphics and Production Specialists
Jude Levinson
Michael Lewis
Ramses Ramirez
Victor Pérez-Varela

Book Designers
London Road Design
Catalin Dulfu
Kurt Krames

Illustrator
Mary Jo Richards

Proofreading and Indexing
York Production Services

Cover Design
Joann Vuong

About the Author

Patrick Volkerding is the Creator of Slackware, an acclaimed Linux distribution. He and Kevin Reichard collaborated on Linux Configuration and Installation, now in its fourth edition.

Kevin Reichard is a UNIX/Linux expert and a prolific computer book author. He and Patrick Volkerding collaborated on Linux Configuration and Installation, now in its fourth edition.

Preface

Welcome to *Linux System Commands*! Whether you're a novice Linux user or an advanced Linux hack, we think you'll find this book very useful.

This book is meant for a variety of Linux users:

- The curious user seeking an alternative to the Microsoft/Apple personal-computer operating systems

- The programmer who wants a version of UNIX for the office or home

- The Webmaster who wants a stable Internet server

- The end user who wants a stable operating system with all of the tools for local and Internet usage

- The networking engineer who wants to set up a Linux server

- The student who wants to know more about a state-of-the-art operating system

Whoever you are, you'll be very happy using Linux as an operating system.

This Book's Purpose

Commands are at the heart of the Linux operating system. Many Linux experts prefer commands instead of graphical tools for configuring and using their Linux systems. Why wait for a window to open; why click on several levels of menus when you can type a quick command?

The purpose of this book is to provide you with a reference to the most common Linux commands and many of the most common options to use with them. Think of this book as you would think of a dictionary when you write or a mechanic's manual when you fix a car. Open the book when you need to be reminded of how to use the tools you need to get your Linux system working the way you would like.

A Little Linux History

Linux began life as a small student project at the University of Helsinki in Finland. Linux Torvalds wanted a small, UNIX-like operating system, and so he set out to write one. He received help from volunteers all around the globe who collaborated via bulletin board, electronic mail, and the Internet to create the Linux operating system.

The crew ended up creating a rather remarkable operating system that works very well, is very stable, and rivals offerings from Microsoft, Apple, and Sun. Linux offers the following features:

- **Multitasking** — Linux natively runs more than one task (program) at a time in a UNIX-like fashion. It also supports preemptive multitasking, which allows priorities to be set for different processes.

- **Multiuser** — Many users can be networked into a single Linux server. Linux is the least expensive, and perhaps best-featured, multiuser operating system on the planet today.

- **User-friendly** — The X Window System interface and a bunch of great tools make Linux easy to use.

Today, Linux claims millions of users, and that number keeps growing every day. One reason for Linux's popularity is cost. Linux itself is free of charge. Many Linux books come with free Linux CDs, so you can get a full-blown, powerful operating system for the price of the book. Even those companies that create Linux distributions and sell them on CD-ROM offer those same distributions free-of-charge for download on the Internet. Distributions, such as Slackware Linux and Red Hat Linux, use different installation processes and often different administration tools.

Acquiring Linux

This book does not feature a CD-ROM that contains Linux. However, we strongly urge you to check out one of the other titles in the M&T Books Slackware series, all of which contain Slackware Linux on an accompanying CD-ROM.

The Free Software Foundation

Linux is the product of many devoted volunteers, many of whom also gave their time to the Free Software Foundation (FSF). The FSF is an idealistic group lead by Richard Stallman whose belief is that all software should be free. In support of this belief, they issue a lot of useful software to the world, either directly or under the auspices of the GNU License.

The result is that a slew of GNU commands are incorporated into Linux. We've noted them with an icon in the book. These GNU commands are typically clones of the most popular UNIX commands. They are created in such a way that UNIX licensing schemes don't kick in. As such, they're very useful, and they tend to work very well.

You can reach the Free Software Foundation at:

Free Software Foundation
59 Temple Place, Suite 330
Boston, MA 02111-1307
1-617-542-5942 (voice)
1-617-542-2652 (fax)
gnu@prep.ai.mit.edu
http://www.gnu.org/

Conventions Used in This Book

We took a consistent approach to the commands listed in Chapters 5-11 of this book. We think this consistency will help you expand your Linux usage and master new commands and concepts. All the commands are set up in the same fashion and consist of the following:

- A headline, a sample command-line usage
- The purpose of the command (in some detail)
- A listing of the most common command-line options
- Any commands needed by the command, if it requires further input (e.g., `mail` or `ftp`)
- An example (or examples) of actual usage (for most commands, but not all of them)
- Related commands (if applicable)

In addition, the text itself features the following conventions:

- Commands to be entered directly into a Linux system are in a `monospaced` font. This includes the names of commands and command lines in their entirety.
- Options, when not presented as part of an entire command line, are listed in `monospace` font.
- Variables are listed in `monospace` font.
- New concepts are marked with *italic* text.

The following icons are used throughout the book:

●—X Window System Command ———————————

This special icon is used to indicate that a command is an X Window System command.

●—GNU Command ——————————————————

This special icon is used to indicate that a command is a GNU command.

●—CROSS-REFERENCE——————————————————

This icon is used to cross-reference material in other parts of the book as well as information that can be found on the online manual pages.

●—NOTE——————————————————————

This icon tells you that something is important. For example, it can be a concept that may help you master the task at hand, or something fundamental for understanding subsequent material.

●—TIP—————————————————————

This icon indicates a more efficient way of doing something, or a technique that may not be obvious.

How to Contact Us

We would like your feedback. After you have had a chance to use this book; please take a moment to register it at `http://my2cents.idgbooks.com`. (Details are listed on the *my2cents* page in the back of the book.)

You can drop us a line via email at:

`reichard@mr.net`

Because of the amount of email we receive, we can't guarantee an immediate response. You can also visit our other Web sites. The Slackware Linux Web site is:

`www.slackware.com`

Kevin Reichard's Web site is:

`www.kreichard.com`

Brief Contents

Contents

Linux® System Commands

Patrick Volkerding
Kevin Reichard

M&T Books

An imprint of IDG Books Worldwide, Inc.

Foster City, CA • Chicago, IL • Indianapolis, IN • New York, NY

I

Illuminating Linux Procedures

in plain english in plain english
n english in plain english in p
lain english in plain english in
a plain english in plain english
n english in plain english in p
a plain english in plain english
n english in plain english in p
lain english in plain english in
a plain english in plain english
n english in plain english in p
lain english in plain english in
a plain english in plain english
n english in plain english in p
a plain english in plain english

One frustrating aspect of working with any operating system is when you don't have the knowledge necessary to make what you want happen on an unfamiliar operating system. This is why we're beginning this book with four chapters that illuminate some specific Linux procedures. Each chapter fills a specific role in your Linux usage, ranging from an introduction of Linux in Chapter 1 to specific reference works in Chapters 2, 3, and 4.

Why are we including a DOS reference chapter? Isn't DOS dead? DOS is still the foundation of Windows 95/98, and if you're a power user, you most likely do much of your work with DOS commands rather than a graphical interface. If you have DOS experience and want to know about similar tools in Linux, then Chapter 3 is for you.

in plain english in p
sh in plain english in
glish in plain english
in plain english in p
sh in plain english in
glish in plain english
in plain english in p
glish in plain english
in plain english in p
sh in plain english in
glish in plain english
in plain english in p
sh in plain english in
glish in plain english
in plain english in p
lish in plain english
in plain english in p
sh in plain english in
glish in plain english
in plain english in p
sh in plain english in
lish in plain english
in plain english in p
glish in plain english

Linux Structures and Commands

Depending on your background, Linux is either an amazingly complex operating system (that is, if your background is in the Microsoft Windows or Macintosh worlds) or just another simple, command-line-driven operating system (if your background is in the MS-DOS or UNIX worlds). The truth lies somewhere in between. Yes, Linux can be inscrutable at times, and yes, it is built around the command line, even if you're running the X Window System. However, as far as operating systems go, Linux isn't any more complex than MS-DOS or UNIX, and it actually has some tools that rival those of Windows and the Macintosh.

As you prepare to plumb the depths of the Linux operating system, two concepts will make your life easier:

- **Linux is really a collection of small, easy-to-use commands.** If you can simplify your tasks and break them down into discrete elements, you can do just about anything.

1

- **Even GUI programs are more like utilities than full applications.** Even when you're working with XFree86, the Linux version of the X Window System (a popular graphical interface in the UNIX world), you're still basically working with a collection of small, easy-to-use commands.

Because the core of Linux is its commands, anyone who wants to master Linux should be eager to master its command structure first. That's where this book comes in: *Linux System Commands* is a listing of the Linux command structure. Before you can use these commands, however, you need to know how Linux deals with commands and how to enter these commands into the system.

The Command Line

As already mentioned, Linux is a *command-line-driven operating system.* Commands are given to the operating system on the command line. You know that Linux is ready to accept a command when you see the following prompt on your screen:

$

For the root user (also called the super user), the default is as follows:

#

A prompt can appear in a full screen when you're running in terminal mode, or it can appear in a Terminal window when you're running the X Window System, as shown in Figure 1-1.

The dollar sign is called a *prompt,* and it's the mechanism Linux uses to tell you that it's ready to accept a command. At the prompt, you can enter a single command or a combination of commands and options, the sum of which is called a *command*

A *command* is exactly that. No matter what you enter at the prompt, Linux interprets it as a command, or an order to do something. You can use commands directly to do something, such as moving and copying files. You can also use commands to run other programs, such as elvis or emacs. Linux has a specific set of commands, so if you type something that doesn't match one of its commands, it tells you it can't find the command. (You can actually see the list of commands when you look in directories, but we're getting ahead of ourselves here.) Literally hundreds of commands are in the Linux operating system.*line.*

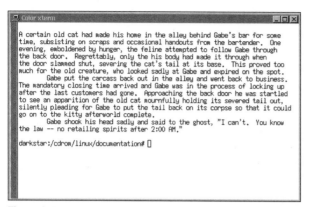

Figure 1-1 *Xterm running in the X Window System.*

Commands have *options,* which serve to better specify the behavior of a command. These options can tell a command to perform an action only under certain circumstances. This can be seen best with a general command and some of its options.

The ls command is one of the most basic and most used commands. By itself, it merely lists the files in a given directory, as shown in Figure 1-2.

Figure 1-2 *The ls command used by itself lists the files in a given directory.*

The figure shows us that this particular directory contains a set of directories. (The names of the files and directories in this chapter aren't important; you simply need to know the mechanisms for identifying these files and directories, and how they can be applied to almost any command.) However, the ls command by itself refers only to files that are accessible to all users and aren't hidden in some way. Hidden files begin with a dot (.), so you need to tell the ls command to look for all files, including hidden files. This is done with an option. When you add the -a

1

option to the ls command, you get a listing of all files and directories, including hidden files, as shown in Figure 1-3.

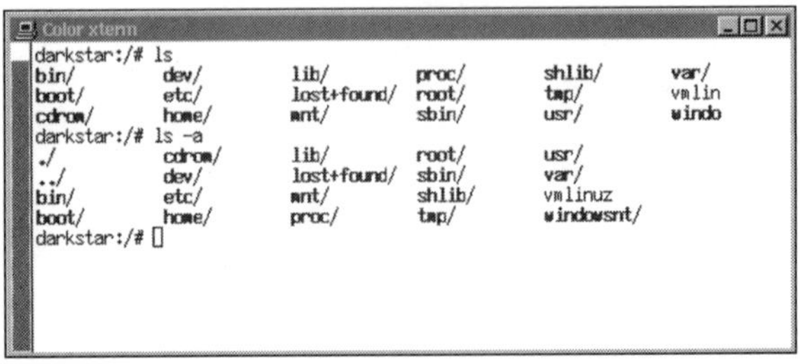

Figure 1-3 *The -a option with the ls command*

Taking the example one step further, you can ask the ls command to return a long listing for the files or directories in the current directory with the –l (the letter *l*, not the number 1) option, as shown in Figure 1-4.

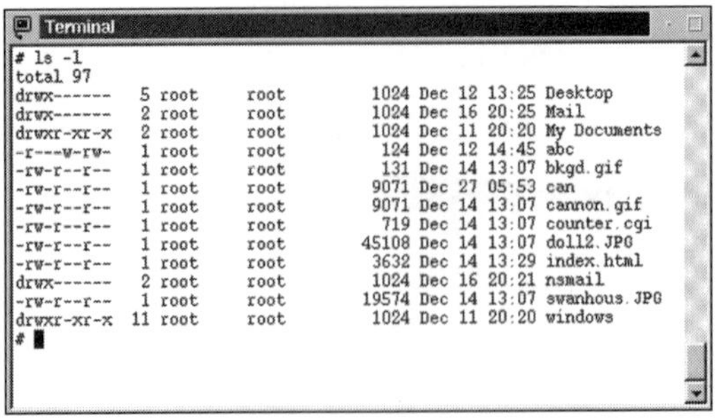

Figure 1-4 *The -l option with the ls command*

Very few Linux commands don't have options or arguments of some sort.

●—CROSS-REFERENCE

Chapters 5-11, which list many commands, devote a lot of space to these options.

Files

The ls command is used to list the files and directories in the current directory or the contents of a specified directory. In some ways, this command is an oddity in the Linux world, because it's not used directly on a file, which is the method Linux uses for organizing information. As you browse through the rest of this book, you'll see that the vast majority of commands are used in conjunction with files.

Most commands allow file names as options because so many items in the Linux operating system are represented by files: data, commands, directories, and devices, to name a few. You saw the ls command used to list files in a directory, and the reason why that command is so handy is that everything in Linux is a file. Commands are actually files that are invoked as programs. Devices attached to your PC are actually represented in the Linux operating system by files (usually located in the /dev directory). When you print a file, you're actually sending a file to a device file representing the printer.

At a basic level, a file is nothing more than an organized area of a storage device (such as a hard disk or a floppy drive), made up of bits. *Bits* are nothing more than digital players in an electronic format, representing either 0 or 1. The Linux operating system takes these bits and formats them in a way that's recognizable to both you and the operating system. Without this organization, the contents of a hard drive would just be random 0's and 1's. This organizational scheme is called the *file system*.

The main function of the Linux operating system is to keep track of and manipulate the file system and its contents. The importance of the ls command can't be overstated, because it lets you know which files are in a portion of the file system at a given time. That's why the most frequently used commands in Linux relate to manipulating files on basic levels, such as elvis for editing files, rm for deleting files, and mv for moving files.

The following are the four major types of files, explained in order of importance in the Linux operating system:

- **Ordinary files:** The rank and file of Linux files, usually containing data that's acted upon by other programs and the operating system itself. An ordinary file can be an ASCII text file, a data file for a program (such as a formatted file for a page-layout program, or a database file for a database manager), a command file (which contains further instructions for a program, but is stored in ASCII text, such as a Perl or Tcl script), or an executable program file.

1

- **Directories:** Files that represent information about other files. Files in the Linux operating system are stored hierarchically, with files stored within collections of other files. Directories are explained in the next section. (From the X Window System, a directory is usually represented as a folder.)

- **Device files:** Represent the devices attached to your PC. These devices are stored in the /dev directory; for instance, a tape drive is represented by /dev/st0.

- **Links:** Multiple names in the file system that represent the same file. Links are particularly valuable for having the same command represented from several different directories or using different names. It saves disk space to not have multiple copies of the same files.

Directories

As you saw earlier, directories are merely files that are used to store other files. Directories are an absolute must for an operating system such as Linux. In Linux, every command is a file, every device is a file, and every program is at least one file (but usually many more). Add up all of these files, and you end up with a mess of a file system, with thousands of individual files. To make matters worse, Linux is designed to be on a network, which means that every user has access to thousands of other files across the network and possibly on a file server. Keeping track of these files would be impossible if they couldn't be stored in some sort of hierarchy. That's where directories come in.

The directory hierarchy in Linux, which you can visualize as a pyramid, is actually pretty simple. There's a *root directory*, which is at the top of the pyramid and is represented by a slash (/). Every directory is a *subdirectory* of the root directory. In addition, there are subdirectories within subdirectories.

As a user, you are "in" a directory at all times. This is called the *current directory.* Your command prompt usually lists the name of the current directory (beginning with a slash, which indicates that the directory hierarchy begins with a root directory).A standard Linux installation, such as Slackware Linux, has a fairly predictable set of directories. When your current directory is the root directory, Linux features a set of subdirectories, such as those shown in Figure 1-5.

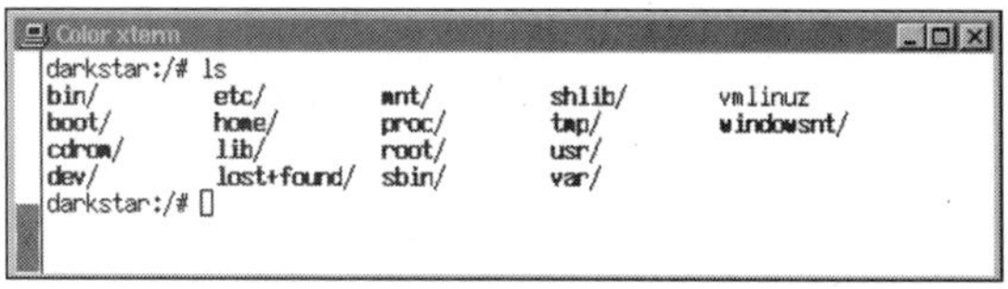

Figure 1-5 *The root directory in a typical Slackware Linux installation*

Some of these directories are found in almost all Linux and UNIX installations, such as etc, sbin, usr, and var. Other directories are unique to Linux. Still others are devoted to users, such as root and home. If you installed Linux on your own, you probably have at least one home directory (root, used when you're logged in as the root user) and more likely two (such as a named directory under home).

Linux features numerous commands for creating your own directories, which are covered throughout the course of this book.

Standard Input/Output and Redirection

The next piece in the Linux puzzle concerns linking commands and files in the form of *standard input and output (I/O)*. Don't be dismayed by this techie term: standard I/O really concerns how command lines are structured, where input can come from and where the results of a command should be sent.

Linux is like every other operating system in that it needs to know where input is going to come from and where output should be sent. Other operating systems, such as Windows and the Macintosh, make assumptions when it comes to input and output. Linux does, too, in some circumstances, but in most other circumstances, you need to put some thought into where your work comes from and where it goes. The basic principles behind standard I/O can be best explained with an example.

The cat command is an amazingly versatile command. It can be used to display the contents of files, add to files, and more. It can also be used as a rudimentary text editor when run on a command line by itself:

```
$ cat
```

1

The cursor will go to the next line, and then you can enter text. Because you have not specified where the text should go, Linux and the `cat` command assume that the input should go to the screen. After the input goes to the screen, it's lost forever, because no mechanism exists for saving the text to disk. Most Linux commands assume that standard input means input from the keyboard, and standard output means display on the terminal. Under these circumstances, `cat` can be used to improve your typing skills, but otherwise is of little use.

However, `cat`'s usefulness increases when you combine it with filenames in a command line. Combining `cat` and a filename displays an existing file on the screen, as shown in Figure 1-6.

```
Color xterm                                              _ □ ×
darkstar:~# cat lodlin16.txt
Quickstart for LOADLIN-1.6
============================

Version 1.6 of LOADLIN (as opposite to prior versions) normally needs no
special configuration and has been reported very stable by all ALPHA testers,
so I guess you will only need

    LOADLIN.EXE,

Copy this file to a DOS partition (e.g C:\LOADLIN).

To boot Linux you need also a compressed kernel image file such as
the "/vmlinuz" or the "/usr/src/zImage". In Slackware distribution you
can find a lot of kernels (bare, scsi, modern, ...) in the directory
..../slackware/kernels of the site you got it from.

Copy the image file to your DOS partion (e.g. C:\).

To boot type at dos prompt:

    1. For a Linux partition (ext2, minix, ...) to mount as root

        loadlin c:\vmlinuz root=/dev/hdb2 ro
                                          ==
```

Figure 1-6   *A file combined with cat*

Instead of using standard input from the keyboard, `cat` uses standard input from a file. The contents of the file haven't been altered; they've merely been displayed on the screen.

You can use `cat` to store keystrokes to a file with the use of redirection symbols. These symbols, which are part of the core operating system, are used to alter standard I/O. You could combine `cat` — or any other Linux command, for that matter — with a redirection symbol to redirect its output to a file. In the following example, the output from `cat`, which is normally sent to the screen, is redirected to a file named kevin.report:

    $ cat > kevin.report

The output is sent one keystroke at a time to the file kevin.report. Typing Ctrl-D stops the redirection and ends the cat command.

Redirection can be used both for input and output. The `cat` command can be told to copy a file to a new filename in the following manner:

```
$ cat kevin.report > pat.report
```

Here, the input is kevin.report and the output is pat.report. Nothing about kevin.report is changed.

A separate redirection symbol is used to append text to an existing file. Here, the contents of kevin.report are appended to an existing file named pat.report:

```
$ cat kevin.report > pat.report
```

If you were to omit a filename as the input, cat would assume that keystrokes should be used for appending. The following command line lets you append keystrokes directly to the end of the file named kevin.report:

```
$ cat > kevin.report
```

The following are useful redirection symbols:

>   Used to send the output of a command to a file or another command. For example, cat > file is used to send the output of the cat command to file.

<   Used to send the input of a file or command to a command. For example, cat < file means that cat should use file as input.

>   Used to append input to an existing file. For example, cat > file tells Linux to append the keystrokes to an existing file named file.

| The pipe symbol, which is used when you want to run a command and then send its output to another command. For instance, cat | grep runs the cat command and sends the output to the grep command, which is then run. (We'll cover pipes right after the next section.)

1

Arguments

Input/output symbols may seem to offer a few different ways to do the same thing. Indeed, < and > can seem interchangeable, depending on how the command line is structured. However, both symbols are needed. Command lines that look similar can actually be dealt with quite differently by the operating system. For instance, this command line

```
$ cat pat.file
```

is functionally the same as

```
$ cat < pat.file
```

The two command lines are actually different, however. In the first, `pat.file` is an argument for the `cat` command. In the Linux world, *arguments* are command-line modifiers that are variables; in this instance, the argument happened to be a file. In the second example, `pat.file` is input to the `cat` command.

The complexity of command lines is unlimited when it comes to redirection symbols. It's not uncommon to see two redirection symbols used as follows, especially in a shell script:

```
$ cat < file1 > file2
```

This tells `cat` to use input from file1 and to send the output to file2.

Pipes

A *pipe,* as noted by |, is merely one additional redirection tool. It has the advantage of working directly with commands, telling one command to use as input the output of another command. Here's how it is used:

```
$ command1 | command2
```

The combination of commands and a pipe symbol is called a *pipeline.* Pipes are often used when preparing files for printing.

X Window System Command-Line Options

X Window System commands appear throughout Chapters 5 to 11. These commands share a common set of command-line options. Rather than listing these options with every command, they are listed in Table 1-1.

Table 1-1   *Window Command-Line Options*

Option	Purpose
-background *red green blue*	Sets the background color to *red green blue*.
-background *color*	Uses *color* for the window background.
-bg *color*	Uses *color* for the window background.
-display host:*disp_num*	Connects to a display, as specified with a *disp_num*-numbered X server (which is almost always 0) on a given host.
-fg *color*	Uses *color* for the window foreground.
-fn *fontname*	Uses a specified *font name*.
-font *fontname*	Uses a specified *font name*.
-foreground_color *red green blue*	Sets the foreground color to *red green blue*.
-foreground *color*	Uses *color* for the window foreground.
-geometry *WidthxHeight+x+y*	Sets the window size (*WidthxHeight*) and position (*x+y*).
-geometry *WidthxHeight*	Sets the window size.
-geometry *+x+y*	Sets the position of a window's upper-left corner.
-height *rows*	Sets the height of the base window in *rows*.
-position *x y*	Sets the location of the upper-left corner of the window, in *x y* pixels.
-reverse	Reverses the foreground and background colors.

Continued

Table 1-1   *Continued*

Option	Purpose
-rv	Reverses the foreground and background colors.
-size *width height*	Sets the window size, in *width* × *height* pixels.
-Wb *red green blue*	Sets the background color to *red green blue*.
-Wf *red green blue*	Sets the foreground color to *red green blue*.
-WG *WidthxHeight+x+y*	Sets the window size (*WidthxHeight*) and position (*x+y*).
-WG *WidthxHeight*	Sets the window size.
-WG *+x+y*	Sets the position of the window's upper-left corner, in *x y* pixels.
-Wh *rows*	Sets the height of the base window in *rows*.
-Wi	Starts the window as an icon rather than as a full window.
-width *columns*	Sets the width of the base window in *columns*.
-Wp *x y*	Sets the location of the upper-left corner of the window in *x y* pixels.
-Wr host:*disp_num*	Connects to a display, as specified with a *disp_num*-numbered X server (which is almost always 0) on a given host.
-Ws *width height*	Sets the base window size in *width* x *height* pixels.
-Wt *fontname*	Uses specified *fontname*.
-Ww *columns*	Sets the width of the base window in *columns*.

in plain english in pl
sh in plain english in
glish in plain english
in plain english in pl
sh in plain english in
glish in plain english
in plain english in pl
glish in plain english
in plain english in pl
sh in plain english in
glish in plain english
in plain english in pl
sh in plain english in
glish in plain english
in plain english in pl
lish in plain english
in plain english in pl
sh in plain english in
glish in plain english
in plain english in pl
sh in plain english in
lish in plain english
in plain english in pl
glish in plain english

Linux Commands Demystified

Human beings don't think in computerese, which is why we need a reference work like this one. Commands tend to be rather obscure, and their purpose isn't always apparent. To further your Linux efforts, we've tried to demystify the Linux commands by compiling the following listing of commands and organizing them by keyword and function. You can look up an italicized keyword in the "If You Want To...." column — for example, *print* — and see which Linux commands help perform that task in the "Use This Linux Command..." column. Then, go to the chapter in this book that covers that category of commands for a complete explanation of the command.

●—CROSS-REFERENCE

To help you find the category of a particular command, refer to Chapter 4, "Linux Commands A to Z," which lists each command and its category.

2

If You Want To...	*Use This Linux Command...*
run the *AppleTalk* filing daemon	afpd
support an *AppleTalk* network	atalkd
control server *access*	xhost
list system and user aliases	listalias
check an *alias* in elm	checkalias
append files	cat
know your machine *architecture*	arch
create an *archive*	cpio, tar
work with *archives*	ar
convert *ASCII* to a bitmap	atobm
convert a bitmap to *ASCII*	bmtoa
show scheduled commands	atq
run a command *at* a specific time	at
list *atoms* related to X	xlsatoms
manage *authorization* information for X	xauth
set *background* attributes for X	xsetroot
set a *background* image for X	xpmroot
print a *banner*	banner
display a file's *basename*	basename
run *batch* commands	batch
display first 10 lines of a text file	head
convert a *bitmap* to ASCII	bmtoa
view and edit *bitmaps*	bitmap
manage the Internet *Bootstrap* Protocol	bootpd, bootptest
search a device for bad *blocks*	badblocks
install the *boot* loader	lilo
compile *C* programs	gcc
compile *C++* programs	g++
convert from Pascal to *C*	p2c

If You Want To...	*Use This Linux Command...*
listen to audio *CDs*	workbone, workman
create *CD* formatted music	mkisofs, mkhybrid
record *CDs*	cdrecord, cdwrite
perform *calculations*	bc, dc, xcalc
view a *calendar*	cal
clear your screen	clear
list running *client applications*	xlsclients
display the contents of the *clipboard*	xclipboard
display a *clock*	oclock, rclock, xclock
show a *color* database	showrgb
display the default *colormap*	xcmap
set *colormap* properties	xstdcmap
cut *columns*, *bytes,* or *characters*	cut
format text into *columns*	column
combine files	cat, join
set *colors* for ls	dircolors
run a *command* at a specific time	at
build *command* lines	xargs
compare files	cmp, diff, diff3, sdiff, zcmp, zdiff
compare compressed files	zcmp, zdiff
compare sorted files	comm
compare text files	diff, diff3, sdiff
compare three text files	diff3
compile C++ programs	gcc, g++
compile Fortran programs	g77
compress an executable file	gzexe
compress a file	compress, bzip2, gzip, znew
connect to another computer	minicom, seyon
convert and copy files	dd

2

If You Want To...	*Use This Linux Command...*
copy files	cp, cat
count words, lines, and bytes	wc
return the *current* date	date
change the *date* on your system	date
debug programs	gdb
decode uuencoded files	uudecode
delete files	rm
delete directories	rmdir
change the *directory*	cd
make a *directory*	mkdir
print the current *directory*	pwd
list *disk* free space	df
lock the X *display*	xlock
view X *display* information	xdpyinfo
query the *DNS* server	dnsquery
show the *domain* name	dnsdomainname
make a *DOS* (FAT16) file system	mkdosfs
convert *DOS* files to Linux files	fromdos
echo input	echo
edit a text file	ed, elvis, emacs, joe, jove, vi, vim, xedit
eject removable media	eject
create *electronic mail*	elm, mail, mailx, metasend, pine
format *electronic mail*	formail
notify of incoming *electronic mail*	biff, newmail, xbiff, wnewmail
send multimedia *electronic mail*	metasend
print *electronic mail*	printmail
read *electronic mail*	elm, mail, mailx, pine, readmsg
reply via *electronic mail*	Rnmail

If You Want To...	*Use This Linux Command...*
retrieve *electronic* mail from server	`fetchmail`
send batches of *electronic mail*	`fastmail`
split MIME content from *electronic mail*	`splitmail`
launch an *electronic-mail server*	`imapd, in.pop3d, ipop3d, sendmail`
display the last 10 lines of a text file	`tail`
encode a file	`uuencode`
return *environment variables*	`printenv`
display *environment variables*	`env`
view X *event* information	`xev`
make *FIFO*	`mkfifo`
calculate number of bytes to verify *files*	`cksum`
make a Linux *file system*	`mkfs`
make a Linux *swap area*	`mkswap`
check and repair a *file system*	`fsck`
find files	`find`
change *finger* information	`chfn`
return *finger* information	`finger`
launch a *font server*	`xfs`
view *font server* information	`fsinfo`
list *fonts*	`fslsfonts, showfont, xfd, xfontsel, xlsfonts`
format a text file	`fmt, groff`
format a floppy disk	`fdformat`
generate *fractals*	`xfractint`
launch an *FTP* server	`ftpd`
edit *graphics*	`gimp, xv`
change *group* ownership	`chgrp`
change current *group* permissions	`newgrp`

2

2

If You Want To...	*Use This Linux Command...*
create a new *group*	`groupadd`
view online *help*	`apropos`, `info`, `man`, `whatis`, `xman`
change *HFS* file attributes	`hattrib`
change the *HFS* working directory	`hcd`
copy files to or from an *HFS* volume	`hcopy`
delete both forks of an *HFS* file	`hdel`
display an *HFS* directory in long format	`hdir`
create a new *HFS* file system	`hformat`
list files in an *HFS* directory	`hls`
create a new *HFS* directory	`hmkdir`
mount a new *HFS* volume	`hmount`
print the full path to an *HFS* working directory	`hpwd`
rename an *HFS* file or directory	`hrename`
remove an empty *HFS* directory	`hrmdir`
remove an *HFS* volume	`humount`
display or change the current *HFS* volume	`hvol`
launch a shell for manipulating *HFS* volumes	`hfs`
launch an X shell for manipulating *HFS* volumes	`xhfs`
return *host* information	`host`
show current *host name*	`hostname`
open a telnet connection to *IBM 3270* host	`x3270`
edit *images*	`gimp`, `xv`
launch an *IMAP* mail server	`imapd`
install Slackware packages	`installpkg`
launch an *Internet* server	`inetd`

If You Want To...	Use This Linux Command...
eject/change protection on a Zip/*Jaz* disk	`mzip`
join sorted files	`join`
log *kernel* messages	`klogd`
display *kernel* symbols	`ksyms`
manage *kernel* modules	`kerneld`
rebuild *kernel* module tables	`depmod`
load *kernel* modules	`insmod, modprobe`
return information about a *kernel* module	`modinfo`
view *keyboard* information	`dumpkeys, kdb_mode`
modify X *keymaps*	`xmodmap`
save *keystrokes* to a file	`script`
view *keyword* information	`whatis`
link files	`ln`
list files	`ls`
log in remotely	`rlogin`
log in to the system	`login`
view your *login* name	`logname`
change HFS (*Macintosh*) file attributes	`hattrib`
change the *HFS* (*Macintosh*) working directory	`hcd`
copy files to or from an HFS (*Macintosh*) volume	`hcopy`
delete both forks of an HFS (*Macintosh*) file	`hdel`
display an HFS (*Macintosh*) directory in long format	`hdir`
create a new HFS (*Macintosh*) file system	`hformat`
list files in an HFS (*Macintosh*) directory	`hls`

2

If You Want To...	*Use This Linux Command...*
create a new HFS (*Macintosh*) directory	`hmkdir`
mount a new HFS (*Macintosh*) volume	`hmount`
print the full path to an HFS (*Macintosh*) working directory	`hpwd`
rename an HFS (*Macintosh*) file or directory	`hrename`
remove an empty HFS (*Macintosh*) directory	`hrmdir`
remove an HFS (*Macintosh*) volume	`humount`
display or change the current HFS (*Macintosh*) volume	`hvol`
launch a shell for manipulating HFS (*Macintosh*) volumes	`hfs`
launch an X shell for manipulating HFS (*Macintosh*) volumes	`xhfs`
create electronic *mail*	`elm, mail, metasend, pine`
encode electronic *mail*	`mimencode, mmencode`
format electronic *mail*	`formail`
notify of incoming electronic *mail*	`biff, newmail, xbiff, wnewmail`
create multimedia electronic *mail*	`metasend`
print electronic *mail*	`printmail`
read electronic *mail*	`elm, mail, pine, readmsg`
reply via electronic *mail*	`Rnmail`
retrieve electronic *mail*	`fetchmail`
retrieve electronic *mail* via POP	`popclient`
send batches of electronic *mail*	`fastmail`
split MIME electronic *mail*	`splitmail`
launch a *mail* server	`imapd, sendmail`
list free *memory*	`free`
merge files	`paste`

If You Want To...	*Use This Linux Command...*
merge three files	merge
MIME-encode electronic mail	mimencode, mmencode
change file permission *mode*	chmod
unload a *module*	rmmod
mount a disk	mount
mount a floppy disk	fdmount
control a tape drive	mt
run a *mouse* in terminal mode	gpm
move files	mv
create *multimedia* electronic mail	metasend
display *network* statistics	netstat
check that remote computer is accessible	ping
list *network* users	rusers
check for unread Usenet *news*	checknews
post Usenet *news*	Pnews, postnews
read Usenet *news*	trn, tin, nn, rn
list Usenet *newsgroups*	getlist, newsgroups
synchronize Usenet *newsgroups*	actsync
run commands with new priority	nice
dump files in *octal*	od
set X *options*	xset
change *ownership* of file	chown
install Slackware *packages*	installpkg
maintain Slackware *packages*	pkgtool
make Slackware *packages*	makepkg
remove Slackware *packages*	removepkg
change a *password*	passwd
partition a drive	cfdisk, fdisk
monitor *PC Card* devices	cardinfo

2

If You Want To...	*Use This Linux Command...*
monitor *PCMCIA* devices	cardinfo, cardmgr
display an X *pixmap*	sxpm
plot data	gnuplot
view a *PostScript* file	ghostview, gs
print a file	lpr
prepare a file for *printing*	pr
delete a *print* job	lprm
view *process* status information	ps
end a *process*	kill, killall, xkill
reprioritize a *process*	snice
return a *process* ID	pidof
list the *processes* eating the most CPU time	top
display X window or font *properties*	xprop
refresh your screen	xrefresh
remove files	rm
remove directories	rmdir
set an X *resource* database	xrdb
list X *resources*	appres, listres, viewres
reverse file lines	rev
set *root window* attributes	xsetroot
set the *root window* image	xpmroot
change *root* directory for a command	chroot
schedule tasks	crontab
magnify X *screen*	xmag
create a *screen* capture in X	xwd, xv
display a *screen* capture in X	xwud, xv
search files	egrep, fgrep, grep
search compressed files	zegrep, zfgrep, zgrep
launch X *session* manager	xsm

If You Want To...	*Use This Linux Command...*
view X *server* performance	x11perf
compare X *server* performance	x11perfcomp
enable/disable *shadow* passwords	shadowconfig
change your *shell*	chsh
launch a *shell*	ash, bash, tcsh, zsh
create *shell* archives	shar
unpack a *shell* archive	unshar
run two *shells* in the same window	splitvt
shut down a system	shutdown
install *Slackware*	setup
sort files	sort
check *spelling*	ispell
split a file	csplit, split
launch a *spreadsheet*	xspread, sc
trace *system* calls	strace
display *system* load information	tload, xload
display *system* usage	uptime, w
run a *Tcl* command shell	wish
launch a *terminal* emulator	rxvt, xterm
change *terminal* settings	stty, setterm
run the *TeX* formatter	latex
view *textinfo* information	info
find *text* in a binary file	strings
transfer files	ftp, tftp, ncftp
send data to *two* locations	tee
determine the file *type*	file
unmount file systems	umount
uncompress a file	uncompress, zcat
unzip a file	bzip2, gunzip, gzip, zcat
unzip a zipped file	bzip2, unzip

2

If You Want To...	*Use This Linux Command...*
monitor *UPS*	`powerd`
synchronize *Usenet* newsgroups	`actsync`
create new *users*	`newusers, useradd, adduser`
list information for current *users*	`who, rwho`
modify a *user* account	`usermod`
substitute a *user*	`su`
configure a *video card*	`SuperProbe`
view files	`cat, less, more`
view compressed files	`zmore, zcat, zless`
report *virtual memory* usage	`vmstat`
set text to specified *width*	`fold`
display *window* information	`xwininfo`
browse the *World Wide Web*	`lynx, netscape`
launch *X Window System*	`startx`
edit *X* resources	`editres`
generate *XF86Config* files	`XFf86Setup, xf86config`
receive via *xmodem*	`rx`
send via *xmodem*	`sx`
receive via *ymodem*	`rb`
send via *ymodem*	`sb`
receive via *zmodem*	`rz`
send via *zmodem*	`sz`

in plain english in p
sh in plain english in
glish in plain english
in plain english in p
sh in plain english in
glish in plain english
in plain english in p
glish in plain english
in plain english in p
sh in plain english in
glish in plain english
in plain english in p
sh in plain english in
glish in plain english
in plain english in p
lish in plain english
in plain english in p
sh in plain english in
glish in plain english
in plain english in p
sh in plain english in
lish in plain english
in plain english in p
glish in plain english

3

Linux/DOS Cross-Reference

DOS and Linux have more similarities than you might expect — both DOS and Linux have their roots in UNIX, and the commands and file systems generally behave the same way in all three operating systems. If your background is in DOS or Windows — Windows essentially is a graphical interface to DOS — you certainly can make the leap to Linux. This chapter lists some popular DOS commands and their Linux counterparts.

DOS COMMAND	Linux COMMAND COUNTERPART
APPEND	*None*
ASSIGN	*None*
ATTRIB	chmod
BACKUP	cpio, tar
BREAK	*None*
CALL	exec
CD	cd
CHCP	*None*
CHDIR	cd
CHKDSK	fsck
CHOICE	*None*
CLS	clear, reset
COMMAND	bash, csh, sh
COMP	cmp, diff, diff3, sdiff
COPY	cp, cat
CTTY	stty
DATE	date
DBLSPACE	*None*
DEFRAG	*None*
DEL	rm
DELTREE	rmdir, rm
DIR	ls
DISKCOMP	*None*
DISKCOPY	dd
DOSKEY	history (Korn and bash shells)
DOSSHELL	*None*
ECHO	echo
EDIT	elvis, emacs, joe, jed, jove, pico, vi
EXIT	exit
EXPAND	gunzip, uncompress, bunzip2

DOS COMMAND	Linux COMMAND COUNTERPART
FASTHELP	apropos, man, xman, whatis
FASTOPEN	*None*
FC	cmp, diff, diff3, sdiff
FDISK	fdisk
FIND	find
FOR	for (shell command)
FORMAT	mkfs
GOTO	goto (C shell)
GRAFTABL	*None*
GRAPHICS	*None*
HELP	apropos, man, whatis
IF	if (shell command)
INTERLNK	*None*
INTERSVR	*None*
JOIN	*None*
LABEL	*None*
LOADFIX	*None*
LOADHIGH	*None* (not needed)
MEM	free
MIRROR	*None*
MKDIR	mkdir
MODE	stty, setterm
MORE	less, more
MOVE	mv
MSAV	*None*
MSBACKUP	cpio, tar
MSD	*None*
NLSFUNC	*None*
PATH	echo $PATH
PAUSE	sleep

DOS COMMAND	Linux COMMAND COUNTERPART
POWER	*None*
PRINT	lpr
PROMPT	PS1
RECOVER	*None*
REM	#
RENAME	mv
REPLACE	*None*
RESTORE	cpio, tar
RMDIR	rmdir
SET	export, setenv
SETVER	*None*
SHARE	*None*
SHIFT	shift
SMARTDRV	*None*
SORT	sort
SUBST	*None*
SYS	*None*
TIME	date
TREE	*None*
TYPE	cat, less, more
UNDELETE	*None*
UNFORMAT	*None*
VER	uname
VERIFY	*None*
VOL	*None*
VSAFE	*None*
XCOPY	cp

Linux Commands
A to Z

4

Here is an alphabetical listing of the commands described in Chapters 5 through 11. This listing doesn't constitute the entire Linux command set — check out the online Linux man and info pages for that — but it does list the commands that you'll probably use most of the time.

Element	Chapter
actsync	Internet/Electronic-Mail Commands
afpd	Networking Commands
agetty	General-Purpose Commands
ansi2knr	Programming Commands
answer	Internet/Electronic-Mail Commands
appres	General-Purpose Commands
apropos	General-Purpose Commands
ar	Programming Commands
arch	General-Purpose Commands
as	Programming Commands
ash	General-Purpose Commands
atalkd	Networking Commands
atobm	General-Purpose Commands
audiocompose	Internet/Electronic-Mail Commands
audiosend	Internet/Electronic-Mail Commands
banner	General-Purpose Commands
basename	File-Management Commands
bash	General-Purpose Commands
bc	General-Purpose Commands
bdftopcf	General-Purpose Commands
biff	Internet/Electronic-Mail Commands
bison	Programming Commands
bitmap	General-Purpose Commands
bmtoa	General-Purpose Commands
bootpd	Networking Commands
bootptest	Networking Commands
bpe	Text-Processing Commands
bzip2	File-Management Commands
cal	General-Purpose Commands

Element	Chapter
cat	Text-Processing Commands
cc	Programming Commands
cd	File-Management Commands
cdrecord	General-Purpose Commands
cdwrite	General-Purpose Commands
checkalias	Internet/Electronic-Mail Commands
checknews	Internet/Electronic-Mail Commands
chfn	Internet/Electronic-Mail Commands
chgrp	File-Management Commands
chmod	File-Management Commands
chown	File-Management Commands
chroot	File-Management Commands
chsh	General-Purpose Commands
cksum	General-Purpose Commands
clear	General-Purpose Commands
cmp	Text-Processing Commands
colcrt	General-Purpose Commands
colrm	Text-Processing Commands
column	Text-Processing Commands
comm	Text-Processing Commands
compress	File-Management Commands
cp	File-Management Commands
cpp	Programming Commands
csh	General-Purpose Commands
csplit	Text-Processing Commands
ctags	Programming Commands
cut	Text-Processing Commands
date	General-Purpose Commands
dc	General-Purpose Commands

4

Element	Chapter
dd	File-Management Commands
diff	Text-Processing Commands
diff3	Text-Processing Commands
dir	File-Management Commands
dircolors	General-Purpose Commands
dnsdomainname	Networking Commands
dnsquery	Networking Commands
dumpkeys	General-Purpose Commands
echo	General-Purpose Commands
egrep	Text-Processing Commands
elm	Internet/Electronic-Mail Commands
elvis	Text-Processing Commands
emacs	Text-Processing Commands
env	General-Purpose Commands
etags	Programming Commands
expand	Text-Processing Commands
fastmail	Internet/Electronic-Mail Commands
faucet	Networking Commands
fetchmail	Internet/Electronic-Mail Commands
fgrep	Text-Processing Commands
file	File-Management Commands
find	File-Management Commands
finger	Internet/Electronic-Mail Commands
flex	Programming Commands
fmt	Text-Processing Commands
fold	Text-Processing Commands
formail	Internet/Electronic-Mail Commands
frm	Internet/Electronic-Mail Commands
fromdos	File-Management Commands

Element	Chapter
fsinfo	General-Purpose Commands
fslsfonts	General-Purpose Commands
fstobdf	General-Purpose Commands
ftp	Internet/Electronic-Mail Commands
ftpcount	Internet/Electronic-Mail Commands
funzip	File-Management Commands
fuser	Networking Commands
g77	Programming Commands
gawk	Programming Commands
gcc	Programming Commands
gdb	Programming Commands
getfilename	File-Management Commands
getkeycodes	General-Purpose Commands
getlist	Internet/Electronic-Mail Commands
getpeername	Networking Commands
getty	General-Purpose Commands
gimp	General-Purpose Commands
gnuplot	General-Purpose Commands
gprof	Programming Commands
grep	Text-Processing Commands
grodvi	Text-Processing Commands
groff	Text-Processing Commands
grolj4	Text-Processing Commands
grops	Text-Processing Commands
grotty	Text-Processing Commands
gs	Text-Processing Commands
gunzip	File-Management Commands
gv	Text-Processing Commands
gzexe	File-Management Commands

4

Element	Chapter
gzip	File-Management Commands
hattrib	File-Management Commands
hcd	File-Management Commands
hcopy	File-Management Commands
hdel	File-Management Commands
hdir	File-Management Commands
head	Text-Processing Commands
hformat	File-Management Commands
hfs	File-Management Commands
hls	File-Management Commands
hmount	File-Management Commands
hose	Networking Commands
host	Networking Commands
hostname	Networking Commands
hpwd	File-Management Commands
hrename	File-Management Commands
hrmdir	File-Management Commands
humount	File-Management Commands
hvol	File-Management Commands
id	General-Purpose Commands
imake	Programming Commands
info	General-Purpose Commands
ispell	Text-Processing Commands
joe	Text-Processing Commands
join	Text-Processing Commands
jove	Text-Processing Commands
kdb_mode	General-Purpose Commands
kill	General-Purpose Commands
killall	General-Purpose Commands

Element	Chapter
latex	Text-Processing Commands
less	Text-Processing Commands
listres	General-Purpose Commands
ln	File-Management Commands
locate	File-Management Commands
locatedb	File-Management Commands
lockfile	File-Management Commands
login	General-Purpose Commands
logname	General-Purpose Commands
look	Text-Processing Commands
lpq	Text-Processing Commands
lpr	Text-Processing Commands
lprm	Text-Processing Commands
ls	File-Management Commands
lynx	Internet/Electronic-Mail Commands
mail	Internet/Electronic-Mail Commands
mailx	Internet/Electronic-Mail Commands
make	Programming Commands
makedepend	Programming Commands
makestrs	Programming Commands
makewhatis	General-Purpose Commands
man	General-Purpose Commands
manpath	General-Purpose Commands
mattrib	Mtools Commands
mbadblocks	Mtools Commands
mc	File-Management Commands
mcd	Mtools Commands
mcookie	General-Purpose Commands
mcopy	Mtools Commands

4

Element	Chapter
mdel	Mtools Commands
mdir	Mtools Commands
merge	File-Management Commands
messages	Internet/Electronic-Mail Commands
metamail	Internet/Electronic-Mail Commands
metasend	Internet/Electronic-Mail Commands
mformat	Mtools Commands
mimencode	Internet/Electronic-Mail Commands
minicom	General-Purpose Commands
mkdir	File-Management Commands
mkdirhier	File-Management Commands
mkdosfs	File-Management Commands
mkfifo	File-Management Commands
mkfontdir	File-Management Commands
mkfs	File-Management Commands
mkmanifest	File-Management Commands
mknod	File-Management Commands
mlabel	Mtools Commands
mmd	Mtools Commands
mmencode	Internet/Electronic-Mail Commands
mmount	Mtools Commands
mmove	Mtools Commands
more	Text-Processing Commands
mrd	Mtools Commands
mread	Mtools Commands
mren	Mtools Commands
msgfmt	Programming Commands
mtest	Mtools Commands
mtype	Mtools Commands

4

Element	Chapter
mv	File-Management Commands
mwrite	Mtools Commands
mzip	General-Purpose Commands
netstat	Networking Commands
newgrp	File-Management Commands
newmail	Internet/Electronic-Mail Commands
newsgroups	Internet/Electronic-Mail Commands
nice	General-Purpose Commands
nohup	General-Purpose Commands
nroff	Text-Processing Commands
objcopy	Programming Commands
oclock	General-Purpose Commands
od	File-Management Commands
p2c	Programming Commands
passwd	General-Purpose Commands
paste	Text-Processing Commands
pathchk	General-Purpose Commands
perl	Programming Commands
pico	Text-Processing Commands
pidof	General-Purpose Commands
pine	Internet/Electronic-Mail Commands
ping	Networking Commands
pname	General-Purpose Commands
Pnews	Internet/Electronic-Mail Commands
popclient	Internet/Electronic-Mail Commands
postnews	Internet/Electronic-Mail Commands
pr	Text-Processing Commands
printenv	General-Purpose Commands
printf	Text-Processing Commands

Element	Chapter
printmail	Internet/Electronic-Mail Commands
procmail	Internet/Electronic-Mail Commands
ps	General-Purpose Commands
psbb	Text-Processing Commands
pwd	File-Management Commands
rb	General-Purpose Commands
rclock	General-Purpose Commands
rcp	Networking Commands
rdjpgcom	General-Purpose Commands
readmsg	Internet/Electronic-Mail Commands
reconfig	General-Purpose Commands
ref	Programming Commands
refer	Text-Processing Commands
renice	General-Purpose Commands
reset	General-Purpose Commands
resize	General-Purpose Commands
rev	Text-Processing Commands
richtext	Internet/Electronic-Mail Commands
rlogin	Networking Commands
rm	File-Management Commands
rmail	Internet/Electronic-Mail Commands
rmdir	File-Management Commands
Rnmail	Internet/Electronic-Mail Commands
rpcgen	Programming Commands
rsh	Networking Commands
rstart	Networking Commands
runscript	General-Purpose Commands
ruptime	General-Purpose Commands
rusers	Networking Commands

Element	Chapter
rwall	Networking Commands
rwho	Networking Commands
rx	General-Purpose Commands
rxvt	General-Purpose Commands
rz	General-Purpose Commands
sb	General-Purpose Commands
script	General-Purpose Commands
sdiff	Text-Processing Commands
sed	Text-Processing Commands
selection	Text-Processing Commands
seyon	General-Purpose Commands
shar	General-Purpose Commands
shelltool	General-Purpose Commands
showaudio	Internet/Electronic-Mail Commands
showexternal	Internet/Electronic-Mail Commands
showfont	General-Purpose Commands
shownonascii	Internet/Electronic-Mail Commands
showpartial	Internet/Electronic-Mail Commands
showpicture	Internet/Electronic-Mail Commands
showrgb	General-Purpose Commands
shrinkfile	File-Management Commands
size	File-Management Commands
skill	General-Purpose Commands
sleep	General-Purpose Commands
sliplogin	Networking Commands
smproxy	General-Purpose Commands
snice	General-Purpose Commands
sockdown	Networking Commands
soelim	Text-Processing Commands

Element	Chapter
sort	Text-Processing Commands
split	Text-Processing Commands
splitmail	Internet/Electronic-Mail Commands
splitvt	General-Purpose Commands
sq	File-Management Commands
startx	General-Purpose Commands
strace	General-Purpose Commands
strings	General-Purpose Commands
strings-gnu	General-Purpose Commands
strip	Programming Commands
stty	General-Purpose Commands
su	General-Purpose Commands
sum	File-Management Commands
sunst	General-Purpose Commands
sx	General-Purpose Commands
sxpm	General-Purpose Commands
sz	General-Purpose Commands
tac	Text-Processing Commands
tail	Text-Processing Commands
talk	Networking Commands
tcsh	General-Purpose Commands
tee	General-Purpose Commands
telnet	Networking Commands
test	File-Management Commands
tftp	Internet/Electronic-Mail Commands
tload	General-Purpose Commands
top	General-Purpose Commands
tr	Text-Processing Commands
trn	Internet/Electronic-Mail Commands

Element	Chapter
troff	Text-Processing Commands
true	General-Purpose Commands
ul	General-Purpose Commands
unexpand	Text-Processing Commands
uniq	Text-Processing Commands
unshar	General-Purpose Commands
unsq	File-Management Commands
unzip	File-Management Commands
unzipsfx	File-Management Commands
updatedb	File-Management Commands
uptime	General-Purpose Commands
users	General-Purpose Commands
uucp	Networking Commands
uudecode	Internet/Electronic-Mail Commands
uuencode	Internet/Electronic-Mail Commands
uustat	Internet/Electronic-Mail Commands
uux	Internet/Electronic-Mail Commands
vi	Text-Processing Commands
viewres	General-Purpose Commands
vim	Text-Processing Commands
vrfy	Internet/Electronic-Mail Commands
w	General-Purpose Commands
wc	Text-Processing Commands
whatis	General-Purpose Commands
who	General-Purpose Commands
whoami	General-Purpose Commands
wish	General-Purpose Commands
wnewmail	Internet/Electronic-Mail Commands
workbone	General-Purpose Commands

Element	Chapter
workman	General-Purpose Commands
write	Networking Commands
x11perf	General-Purpose Commands
x11perfcomp	General-Purpose Commands
x3270	Networking Commands
xargs	General-Purpose Commands
xauth	General-Purpose Commands
xbiff	Internet/Electronic-Mail Commands
xcalc	General-Purpose Commands
xclipboard	General-Purpose Commands
xclock	General-Purpose Commands
xcmap	General-Purpose Commands
xcmsdb	General-Purpose Commands
xconsole	General-Purpose Commands
xcutsel	General-Purpose Commands
xdm	General-Purpose Commands
xdpyinfo	General-Purpose Commands
xedit	Text-Processing Commands
xev	General-Purpose Commands
xeyes	General-Purpose Commands
xf86config	General-Purpose Commands
xfd	General-Purpose Commands
xfilemanager	File-Management Commands
xfm	File-Management Commands
xfontsel	General-Purpose Commands
xfractint	General-Purpose Commands
xfs	General-Purpose Commands
xgc	General-Purpose Commands
xgettext	Programming Commands

Element

Chapter

Element	Chapter
xhfs	File-Management Commands
xhost	General-Purpose Commands
xieperf	General-Purpose Commands
xinit	General-Purpose Commands
xkill	General-Purpose Commands
xload	General-Purpose Commands
xlock	General-Purpose Commands
xlogo	General-Purpose Commands
xlsatoms	General-Purpose Commands
xlsclients	General-Purpose Commands
xlsfonts	General-Purpose Commands
xmag	General-Purpose Commands
xman	General-Purpose Commands
xmessage	General-Purpose Commands
xmh	Internet/Electronic-Mail Commands
xmkmf	Programming Commands
xmodmap	General-Purpose Commands
xon	General-Purpose Commands
xpaint	General-Purpose Commands
xpmroot	General-Purpose Commands
xrdb	General-Purpose Commands
xrefresh	General-Purpose Commands
xset	General-Purpose Commands
xsetroot	General-Purpose Commands
xsm	General-Purpose Commands
xsmclient	General-Purpose Commands
xspread	General-Purpose Commands
xstdcmap	General-Purpose Commands
xterm	General-Purpose Commands

Element	Chapter
xv	General-Purpose Commands
xvidtune	General-Purpose Commands
xvpictoppm	General-Purpose Commands
xwd	General-Purpose Commands
xwininfo	General-Purpose Commands
xwud	General-Purpose Commands
xxgdb	Programming Commands
yacc	Programming Commands
yes	General-Purpose Commands
ytalk	Networking Commands
zcat	File-Management Commands
zcmp	Text-Processing Commands
zdiff	Text-Processing Commands
zegrep	Text-Processing Commands
zfgrep	Text-Processing Commands
zforce	File-Management Commands
zgrep	Text-Processing Commands
zmore	Text-Processing Commands
znew	File-Management Commands
zoo	File-Management Commands
zsh	General-Purpose Commands

4

II

The Commands

This section, which consists of seven chapters, covers the major Linux commands, sorted by group and function. The format of each of the commands presented in these chapters is the same. The name of the command is given, followed by an example command line and an explanation of the command's purpose. Also provided, if applicable, are the available command-line options, examples, and related commands. Also, we note whether a command is a GNU command or an X Window System command.

in plain english in pl
sh in plain english in
glish in plain english
in plain english in pl
sh in plain english in
glish in plain english
in plain english in pl
glish in plain english
in plain english in pl
sh in plain english in
glish in plain english
in plain english in pl
sh in plain english in
glish in plain english
n plain english in pl
lish in plain english
in plain english in pl
sh in plain english in
glish in plain english
in plain english in pl
sh in plain english in
lish in plain english
n plain english in pl
glish in plain english

General-Purpose Commands

The general-purpose commands are used for your everyday computing chores. They are the workhorses of the Linux operating system: they aren't flashy, but they're accessible by all users, and after you get to know them, you'll be surprised how often you use them.

agetty
Handle Login Requests

agetty option(s)
arguments

Purpose

The agetty command is a tty-management package optimized
for the Linux environment and dial-up lines. It opens a tty port,
prompts for a login name, and invokes the login command.
Typically, you don't call agetty on your own; it's usually called
by the /etc/inittab file when you boot a system.

Arguments

baud_rate   Sets a comma-separated list of one or more baud
             rates; it's invoked when agetty receives a BREAK
             character.

port   Specifies a path name relative to the /dev directory.

term   Sets the TERM variable, overriding the settings from
             init.

Options

-f issue_file   Displays *issue_file* instead of the default
                     /etc/issue file.

-h   Enables hardware (RTS/CTS) flow control. By
                     default, agetty determines whether software
                     (XON/XOFF) flow control is appropriate.

-i   Disables the transmission of the /etc/issue file
                     before writing the login prompt.

-I initstring   Sets an initial string to send to tty or a
                     modem; this can include modem initializa-
                     tion strings.

-l login_program   Invokes *login_program* instead of the default
                     /bin/login.

-L   Forces the line to be a local hard-wired
                     serial line.

-m	Detects the baud rate from the CONNECT status message issues by Hayes-compatible modems.
-n	Does not prompt the user for a login name. It was originally envisioned as a tool for using Linux as a Bulletin Board Service (BBS); however, in this day and age of increased security awareness, this option might be considered to be on the dangerous side.
-t *timeout*	Times out in *timeout* seconds if no username can be read.
-w	Waits for the user to send a carriage-return or line feed character before sending the /etc/issue file and the login prompt. Most often used with the –I option.

Related Commands

```
getty
stty
tty
```

appres **List X Resources** **(X Window System** **Command)**	**appres** *class* *toolkitoptions*

Purpose

The appres command lists the X resources specified by an application. You can specify a general application, or you can specify a particular widget.

● **TIP**

The output can be quite voluminous, so you may want to pipe the output to another file.

Example

```
$ appres XTerm
*mainMenu*interrupt*Label:        Send INT Signal
*mailMenu*logging*Label:          Log to File
*mainMenu*quit*Label:    Quit
...
```

Related Commands

```
listres
xrdb
```

5

apropos Search Whatis Database	apropos *keyword*

Purpose

The apropos command searches the whatis database for information concerning a specified keyword and returns the information in the default EDITOR. The whatis database contains short text summaries of commands.

Example

```
$ apropos xterm
xterm (1x)          – terminal emulator for X
```

Related Commands

```
man
whatis
xman
```

arch
Return Machine
Architecture

arch

Purpose

The arch command lists the machine architecture of the PC running Linux. This can be i386, i486, or i586 (for Pentium-based PCs).

Example

```
$ arch
i586
```

Related Command

```
uname
```

ash
Start Ash Shell

ash

Purpose

The ash command launches the ash shell, one of the many Linux command-line shells.

● CROSS-REFERENCE

See Chapter 12 for more information on shells.

atobm
Convert Bitmap Images

atobm *option(s)*
filename

Purpose

The atobm command converts ASCII strings to a bitmap file. See the bitmap command for more explanation about X Window System bitmap files.

Options

-chars *cc*	Sets the characters to use to specify the 0's and 1's that make up the bitmap file. The default is to use dashes (-) for 0's and pound signs (#) for the 1's.
-name *variable*	Sets the variable name used when writing the converted bitmap filename. The default is to use the base name of the filename command-line argument.
-xhot *number*	Sets the "hot spot" X coordinate.
-yhot *number*	Sets the "hot spot" Y coordinate.

Related Commands

bitmap
bmtoa

banner
Print Banner

banner *option message*

Purpose

The banner command prints a banner of string of characters using asterisks. The total width of the banner is 132 characters, and the banner is printed sideways. If no character string is given, you will be prompted to enter a string.

You can change the width of the banner using the -w*n* option, where *n* is replaced by the width of the banner in characters. (This command was popular in the old days, when the output of banner could be directed to typewriter-style printers that printed on rolls of paper.)

Option

-w *num*   Sets the width of the banner to *num* characters.

Example

```
$ banner kevin
```

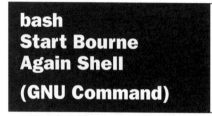

bash Start Bourne Again Shell (GNU Command)	bash *option(s)*

Purpose

The bash command launches the Bourne Again SHell, a clone of the popular UNIX Bourne shell.

● **CROSS-REFERENCE**

See Chapter 12 for more details on bash. Type man bash to see the bash man page.

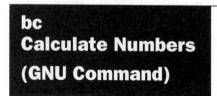

bc Calculate Numbers (GNU Command)	bc *option(s) files*

Purpose

The bc command acts as an online calculator and as a tool for unlimited-precision arithmetic. It can be used to enter numerals directly. It can be embedded into shell scripts, using a syntax similar to the C programming language. It can also be used to convert numerals to different bases.

After entering the bc command on a command line, arithmetic functions can be entered directly. When you're through using the bc command, type quit.

Options

-l   Adds functions from the math library.

-s   Overrides extensions, achieving POSIX conformity.

-w   Prints a warning when using extensions to POSIX bc.

Common Operators

+   Addition.

–   Subtraction.

/   Division.

*   Multiplication.

%   Remainder.

^   Exponentiation.

sqrt(n)   Square root.

Value Storage

scale=n   Sets scale using n decimal spaces; the default is 0. This is best used with base 10. The default also means that the output is in integers. The current value can be viewed by entering only scale (and no value) by itself. For digits between 10 and 15, use the letters A through F.

ibase=n   Sets the input base (the default is 10). The current value can be viewed by entering only ibase (and no value) by itself. For digits between 10 and 15, use the letters A through F.

obase=x   Sets the output base (the default is 10). The current value can be viewed by entering only obase (and no value) by itself. For digits between 10 and 15, use the letters A through F.

last   Returns the last value.

Keywords

```
for (exp) [statements]
```
Performs the *statements* if *exp* is true.

```
if (exp) [statements]
(else [statements])
```
Performs the *statement* if the *exp* is true. Can also be used with the else *extension*; in this case, the alternate statements will be performed.

```
while (exp) [statements]
```
Repeats the *statement* if *exp* is true.

```
break
```
Ends a for or while statement.

```
continue
```
Jumps to the next iteration in a for statement. This is a GNU extension.

```
define a(b)
```
Defines the function *a* with the argument *b*.

GNU Extensions

```
halt
```
Halts the bc command.

```
limits
```
Returns the local limits on the bc command.

```
print list
```
An odd command used to print a series of special characters. The *list* is a list of comma-delimited expressions and strings, printed in order. Strings can include special characters, including the following:

"\a"	bell
"\b"	backspace
"\f"	form feed
"\n"	newline
"\r"	return
"\q"	double quote
"\t"	tab
"\\"	backslash

Other Operators and Keywords

```
assignment    = + =- =* =/ =^ =
relational    < <= > >= == !=
unary         - ++ --
```

Math-Library Functions

s   Sine.

c   Cosine.

a   Arctangent.

e   Exponential; base e.

l   Natural logarithm.

j(n,x)   Bessel function.

Other Symbols

/* */   Comment lines.

{ }   Brackets statements.

[ ]   Array index.

Example

```
$ bc
scale=5
sqrt((55*6)/5)
8.12402
quit
```

Related Command

dc

---

bdftopcf Convert Bitmap Fonts (X Window System Command)	bdftopcf *option(s)* *fontfile.bdf*

Purpose

The bdftopcf command converts fonts from the X Bitmap Distribution Format (BDF) to the Portable Compiled Format

(PCF), which is more easily used by the X font server. PCF fonts can be read by any machine.

Options

-i	Inhibits computation of ink metrics. Bypassing computation can speed processing.
-l	Sets the font bit order to least significant bit (LSB) first.
-L	Sets the font byte order to LSB first.
-m	Sets the font bit order to most significant bit (MSB) first.
-M	Sets the font byte order to MSB first.
-o *outputfile*	Specifies the name of the output file.
-p*n*	Padding for the font glyph is set to *n*. Each glyph has each scanline padded to 1, 2, 4, or 8 bytes.
-t	Convert fonts to "terminal fonts" when possible. This option allows fonts to be rendered more quickly by the font server.
-u*n*	Sets the font scanline unit to *n*. This option is necessary when the font bit order is different than the font byte order; *n* can be 1, 2, or 4 bytes.

Example

```
$ bdftopcf -t -o fontfile.pcf fontfile.dbf
```

bitmap
Bitmap Editor
(X Window System Command)

bitmap option(s)
filename basename

Purpose

The bitmap command is used to create and edit bitmaps. Bitmaps are image files laid out in a grid and used in the X Window

System for a variety of purposes, from icons and cursors to Web-page graphic elements. They are stored as actual C code, which can be inserted directly into programs.

This program can specify a "hot spot" for use with a cursor, which tells the window manager where the cursor is specifically pointing, such as a tip of an arrow or the middle of cross hairs.

The basename is used with the C code input file. To see how the image will actually appear, press Alt + I.

●—TIP

Several commands are available when this program is actually running, such as inverting the present image and marking a section of the bitmap. These are available through buttons on the left side of the window.

Options

`-size WIDTHxHEIGHT`	Specifies the size of the bitmap grid.
`-sw dimension`	Specifies the width of squares, in pixels.
`-sh dimension`	Specifies the height of squares, in pixels.
`-gt dimension`	Sets the grid tolerance; if the size of the dimensions falls below the dimension, the grid will be turned off.
`-grid`	Turns off the grid lines.
`+grid`	Turns on the grid lines.
`-axes`	Turns off the major axes.
`+axes`	Turns on the major axes.
`-dashed`	Turns off the dashing for the frame and grid lines.
`+dashed`	Turns on the dashing for the frame and grid lines.
`-stippled`	Turns off the stippling of highlighted squares.
`+stippled`	Turns on the stippling of highlighted squares.
`-proportional`	Turns off proportional mode, in which the square width is equal to square height.
`+proportional`	Turns on proportional mode, in which the square width is equal to square height.

-dashes *filename*	Sets the bitmap filename to be used as a stipple for dashing.
-stipple *filename*	Sets the bitmap filename to be used as a stipple for highlighting.
-hl *color*	Sets the color used for highlighting.
-fr *color*	Sets the color used for the frame and grid lines.

Related Commands

    atobm
    bmtoa

bmtoa
Converts Bitmaps
(X Window System
Command)

bmtoa *option filename*

Purpose

The bmtoa command converts X Window System bitmap files to ASCII strings. See the bitmap command for more information on X Window System bitmap files.

Option

-chars *cc*   Sets the characters to use to specify the 0's and 1's that make up the bitmap file. The default is to use dashes (-) for 0's and pound signs (#) for the 1's.

Example

    $ bmtoa bitmap_file

Related Commands

    atobm
    bitmap

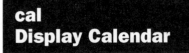

cal
Display Calendar

cal *option(s) month*
year

Purpose

The cal command displays a calendar for the current month, for a specific month and year when the month and year are specified, or a calendar for 12 months of a specific year when only the year is specified. The year can be between 1 and 9999, while the month can be between 1 and 12.

● **TIP**

The cal command is based on the British/American convention. To see the Gregorian calendar, use a command line of cal 1752.

Options

month   Specifies a month.

year   Specifies a year.

-j   Returns Julian dates, where days are numbered between 1 and 365 (except for leap years).

Examples

The following example displays the current month:

cal

This example displays a calendar for July 1997.

cal 7 1997

This example displays a calendar for the entire year 1997.

cal 1997

This example displays a calendar for the entire year 1752.

cal 1752

Related Command

date

cdrecord Create CDs	cdrecord *option(s)* *device settings*

Purpose

The cdrecord command records data or audio tracks on a CD recorder that conforms to Orange Book standards. You'll need to know what device is housing the CD recording, although, in most cases, it will be the SCSI device.

Track options are used to identify the format that the music tracks are stored in. Also, settings are used to define driver names and blanking options.

Options

-checkdrive	Checks whether there is a driver currently assigned.
-debug	Prints additional debugging information.
defpregap=*num*	Sets the default pregap size for all tracks except track number one. This should be used only with TEAC drives when creating track-at-once disks.
-dummy	Runs through a recording process but doesn't turn on the laser. This is done to make sure that the CD can be recorded properly.
-eject	Ejects the CD after the recording is made.
-fix	Fixates (finalizes) the CD after it's completed.
-ignsize	Ignores the known size of the media. Not recommended for anything other than debugging circumstances.
-inq	Performs an inquiry on the drive and exits.
-load	Loads the media and then exits.
-multi	Records multisession CDs. This isn't recommended for most situations.
-nofix	Does not fixate (finalize) the CD. Useful when you're creating an audio CD in steps. At some point, you'll need to fixate the CD before playing it, however.

-prcap	Prints the drive capabilities, as deduced from mode page 0x2A.
-reset	Resets the SCSI bus.
-scanbus	Scans all SCSI devices on all SCSI busses and prints the inquiry strings.
-toc	Prints a table of contents or PMA for a CD.
-v	Increases the verbosity level, which means that you'll receive more information about progress made during the recording process.
-V	Increases the verbosity level regarding SCSI command transport; useful in debugging.

Settings

blank=type	Blanks a CD-RW either before recording or existing. The *type* can be one of the following:

all	Blanks the entire disk.
fast	Blanks the PMA, TOC, and the pregap. This is considered to be a minimal blanking.
track	Blanks a specific track.
session	Blanks the last session.
trtail	Blanks the tail of a track.
unclose	Uncloses the last session.
unreserve	Unreserves a reserved track.
help	Lists all blanking types.

dev=target	Sets the SCSI target for the command.
driver=name	Specifies a user-supplied driver name.
fs=num	Sets the FIFO (ring buffer) size to *num*.
speed=num	Sets the speed factor, as a multiple of the audio speed: 150Kbps for CD-ROMs and 172Kbps for audio CDs.
timeout=num	Sets the SCSI command timeout to *num*.

Track Options

-audio	Writes all tracks in CD-DA audio format.
-cdi	Writes all tracks in CDI format.
-data	Records all tracks in CD-ROM mode 1 format. The file with track data should contain an ISO-9660 or Rock Ridge file system image. This is the default.
-isosize	Uses the ISO-9660 file system size as the size of the next track.
-mode2	Writes all tracks in CD-ROM mode 2 format.
-pad	Adds 15 sectors of zeroed data to the end of this and each subsequent data track.
padsize=num	Sets the amount of data (specified as num) to be appended to the next track. The value is reset to 0 for each new track.
-nopad	Avoids padding tracks. (This is the default.)
pregap=num	Sets the pregap size for the next track to num. This should only be used with TEAC drives when creating track-at-once disks.
-preemp	Indicates in the table of contents that all entries have been sampled with 50/15 second preemphasis.
-nopreemp	Indicates in the table of contents that all entries have been mastered with linear data. (This is the default.)
-swab	Assumes that audio data is in byte-swapped (little-endian) order.
tsize=num	Specifies the valid amount of data on a raw disk.
-xa1	Writes all tracks in CD-ROM XA mode 1 format.
-xa2	Writes all tracks in CD-ROM XA mode 2 format.

Related Command

cdwrite

cdwrite
Create CDs

cdwrite *option(s) source*

Purpose

The cdwrite command records data or audio tracks on a CD recorder that conforms to Orange Book standards, writing single-session, Red Book, or Yellow Book disks. You'll need to know which device is housing the CD recording, although, in most cases, it will be the SCSI device. Track options let you define how the tracks are formatted.

●—NOTE

The cdwrite command is no longer supported. You should use the cdrecord command instead.

Options

-e, --eject	Ejects the disk when the recording is finished.
-D *device*, --device *device*	Sets the device name for the CD writer. This is usually the generic address for your SCSI device.
-s *speed*, --speed *speed*	Sets the writing speed (1 as single speed, 2 as double speed, and so forth).
-y, -dummy	Goes through the motions of recording a CD, but turns off the laser. Useful when testing a recording.
--hp	Sets Hewlett-Packard mode.
--ims	Sets IMS mode.
--kodak	Sets Kodak mode.
--philips	Sets Philips mode.
--yamaha	Sets Yamaha mode.
-v, --verbose	Returns a progress display as each track writes.
-h, --help	Prints a short help message and exits.

Track Options

-a, --audio	Writes subsequent tracks in Red Book audio format.
-b *bytes*, --bytes *bytes*	Specifies the length of the data for the next track.
-d, --data	Writes subsequent tracks in Yellow Book data format. This is the default.
-p, -preemp	Indicates in the table of contents that all entries have been sampled with 50/15 second preemphasis.
-n, -nopreemp	Indicates in the table of contents that all entries have been mastered with linear data. (This is the default.)
-P, -pad	Adds 15 sectors of zeroed data to the end of this and each subsequent data track.
-N, -nopad	Avoids padding tracks. (This is the default.)

Related Command

cdrecord

chsh **Change Shell**	chsh [-s *shell*] *user*

Purpose

The chsh command changes your login shell. The root user can specify a shell, or can choose a shell from a list of available shells. Regular users can only pick a shell from available shells in /etc/shells.

Option

-s   Specifies a new shell for the user and suppresses interactive mode.

Example

```
$ chsh -s /bin/csh
```

cksum Check Files	cksum *file(s)*

Purpose

The cksum command performs a cyclic redundancy check (CRC) on the specified file(s) to make sure that the files are not corrupted.

Example

```
$ cksum CHANGES.TXT
4005661398    2344   CHANGES.TXT
```

clear Clear Screen	clear

Purpose

The clear command clears the screen if you're working in terminal mode.

Example

```
clear
```

colcrt Correct Formatting	colcrt *option(s) file*

Purpose

The colcrt command corrects the formatting of escape characters and reverse line feeds generated by the tbl or nroff commands. This command applies if you're working with Linux in terminal mode. It's not usually used on its own, but rather as part of a longer command line.

Options

–	Turns off underlining.
–2	Turns on double spacing.

Related Commands

```
tbl
nroff
```

5

csh C Shell	csh

Purpose

The csh command launches the C shell, one of the many Linux command-line shells.

● **CROSS-REFERENCE**

See Chapter 12 for more information on shells.

date Display Date and Time	date *options* +*format* date *option string* (for privileged users)

Purpose

The date command displays the current date and time. The many formats allow you to control the date format. A privileged user can also use the date command to set a system date. The date can be in numeric or nonnumeric format. A numeric string must be in the format *Mmddhhmmyy*.

● **TIP**

A privileged user, such as the root user, can use the command to set the system date.

Options

+*format*	Displays the date in a specific format; format options are listed in the following section.
-s	Sets the date. The option is available only to privileged users.
-u	Returns the time in universal time, also known as Greenwich Mean Time (GMT).

Formats

%a	Abbreviates the day of the week (Sun, Mon, and so on).
%A	Spells out the day of the week (Sunday, Monday, and so on).
%b	Abbreviates the month (Jan, Feb, and so on). The same as %h.
%B	Spells out the month (January, February, and so on).
%c	Returns the time for a specific country.
%d	Returns the day in two digits (01 through 31).
%D	Returns the date in *mm/dd/yy* format.
%e	Returns the day as a numeral (1 through 31).
%h	Abbreviates the month (Jan, Feb, and so on). The same as %b.
%H	Returns the hour in military time (00 through 23).
%I	Returns the hour in nonmilitary time (00 through 12).
%j	Returns the date in Julian format (1 through 365).
%k	Returns the hour in military time, without leading zeroes (1 through 23).
%l	Returns the hour in nonmilitary time, without leading zeroes (1 through 12).
%m	Returns the month as two numerals (01 for January, 02 for February, and so on).
%M	Returns the number of minutes (0 through 59).
%n	Inserts a newline.
%p	Changes time of day to a.m. and p.m. (as opposed to the default AM and PM).
%r	Returns *hh:mm:ss:a/pm* in 12-hour format.
%s	Returns the number since "The Epoch," 1970-01-01 00:00:00 UTC.
%S	Returns the number of seconds (0 through 59).

%t   Inserts a tab.

%T   Specifies time returns in *hh:mm:ss* format.

%U   Returns the week number for the current year, with Sunday as the first day of the week.

%w   Returns the day of the week as a numeral (Sunday is 0).

%W   Returns the week as a number (0 through 51), with the week beginning on a Monday.

%x   Returns a country-specific date format.

%X   Returns a country-specific time format.

%y   Returns the year in two digits (99).

%Y   Returns the year in four digits (1999).

%Z   Returns a time-zone name.

Example

This example sets the date to January 1 (0101), 1999 (99), at 3:30 p.m. (1530).

```
$ date 0101153099
```

dc
Calculate Numbers
(GNU Command)

dc *filename(s)*

Purpose

The dc command is a reverse-Polish disk calculator supporting unlimited-precision arithmetic. It reads from standard input, although you can supply filenames as input. It supports many of the same options as the bc command.

●—CROSS-REFERENCE

See the bc command in this chapter for more information on the available options.

Related Command

bc

dircolors
Directory Colors
(GNU Command)

dircolors *option(s)*

Purpose

The dircolors command sets the colors for the ls command. It generates an LS_COLORS environment variable and a set of aliases. (For ash and older versions of sh, which don't support aliases, it generates shell functions.)

5

●─TIP ──

The same options and escape sequences used in ls can be used by dircolors. Check out the listing for the ls command in Chapter 6 for more information.

Options

-a, -s	Generates shell functions instead of aliases; used with sh or ash.
-b, -k	Supports aliases instead of shell functions; used with bash or ksh.
-c, -t	Works with a C-style shell; used with csh or tcsh.
-z	Differentiates between string and list environment variables; used with zsh.
-P	Doesn't include the path of the ls binary.
-S	Sets colorization to *no* if the terminal does not occur in any TERM statement.

Supported Statements

TERM *terminal-type*	Establishes a terminal-specific section.
COLOR *option*	Sets the circumstances where color is enabled. *Option* is one of the following:

yes	Always enabled.
all	Always enabled.
no	Never enabled. (This is the default.)

	none	Never enabled. (This is the default.)
	tty	Enabled only if output is a terminal.
OPTIONS *options*		Adds command-line options to ls.
NORMAL *color*		Sets the color for nonfilename text.
FILE *color*		Sets the color for a regular file.
DIR *color*		Sets the color for a directory.
LINK *color*		Sets the color for a symbolic link.
ORPHAN *color*		Sets the color for an orphaned symbolic link.
MISSING *color*		Sets the color for a missing file.
FIFO *color*		Sets the color for a named pipe (FIFO).
SOCK *color*		Sets the color for a socket.
BLK *color*		Sets the color for a block device special file.
CHR *color*		Sets the color for a character device special file.
EXEC *color*		Sets the color for an executable file.
LEFTCODE *color*		Specifies the left code for non-ISO 6429 terminals.
RIGHTCODE *color*		Specifies the right code for non-ISO 6429 terminals.
ENDCODE *color*		Specifies the end code for non-ISO 6429 terminals.
extension color		Sets the color for a file ending in *extension*.
.extension color		Sets the color for a file ending in *.extension*.

Related Command

ls

dumpkeys
Keyboard Information

dumpkeys *option(s)*

Purpose

The dumpkeys command returns information about the current keyboard driver.

Options

`-c`*charset*	Specifies a *charset* to interpret the returned values; *charset* must be `iso-8859-1` (ASCII English; the default), `iso-8859-2`, `iso-8859-3`, `iso-8859-4`, or `iso-8859-8`.
`--compose-only`	Returns information about key combinations.
`-f`	Prints the entire output for each key in canonical format.
`--funcs-only`	Returns information about function keys.
`-i`	Prints limited information about each key: acceptable keycode keywords, the number of actions that can be bound to a key, the ranges of the action codes, and the number of function keys supported by the Linux kernel.
`--keys-only`	Returns information about key bindings, not string definitions.
`-l`	Prints information about each key: acceptable keycode keywords, the number of actions that can bc bound to a key, the ranges of the action codes, the number of function keys supported by the Linux kernel, and the supported action symbols and their numeric values.
`-n`	Returns information in hexadecimal format.

echo **Echoes Input**	**echo** *option string*

Purpose

The echo command echoes text or a value to standard output, normally the screen. It actually exists in three versions:

1. As a Linux command (`/bin/echo`)
2. As a C shell command
3. As a Bourne shell command

The three versions are used interchangeably. The only real difference is that the C shell version is much more limited (it doesn't support control characters in the same way or the -n option).

Option

-n   Avoids printing of a newline at the end of the text.

Control Character

\a   Alert (bell).

\b   Backspace.

\c   No newline.

\f   Form feed.

\n   Newline.

\r   Carriage return.

\t   Horizontal tab.

\v   Vertical tab.

\\   Backslash.

\nnn   ASCII code of any character (in octal format).

Example

This prints the string *Good afternoon* to the screen:

```
$ echo "Good afternoon"
```

This sends the string *We are testing the printer* to the printer:

```
$ echo "We are testing the printer" | lp
```

env
Change Environment for a Command

env options [variable=value] command

Purpose

The env command changes environment variables temporarily for a command or displays the current environment variables with their values. Your Linux system has a set of variables that can be applied to various situations; for instance, instead of every command and program having its own text editor, most of them just summon the EDITOR environment variable and call a system editor. Other variables control the default shell, your terminal type, your command path, and your home directory.

Using env with options, you can temporarily change all or selected environment variables and have the new values used by a command you choose. When you type env with no options, the command lists all current environment variables.

Options

-	Ignores the current environment entirely.
-i	Ignores the current environment entirely.
-u *variable*	Unsets the specified *variable*.

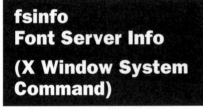

fsinfo **Font Server Info** **(X Window System** **Command)**	**fsinfo** *server* *servername*

Purpose

The fsinfo command returns information about a running X Window System font server.

Related Commands

```
fslsfonts
xfs
```

fslsfonts **List Fonts** **(X Window System** **Command)**	**fslsfonts** *option(s)* *pattern*

Purpose

The fslsfonts command lists the fonts served by a running X font server. You can list all the fonts (which can be quite voluminous), or you can match fonts with a pattern, which supports wildcards. (If you use the * and ? wildcards, you must quote them.)

Options

-1	Formats output in a single column (it is the number one).
-C	Formats output in multiple columns.
-l	Lists font attributes (it is the letter l).
-ll	Lists font properties.
-lll	Works the same as the -lll option with xlsfonts.
-m	Lists the minimum and maximum bounds of each font.
-n *columns*	Sets the number of *columns* for the output.
-server *host:port*	Specifies the X font server.
-w *width*	Sets the *width* for output; the default is 79 characters.
-u	Leaves output unsorted.

Related Commands

```
fsinfo
fstobdf
showfont
xfs
xlsfonts
```

---

fstobdf **Create BDF Font** **(X Window System** **Command)**	**fstobdf** *option(s)*

Purpose

The fstobdf command reads an X font from a font server and generates a BDF (Adobe's Glyph Bitmap Distribution Format) font.

Options

-fn *fontname*	Specifies the font from the X font server.
-server *servername*	Specifies the X font server.

Related Commands

```
bdftopcf
fslsfonts
xfs
```

getkeycodes
Get Keycodes

getkeycodes

5

Purpose

The getkeycodes command returns the scancode-to-keycode mapping table from the kernel.

getty
Manage Login
Sessions

getty *option(s)*
arguments

Purpose

The getty command is a general tty-management package. It opens a tty port, prompts for a login name, and invokes the /bin/login command. Typically, you don't call getty on your own; it's usually called by the /etc/inittab file when you boot a system.

●─CROSS-REFERENCE

See the online manual page for a full listing of the many available options. (Type man getty.)

Related Commands

```
agetty
stty
```

gimp
GNU Image
Manipulation
(GNU Command)

gimp *option(s) file(s)*

Purpose

The gimp command launches one of the most advanced image-manipulation programs available for Linux. The gimp command is short for *GNU Image Manipulation Program*. With a full set of graphics tools, gimp is complex yet powerful software. We're not covering all the capabilities of this software; entire books have been written about this software.

Options

-b commands, --batch commands	Runs in batch mode, cycling through *commands*.
-n, --no-interface	Runs without a user interface.
--display display	Displays on the specified X *display*.
--no-data	Runs without loading patterns, gradients, palettes, and brushes.
--no-splash	Runs without showing a start-up window.
--no-splash-image	Runs without showing an image in the startup window.
--no-shm	Runs without using shared memory between gimp and its plug-ins.
--no-xshm	Runs without using the X Shared Memory extension.

Related Command

xv

gnuplot **Interactive Plotting** **(GNU Command)**	gnuplot *option(s) file(s)*

Purpose

The gnuplot command launches an interactive plotting program. It plots any number of functions and data files, comparing actual data to theoretical curves. In addition, gnuplot supports user-defined and labeled X and Y ranges with optional autoranging, smart axes scaling, and smart tick marks.

Options

-persist	Leaves the plot windows even after gnuplot terminates.
-raise	Raises the plot window after each plot.
-noraise	Minimizes the plot window after each plot.
-gray	Requests grayscale rendering on grayscale or color displays.
-mono	Forces monochrome rendering on color displays.
-clear	Requests that the window be cleared before a new plot is displayed.
-tvtwm	Sets geometry specifications for the window to be made relative to the currently displayed portion of the virtual root.
-pointsize *size*	Sets the size of the points plotted.

id **Personal Identification**	id *option(s)* *username*

Purpose

The id command returns information about yourself or another specified username. This information includes user and group IDs, as well as effective user and group IDs, when applicable.

Options

-g   Returns only group information.

-G   Returns supplementary group information.

-n   Returns names (not numbers) when used with the -g, -G, or -u options.

-r   Returns real user ID and group ID, not effective IDs.

-u   Returns user ID only.

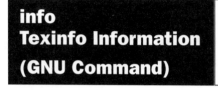

info
Texinfo Information
(GNU Command)

info options topic

5

Purpose

The info command returns hypertext information about a given topic, which can be a command or a subject. This information is stored in GNU texinfo format in an outline fashion.

● CROSS-REFERENCE

See the Texinfo Web site (http://texinfo.org) for information on the texinfo format.

After you launch info with a topic, you can move up and down the outline, looking at related topics. If you launch info without a topic, you'll see the opening info screen (stored in /usr/local/info/dir), explaining how info works and how you can maneuver through the system.

Options

--directory *directory*   Uses *directory* instead of the standard info directory (/usr/local/info/dir).

--dribble *file*   Stores keystrokes in *file*, which can then be used by the --restore option to go back to a specific place in an info session.

-f *file*   Uses *file* instead of the standard info file.

--help	Displays help information about the info command.
-n *node*	Specifies *node* to begin.
-o *file*	Sends information to *file* instead of standard output.
--restore *file*	Runs *file* (created with the --dribble option).
--subnodes	Displays subtopics.
--version	Displays info version.

Related Commands

man
xman

---

kbd_mode
Keyboard Mode

kbd_mode *option(s)*

Purpose

The kbd_mode command returns the current keyboard mode or changes it.

Options

-a	Sets mode to XLATE (ASCII).
-k	Sets mode to MEDIUM-RAW.
-s	Sets mode to RAW.
-u	Sets mode to Unicode.

---

kill
Kill Process

kill *option(s)* PID

Purpose

The kill command ends a process ID (PID). Only owners of the PID or a privileged user (for example, root user) can kill a process.

●—**NOTE**─────────────────────────────────

This command is also built into the bash and csh shells, although it works somewhat differently there.

Options

-1	Lists valid signals that you can send to processes.
-signal	Specifies a *signal* returned by kill -1.

Related Commands
```
killall
ps
```

5

killall Kill All Processes	killall *option(s) name*

Purpose

The killall command kills all processes by name, no matter how many processes are using a command. To kill a process running an executable file, use / somewhere in the command name.

Options

-e	Performs exact matches on the process name (limited to 15 characters).
-g	Kills the process group that the to which specified process belongs.
-q	Suppresses complaints if no processes were killed.
-V	Displays version number and exits.
-w	Waits for specified processes to die.
-i	Confirms that processes should indeed be killed.
-l	Lists valid signals.
-v	Runs in verbose mode; outcomes and IDs are listed.
-signal	Specifies a *signal* returned by killall -1.

Related Commands

```
kill
ps
```

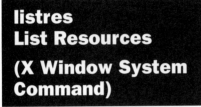

listres List Resources (X Window System Command)	listres *option(s) widget*

Purpose

The listres command returns a list of a widget's resource database. The class in which each resource is first defined, the instance and class name, and the type of each resource is listed. If no specific widgets or the -all option is given, a two-column list of widget names and their class hierarchies is printed.

Options

-all	Returns information for all known widgets and objects.
-nosuper	Ignores resources inherited from a superclass.
-variable	Identifies widgets by the names of the class-record variables, not the class name.
-top *name*	Specifies the *name* of the widget to be treated as the top of the hierarchy.
-format *printf-string*	Specifies the *printf-style* format string to print out the name, instance, class, and type of each resource.

login
Log In System

login *username options*

Purpose

The login command is used to log in to a Linux system. If you don't specify a username on the command line, the login command will prompt for one.

● **NOTE**

The command also performs some administrative acts, such as setting the UID and the GID of the tty, as well as notifying the user if any mail is waiting. A root user can set up the login command to perform some basic authentication (see the manual pages for more information). In addition, the login command can be used to specify where a root user can log in; the list of ttys is at /etc/securetty and is checked by login. Additional security restrictions can be stored in /etc/usertty.

Options

-f   Skips a second login authentication; doesn't work properly under Linux.

-h *host*   Passes the name of a remote *host* to login; used by servers and set by the superuser. This also doesn't work properly in Linux.

-p   Preserves the previous environment used by getty.

logname
Print Login Name
(GNU Command)

logname *option(s)*

Purpose

The logname command returns the login name of the calling process, as found in the file /etc/utmp. If no login name is found, an error message is generated.

Options

--help   Prints a short help message and then exits.

--version   Prints a version number and then exits.

makewhatis Make Whatis	makewhatis *option(s) manpath*

Purpose

The makewhatis command builds and updates the whatis database used by the whatis and apropos databases.

> ●─**NOTE**─────────────
> Perl must be installed for this to work.

Options

-g   Uses a global whatis file instead of one per man directory.

-h   Displays help screen.

-v   Operates in verbose mode.

-u   Updates the database with newer manual pages only. The default is to completely rebuild the database.

-w   Returns the *manpath*.

Related Commands

apropos
man
xman

man Online Manual Page	man *option(s) section title*

Purpose

The man command formats and displays pages from the online manual pages. These pages are the official documentation of the

Linux and UNIX operating systems and come in a strict format. These are useful when seeking out obscure options and obscure commands, but they're not so good when seeking a general explanation of a command.

Normally, you must match a specific command with the man command. However, you can begin searching in sections and narrow your search that way.

Options

-a	Displays all manual pages matching *title*, not just the first page. This is useful when viewing man pages for words such as mount that contain man pages in several different manual sections.
-c	Reformats a man page, even if a formatted page exists.
-C *config_file*	Specifies the man.conf file to use; the default is /usr/lib/man.conf.
-d	Displays debugging information, not the actual man page.
-D	Displays debugging information and the man page.
-f	Calls a summary a la the whatis command.
-h	Prints a one-line summary of the man command.
-k	Same as the apropos command.
-m *system*	Searches for man pages at *system*.
-M *path*	Specifies the path to use when searching for man pages. By default, the environment variable MANPATH is used. If this is not set, the list is looked for at /usr/lib/man.conf.
-p *string*	Specifies preprocessors to run before nroff or troff. Not very applicable to Linux, really.
-P *pager*	Specifies the *pager* to use (that is, the command to format and display the page); the default is /usr/bin/less -is.
-S *section_list*	Specifies the *section_list* to search.
-t	Uses /usr/bin/groff -Tps -mandoc to format the man page.

-w	Displays the locations of the man pages, not the actual pages.
-W	Displays the locations of the man pages, not the actual pages, with one filename per line.

Related Commands

apropos
manpath
whatis
xman

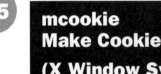

mcookie Make Cookie (X Window System Command)	mcookie *options*

Purpose

The mcookie command creates magic cookies (specifically, a 128-bit random hexadecimal number) for the xauth X authentication system. It's usually used directly with the xauth command.

Options

-v	Runs in verbose mode.
-f *filename*	Adds *filename* to the list of stuff used to generate the random cookie.

●─NOTE───────────────────

In Linux and X Window parlance, the term *cookie* has two meanings. The cookies used by this command and the X authentication system are different from cookies generated by the Netscape Navigator Web browser to store user information, such as session information, to be accessed by a Web server.

Related Command

xauth

minicom
Start Serial
Communications

minicom *option(s)*

Purpose

The minicom command launches a serial-communications package that somewhat resembles Telix. (You're showing your age if you know or used Telix.) It features a dialing directory with auto-redial, support for UUCP-style lock files on serial devices, a separate script language interpreter, capture to file, multiple users with individual configurations, and more. In this age of the Internet, using a serial-communications package — which usually is *not* used for Internet access, but rather is used to connect to a bulletin-board system — seems somewhat quaint.

When you run minicom, several options and commands are available. Check the online manual pages for more information; also, go ahead and investigate minicom after you launch it.

Options

-a   Sets attribute usage.

-c   Sets color usage.

-d   Directly dials a directory input on startup.

-l   Specifies a literal translation of characters with the high bit set.

-m   Overrides the command key with the Alt (Meta) key.

-M   Overrides the command key with the Alt (Meta) key, assuming that the Alt key is the 8th bit of the character high (sends 128 + character code).

-s   Runs the named script at startup.

-p   Uses a specified pseudo terminal instead of a regular terminal.

-C *filename*   Opens capture file called *filename* at startup.

-8   Passes 8-bit characters through without any modification.

-t	Sets a terminal type, overwriting the TERM environment variable.
-o	Skips initialization.
-s	Launches minicom in setup mode, with configuration menus displayed. (Only for root users.)
-z	Displays the terminal status line.

Related Command

seyon

mzip
Eject Zip/Jaz Disk

mzip *option(s) drive*

Purpose

The mzip command ejects a disk and changes the protection mode for a Zip/Jaz drive.

Options

-e   Ejects disk.

-f   Ejects disk even if it's mounted.

-r   Sets the permissions to read-only.

-u   Unprotects the disk temporarily until it is ejected.

-q   Returns the status of the current disk.

-w   Sets the permissions to read-write.

-p   Sets the permissions to write-protected with password protection.

-x   Adds password protection to the disk.

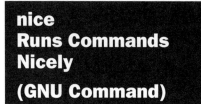

nice
Runs Commands
Nicely
(GNU Command)

nice *option command*
argument(s)

Purpose

The nice command allows you to set priorities for commands; if there's a heavy system load, the command either won't run or won't use up too many system resources. The niceness can be set between 19 (the lowest priority) to -20 (the highest priority), but a privileged user is the only one that can set a negative priority.

●―**NOTE**―――――――――――――――――――――――――

If no arguments exist, the nice command prints the current scheduling priority. In addition, this description of the GNU command is included with most Linux distributions, not the nice shell command.

Option

-ADJUST   Increments priority by 10 (the value of ADJUST).

-adjustment   Adds *adjustment* instead of 10 to the command's priority.

nohup
No Hangups
(GNU Command)

nohup *command*
arguments

Purpose

The nohup command ensures that a command specified on the same command line is run without interruption, even if you log off the system.

●―**NOTE**―――――――――――――――――――――――――

The GNU version of this command is pretty much the same as the nohup command found with most UNIX systems.

oclock
Round Clock
(X Window System Command)

oclock *option(s)*

Purpose

The oclock command launches a round analog clock.

Options

-fg *color*	Sets the *color* for the hands and the jewel of the clock.
-bg *color*	Sets the background *color*.
-jewel *color*	Sets the *color* for the jewel.
-minute *color*	Sets the *color* for the minute hand.
-hour *color*	Sets the *color* for the hour hand.
-bd *color*	Sets the *color* for the window border.
-bw *width*	Sets the *width* for the window border.
-transparent	Pares the clock down to the jewel, the hands, and the border.

Related Commands

rclock
xclock

passwd
Changes Passwords

passwd *name*

Purpose

The passwd changes your password. You can run passwd by itself and be prompted for the old password and then the new password.

● NOTE

A new password must be at least six characters long with both upper- and lowercase letters. In addition, a privileged user can change the password for another user by specifying a username and a new password on the command line.

pathchk
Check Path
(GNU Command)

pathchk *option filename*

Purpose

The pathchk command checks whether a filename is valid (that is, whether directories in the path name are searchable) or portable (meeting length requirements).

Option

-p   Checks for POSIX portability.

pidof
Show Process ID

pidof *option(s) program*

Purpose

The pidof command lists the process ID of a running program. You usually don't use it by itself, but rather in run-level change scripts. It's actually a link to the killall5 command.

Options

-s   Returns only one PID.

-o *pids*   Omits PIDs.

-x   Returns process IDs of shells running the specified scripts.

Related Commands

```
halt
init
killall5
reboot
shutdown
```

---

printenv **Print Environment** **(GNU Command)**	**printenv *variable***

Purpose

The printenv command prints your environment variables. If you specify a variable, this command returns information about that variable; if you don't specify a variable, the printenv command prints information about all variables.

---

ps **Print Status**	**ps *option(s)***

Purpose

The ps command returns information about the status of a process. A long, complicated set of options is available with this command.

● **CROSS-REFERENCE**
  Check the online manual pages for more information about the options.

---

rb **Receive Ymodem**	**rb *option(s)***

Purpose

The rb command is used to receive files using the Ymodem transfer protocol.

Options

-a   Strips carriage returns and all characters beginning with the first Ctrl-Z.

-b   Binary file-transfer override.

-q   Works in quiet mode.

-v   Works in verbose mode, causing a list of filenames to be appended to /tmp/rzlog.

-y   Clobbers any existing files with the same name.

rclock **Clock and Appointment** **Reminder** **(X Window System** **Command)**	**rclock** *option(s)*

Purpose

The rclock command combines an analog clock with an appointment reminder. It enters reverse video if mail is waiting.

Options

-fg *color*	Sets the window's foreground color.
-bg *color*	Sets the window's background color.
-fn *fontname*	Sets the font to use for reminders.
-iconic	Starts iconified.
-adjust *ddhhmm*	Adjusts the clock (*dd* = days, *hh* = hours, *mm* = minutes) without being the root user.
-update *n*	Changes how often, in *n* seconds, that the clock face is updated (the default is 30 seconds).
-mail *n*	Changes how often, in *n* seconds, new mail is checked (the default is 60 seconds).

Related Commands

oclock
xclock

rdjpgcom
Comments in JPEG

rdjpgcom *option*
jpeg_file

Purpose

The rdjpgcom command reads a JPEG file and prints the text comments within. The JPEG format allows for "comment" (COM) blocks, ordinarily used for annotations and titles. The maximum size is 64K, but there's no limit to how many blocks can be in a file.

Option

-verbose   Prints the JPEG image dimensions as well as the comments.

Related Commands

cjpeg
djpeg
wrjpgcom

reconfig
Reconfigures
Xconfig
(X Window System
Command)

reconfig <*Xconfig*
>*XF86Config*

Purpose

The reconfig command converts an old Xconfig file (used in versions of XFree86 before 3.1) to a new XF86Config file.

●─TIP─

You'll need to edit the new XF86Config file before it works.

renice
Change Priorities

renice *priority option*
who

Purpose

The renice command alters the scheduling priority of one or more running processes.

Options

-g   Forces who parameters to be interpreted as process group IDs.

-p   Resets who interpretation to be (the default) process IDs.

-u   Forces who parameters to be interpreted as usernames.

reset
Reset Terminal

reset

Purpose

The reset command resets the terminal. It calls on a number of commands to do so.

Related Commands

```
reset
stty
tput
```

resize
Resize Screen
(X Window System
Command)

resize *option(s)*

Purpose

The resize command sets the TERM and TERMCAP settings to the current screen size of the xterm window. For this to happen, the

command must be part of the command line or redirected to
a file.

Options

-u   Generates Bourne shell commands, even if
                            the Bourne shell is not the current shell.
-c   Generates C shell commands, even if the C
                            shell is not the current shell.
-s [*rows columns*]   Uses Sun console escape sequences instead
                            of the xterm escape codes. If rows and
                            columns are specified, the xterm window
                            will be asked to resize itself.

5

runscript
Runs Minicom
Script

runscript *scriptname*
homedir

Purpose

The runscript command is a script interpreter for the minicom
terminal software. It's usually used to automate logging in to a
remote UNIX server or a bulletin-board system, not for logging on
the Internet. You can also optionally enter your home directory as
the last parameter.

The following commands are recognized within scripts:
expect, send, goto, gosub, return, exit, print, set, inc, dec, if,
timeout, verbose, sleep, break, and call. The actual scripting
language is close to BASIC, and the minicom source code comes
with two example scripts: scriptdemo and unixlogin.

Related Command

minicom

ruptime
Host Status

ruptime *option(s)*

Purpose

The ruptime command shows the host status of a local machine. This is formed from packets broadcast by each host on the network once a minute. Machines for which no status report has been received for 11 minutes are shown as being down.

Options

-a   Counts all users, even users with idle times greater than an hour.

-l   Sorts by load average.

-r   Reverses the sort order.

-t   Sorts by uptime.

-u   Sorts by the number of users.

Related Commands

rwho
uptime

rx
Receive Xmodem

rx *option(s) filename*

Purpose

The rx command receives files using the Xmodem transfer protocol.

Options

a   Strips carriage returns and all characters, beginning with the first Ctrl-Z.

b   Binary file-transfer override.

c   Request 16-bit CRC.

e   Forces sender to escape all control characters; normally XON, XOFF, DLE, CR-@-CR, and Ctrl-X are escaped.

v   Works in verbose mode, causing a list of filenames to be appended to /tmp/rzlog. This command is related to the sx command.

rxvt **Terminal Emulator** **(X Window System** **Command)**	**rxvt** *option(s)*

Purpose

The rxvt command is a color VT100 terminal emulator for the X Window System. It's actually a scaled-down version of the popular xterm terminal emulator, lacking some xterm features (Tektronix 4014 emulation, session logging, and toolkit-style configurability) that you might not miss. The advantage is that rxvt uses much less swap space than xterm. If you're operating in a tight-memory environment, you might want to consider switching from xterm to rxvt.

●—TIP

See the xterm command for more information on resources, because rxvt accepts most of the same resources as xterm.

Options

-7	Runs in 7-bit mode, stripping the 8th bit from all characters typed on the keyboard.
-8	Runs in 8-bit clean mode, allowing the 8th bit of characters typed at the keyboard to be passed to the application.
-bg color	Sets the background color to color.
-bigfont keysym	Sets Alt-keysym as the toggle for increasing the font size, instead of the default Alt->.

-C	Captures system console messages.
-display *display-name*	Opens rxvt on the specified *display-name*.
-e *command* [*options*]	Runs a *command* and its command-line *options* immediately after launching rxvt. If this option is used, it must be the last on the command line.
-fat	Uses a fat scroll bar instead of the default thin scroll bar.
-fg *color*	Sets the foreground color to *color*.
-font *fontname*	Sets the text font to *fontname*.
-geometry *geometry*	Opens the window with the specified X *geometry*.
-ic	Starts iconified.
-ls	Adds - to argv[0] of the window's shell, causing it to be a login shell.
-ls-	Takes away - to argv[0] of the window's shell, causing it to be a login shell. It also tells rxvt to stay iconified if it receives a bell character.
-ma	Opens rxvt from an icon if it receives a bell character.
-meta *string*	Alters Alt+key setting. By default, rxvt sends an escape prefix when it receives an Alt keypress. You can specify *escape*, *8thbit*, or *ignore* for string.
-n *text*	Sets the name in the window icon or the icon manager to *text*. It also sets the window's title in the title bar to *text* unless the -T option is also set.
-pagedown *keysym*	Sets Alt-*keysym* as the toggle for scrolling down a page, instead of the default Alt-Next_Page.
-pageup *keysym*	Sets Alt-*keysym* as the toggle for scrolling up a page, instead of the default Alt-Prev_Page.

-secure *keysym*	Sets Alt-keysym as the toggle for increasing the font size, instead of the default Alt-s.
-sl *number*	Saves *number* of lines of scrolled text, instead of the default 64.
-smallfont *keysym*	Sets Alt-keysym as the toggle for decreasing the font size, instead of the default Alt-<.
-T *text*	Sets the string in the title bar to *text*.
-thin	Uses a thin scroll bar no matter what.

rz	**rz** *option(s)*
Receive Zmodem	

Purpose

The rz command is used to receive batch files using the Zmodem protocol. Path names are supplied by the sending program, and directories are made if necessary (and possible). Normally, the rz command is automatically issued by the calling Zmodem program, but some defective Zmodem implementations may require starting rz the old-fashioned way.

Options

-a	Strips carriage returns and all characters beginning with the first Ctrl-Z.
-b	Binary file-transfer override.
-c	Requests 16-bit CRC.
-D	Output file data to /dev/null; for testing.
-e	Forces sender to escape all control characters; normally, XON, XOFF, DLE, CR-@-CR, and Ctrl-X are escaped.
-p	Skip file if destination file exists.
-q	Works in quiet mode.
-t *time*	Changes timeout to *time* tenths of seconds.
-v	Works in verbose mode, causing a list of filenames to be appended to /tmp/rzlog.
-y	Clobbers any existing files with the same name.

sb **Send Ymodem**	sb *option(s) filename*

Purpose

The sb command sends a file to another system using the Ymodem protocol. This command has a long list of available options.

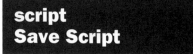

● CROSS-REFERENCE

See the online manual page for more information.

script **Save Script**	script *option filename*

Purpose

The script command saves every character from a terminal session to a specified text filename. If no filename is specified, the characters are saved to typescript.

Option

-a *filename*   Appends keystrokes to existing *filename*.

seyon **Serial** **Communications** **(X Window System** **Command)**	seyon *option(s)*

Purpose

The seyon command is an X Window-based telecommunications package for connection to remote clients and bulletin-board systems. All the options and command are present in the interface, although a few additional options are available that can be set when seyon is launched on the command line.

●—NOTE

This command supports a wide range of resources, as well as a scripting language. See the online manual pages for more information.

Options

`--`	Passes the rest of the command line to the terminal emulator.
`-dial`	Overrides the dialAutoStart resource.
`-emulator terminal-emulator`	Specifies a *terminal emulator* for seyon; if none is specified, then xterm is used.
`-entries entries-list`	Overrides the defaultPhoneEntries resource with *entries-list*.
`-modems device-list`	Overrides the existing modems resource.
`-nodefargs`	Does not pass along terminal-emulation options.
`-noemulator`	Tells seyon not to launch its own terminal emulator.
`-script script`	Executes *script* after seyon is launched.

---

shar
Shell Archives

shar *option(s) filename*

Purpose

The shar command creates shell archives (also known as *shar files*) that are in text format and can be mailed to another user, who can then unpack and execute them with bin/sh.

Options

`-a`	Automatically generates headers.
`-b`	Uses -X as a parameter when compressing. (This is an option to be avoided, for many reasons.)

-B	Treats all files as binary files. (This is an option to be avoided, for many reasons.)
-c	Starts the shar file with a cut line.
-d *XXX*	Uses *XXX* as a file delimiter, instead of the default SHAR_EOF.
-f	Restores by filename only, instead of restoring an entire path.
-F	Forces the prefix character to be prepended to every line, even if it is not required.
-g	Uses -X as a parameter to gzip when compressing. (This is an option to be avoided, for many reasons.)
-l *XX*	Limits shar file to *XX* kilobytes, but does not split files.
-L *XX*	Limits shar file to *XX* kilobytes, but splits files.
-m	Avoids generating touch commands to restore the file-modification dates when unpacking files from the archive.
-M	Determines whether a file is text or binary and archives appropriately, which means that binary files are uuencoded. (This is an option to be avoided, for many reasons.)
-n *name*	Specifies the name of the archive to be included in the header of the shar files.
-o *XXX*	Saves the archives to files XXX.01 through XXX.*nn*, instead of as standard output.
-p	Allows positional parameter options.
-P	Uses temporary files instead of pipes in the shar file.
-s *who@where*	Overrides automatically determined submitter name.
-S	Reads the list of files to be packed from standard input, not the filename.
-T	Treats all files as text.
-V	Produces vanilla shar files, which need only sed and echo in the unsharing environment.

-v	Works in quiet mode, disabling the inclusion of comments to be output when the archive is unpacked.
-w	Does not check with wc -c when an archive is unpacked.
-x	Overwrites existing files without checking.
-X	Checks before overwriting existing files.
-z	Uses gzip and uuencode to compress all files prior to packing. (This is an option to be avoided, for many reasons.)
-Z	Uses compress and uuencode to compress all files prior to packing. (This is an option to be avoided, for many reasons.)

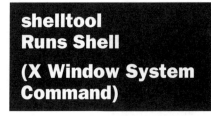

Related Command

unshar

shelltool Runs Shell (X Window System Command)	shelltool *option(s)*

Purpose

The shelltool command runs a shell or a program in a terminal window. Despite what the shelltool documentation says, you don't need OpenWindows installed in your Linux environment to run this command, although little reason actually exists to run it unless you're using OpenWindows applications.

Options

-B *boldstyle*	Sets the style for displaying bold text.
-C	Redirects system console output to shelltool.
-I *command*	Passes *command* to the shell.

| **showfont**
Shows Font
(X Window System
Command) | **showfont** *option(s)* |

Purpose

The showfont command shows a font that's managed by the X font server. You need to have the X font server running for this command to work. The information returned includes font information, font properties, character metrics, and character bitmaps. You can use wildcards to match a wide range of font names.

Options

-bitmap_pad*n*	Sets the bitmap-padding unit of the font (*n* is 0, 1, or 2, where 0 is *ImageRectMin*, 1 is *ImageRectMaxWidth*, and 2 is *ImageRectMax*).
-extents_only	Displays only the character extents, not the bitmaps.
-end *char*	Determines the end of the range of the characters to display (*char* is a number).
-fn *name*	Specifies the font to display.
-lsb	Specifies the bit order of the font as *LSBFirst* (least significant bit first).
-LSB	Specifies the byte order of the font as *LSBFirst* (least significant byte first).
-msb	Specifies the bit order of the font as *MSBFirst* (most significant bit first).
-MSB	Specifies the byte order of the font as *MSBFirst* (most significant byte first).
-pad *n*	Sets the scanpad unit of the font (*n* is 8, 16, 32, or 64).
-server *host:port*	Specifies the X font server to contact.
-start *char*	Determines the start of the range of the characters to display (*char* is a number).

-unit *n*	Sets the scanline unit of the font (*n* is 8, 16, 32, or 64).
-noprops	Does not return font properties.

Related Commands

```
fs
fslsfonts
xlsfonts
```

showrgb
Show Color Database
(X Window System Command)

showrgb *database*

Purpose

The showrgb command reads a database in the dbm database format and converts it back to source form, printing it to the screen.

skill
Reprioritizes Processes

skill *option(s) PID*

Purpose

The skill command signals or reprioritizes a specified process. It sends the terminate signal to a set of processes, or else it can give a signal (preceded with -) instead. To see a list of available signals, use the skill -l or skill -L command line.

Options

-f   Runs in fast mode, where the machine-dependent code responsible for reading processes is allowed to make decisions to improve speed at the expense of error reporting.

-i   Runs in interactive mode, where the user is prompted with each process that is a candidate for action.

-n   Only displays process IDs.

-v   Runs in verbose mode, where successful actions are
      displayed.

-w   Warns when processes are unreachable.

Related Commands

    kill
    nice
    ps
    renice
    signal
    snice

sleep	**sleep** *number*
Pause	
(GNU Command)	

Purpose

The sleep command pauses the system for a specified amount of
time: *number*s seconds, *number*m minutes, *number*h hours, and
*number*d days.

snice	**snice** *priority options*
Reprioritizes	***PID***
Processes	

Purpose

The snice command alters the scheduling priority of selected
processes. By default, the new priority is +4, but an argument
of the form +n (or -n) can be used to specify different values. An
invalid priority is rounded down (or up) to the first acceptable
value.

Options

-f Runs in fast mode, where the machine-dependent code responsible for reading processes is allowed to make decisions to improve speed at the expense of error reporting. (The snice man page states that this option is not very effective.)

-i Runs in interactive mode, where the user is prompted with each process that is a candidate for action.

-n Only displays process IDs.

-v Runs in verbose mode, where successful actions are displayed.

-w Warns when processes are unreachable.

Related Commands

```
kill
nice
ps
renice
signal
skill
```

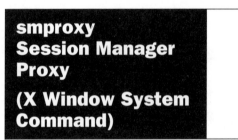

smproxy **Session Manager** **Proxy** **(X Window System** **Command)**	**smproxy** *option(s)*

Purpose

The smproxy command allows X applications that do not support X11R6 session management to participate in an X11R6 session.

Options

-clientId *id*	Sets the session ID used in the previous session.
-restore *saveFile*	Sets the file used to save the state in the previous session.

splitvt
Split Shell

splitvt *option(s) shell*

Purpose

The splitvt command runs two shells in two windows. The shell is your default shell (usually xterm). To move between windows, use Ctrl-W.

Options

-login	Runs the programs under each window as though they were login shells.
-lower *command*	Runs *command* in the lower window.
-nologin	Doesn't allow the programs under each window to run as though they were login shells.
-norc	Doesn't load ~/.splitvtrc.
-rcfile *file*	Loads *file* as the startup file instead of ~/.splitvtrc.
-s *numlines*	Sets *numlines* (number of lines) for the top window.
-t *title*	Sets the title for the xterm title bar.
-upper *command*	Runs *command* in the upper window.

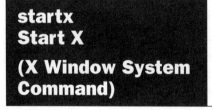

startx
Start X
(X Window System
Command)

startx

Purpose

The startx command launches an X Window System session from a Linux command line. It's really a front end to the xinit command.

When you launch startx, it looks for a file called .xinitrc in your home directory. This file contains information about your X Window setup, as well as which clients you want to run in conjunction with your X environment. Most of these clients should run in the background, except for the last client in the list, which should run in the foreground (this is usually a window manager).

●—**TIP**———————————————————————————————————————

Not many settings are associated with this command; you'll want to check xinit for more information. One option that is useful is the –bpp option, which can be used to set the color depth of your display. For example, to use 16-bit color, you would type **startx –– -bpp 16**.

Related Command

xinit

---

strace **Trace System Call**	strace *option(s)* *command*

Purpose

The strace command is used to trace system calls and signals. You use it to run a specified command; strace then tracks what system calls and signals are used by a process. The resulting information is printed to the screen or to a file (with the -o option). It's a useful command because you don't need the source code to see where a command is having problems.

Options

-a*column*	Aligns in a specific number of *columns*.
-c	Counts time, calls, and errors for each system call and reports a summary.
-d	Shows some debugging output of strace itself.
-eabbrev=*set*	Abbreviates the output from large structures.
-eraw=*set*	Prints undecoded (hexadecimal) arguments for the specified *set* of system calls.
-eread=*set*	Prints all hexadecimal and ASCII information of the specified *set*.
-esignal=*set*	Traces only the specified subset of signals.
-etrace=*set*	Traces only *set* of system calls.
-everbose=*set*	Dereferences structures for the specified *set* of system calls.

-f	Traces child processes.
-i	Prints the instruction pointer at the time of the system call.
-o*filename*	Writes the output to *filename*.
-O *overhead*	Set the overhead for tracing system calls to *overhead* microseconds.
-p*pid*	Attaches to the process *pid* and begins tracing.
-q	Suppresses messages.
-r	Prints a relative timestamp upon entry to each system call.
-s *strsize*	Sets the maximum string size to print (the default is 32).
-S*sortby*	Sorts the output of the output from the -c option by *sortby*.
-t	Begins each line of the trace with the time of day.
-tt	Begins each line of the trace with the time of day, including microseconds.
-T	Returns the time spent in system calls.
-v	Provides verbose output.
-x	Prints non-ASCII strings in hexadecimal string format.
-xx	Prints all strings in hexadecimal string format.

Related Commands
```
ptrace
time
trace
```

strings **Find Strings**	strings *option(s)* *filename(s)*

Purpose
The strings command searches for printable strings in a file. By default, a string must be at least four characters in length before

being displayed. This command is usually used to search for printable text in binary files.

● **NOTE** ───

Most Linux implementations contain two versions of strings: the original UNIX version (strings) and the GNU version (strings-gnu), which is a more advanced version, covered next in this chapter.

Options

-a   Searches through an entire object file for strings. The default is to search only the text and data segments of an object file.

-f   Prints the name of the file containing the string, as well as the string itself.

-n *num* Sets the minimum number of characters in a string to *num*, instead of to the default four.

-o   Prints the decimal offset of the string within the file, as well as the string itself.

Related Commands

hexdump
strings-gnu

---

strings-gnu **Find Strings** **(GNU Command)**	*strings option(s)* *filename(s)*

Purpose

The strings command searches for printable strings in a file. By default, a string must be at least four characters in length before being displayed. This command is usually used to search for printable text in binary files.

● **NOTE** ──

Most Linux implementations contain two versions of strings: the original UNIX version (strings), which is covered in this chapter, and the GNU version (strings-gnu), which is a more advanced version.

Options

-a Searches through an entire object file for strings. The default is to search only the text and data segments of an object file.

-f Prints the name of the file containing the string, as well as the string itself.

-n *num* Sets the minimum number of characters in a string to *num*, instead of to the default four.

-o Prints the decimal offset of the string within the file, as well as the string itself.

-t {o,x,d} Prints the decimal offset of the string within the file, as well as the string itself. The single character argument specifies the radix of the offset — octal, hexadecimal, or decimal.

--target=*bfdname* Specifies an object code format other than your system's default format.

stty Change Terminal Settings (GNU Command)	stty *setting option(s)*

Purpose

The stty command returns and changes terminal settings. With no arguments, stty returns the current settings: baud rate, line discipline number, and line settings that have been changed from the values set by stty sane.

Non-Option Settings

The opposite behavior can be toggled, if you precede the setting with -.

clocal	Disables modem control signals.
cread	Allows input to be received.
crtscts	Enables RTS/CTS handshaking.
cs5 cs6 cs7 cs8	Sets character size to 5, 6, 7, or 8 bits.
cstopb	Uses 2 stop bits per character (one with -).
hup	Sends a hang-up signal when the last process closes the tty.
hupcl	Sends a hang-up signal when the last process closes the tty.
parenb	Generates parity bit in output and expect parity bit in input.
parodd	Sets odd parity (even parity when preceded with -).

Input Settings

The opposite behavior can be toggled, if you precede the setting with -.

brkint	Breaks cause an interrupt signal.
icrnl	Translates carriage return to newline.
ignbrk	Ignores breaks.
igncr	Ignores carriage return.
ignpar	Ignores parity errors.
imaxbel (np)	Enables beeping and not flushing input buffer if a character arrives when the input buffer is full.
inlcr	Translates newline to carriage return.
inpck	Enables input parity checking.
istrip	Strips high (8th) bit of input characters.
iuclc (np)	Translates uppercase characters to lowercase.
ixany (np)	Allows any character to restart output.
ixon	Enables XON/XOFF flow control.

ixoff tandem   Enables sending of stop character when the system input buffer is almost full, and sending of start character when it becomes almost empty again.

parmrk   Marks parity errors with a 255-0-character sequence.

Output Settings

The opposite behavior can be toggled, if you precede the setting with -.

bs1 bs0 (np)	Sets backspace delay style.
cr3 cr2 cr1 cr0 (np)	Sets carriage-return delay style.
ff1 ff0 (np)	Sets form-feed delay style.
nl1 nl0 (np)	Sets newline delay style.
ocrnl (np)	Translates carriage return to newline.
ofdel (np)	Uses delete characters for fill instead of null characters.
ofill (np)	Uses fill (padding) characters instead of timing for delays.
olcuc (np)	Translates lowercase characters to uppercase.
onlcr (np)	Translates newline to carriage return-newline.
onlret (np)	Uses newline as a carriage return.
onocr (np)	Does not print carriage returns in the first column.
opost	Postprocesses output.
tab3 tab2 tab1 tab0 (np)	Sets horizontal tab delay style.
vt1 vt0 (np)	Sets vertical tab delay style.

Options

-a   Prints current settings.

-g   Prints settings in a form that can be used by another stty command.

su option(s)

**su
Substitute User
(GNU Command)**

Purpose

The su command runs a shell with a substitute user and substitute group IDs. Basically, it allows you to log in to the system as a
new user on a temporary basis, with a real and effective user ID,
group ID, and supplemental groups. The shell is taken from password entry, or /bin/sh if none is specified there. If the user has a
password, su prompts for it unless the user has a real user ID 0
(the superuser).

> **●─NOTE**
>
> When this command is run, the current directory remains the same. If
> one or more arguments are given, they are passed as additional argu-
> ments to the shell.

Options

-	Makes the shell a login shell.
-c *command*	Passes *command* to the shell, instead of starting an interactive shell.
-f	Passes the -f option to the shell. Use this with the C shell and not the Bourne Again Shell.
-m	Leaves the HOME, USER, LOGNAME, or SHELL alone.
-s *SHELL*	Runs *SHELL* instead of the user's shell.

**subst
Substitute Definition**

**subst *[-e editor]* -f
substitutions victim**

Purpose

The subst command substitutes definitions into filename(s). It's
used mainly for customizing software to local conditions. Each

victim file is altered according to the contents of the substitutions file.

The *substitutions* file contains one line per substitution. A line consists of two fields separated by one or more tabs. The first field is the name of the substitution, the second is the value. Neither should contain the character #, and use of text-editor metacharacters like & and \ is also unwise; the name in particular should be restricted to alphanumeric characters. A line starting with # is a comment and is ignored.

In the *victim* file, each line on which a substitution is to be made (a target line) must be preceded by a prototype line. Substitutions are done using the sed editor, unless the -e *editor* option is used to identify a different editor (replace *editor* with the name of a text editor command).

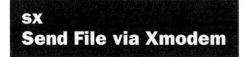

sx	sx *option(s)*
Send File via Xmodem	*filename*

Purpose

The sx command sends a file to another system using the Xmodem protocol. This command has a long list of available options.

●—CROSS-REFERENCE

See the online manual page for more information.

Options

-a	Translates new line (NL) characters in the file being sent to carriage return/line feed (CR/LF).
-k	Uses 1024-byte blocks instead of 128-byte blocks to send the file.
-q	Suppresses verbose output.
-t *timeout*	Changes timeout value to *timeout* (10ths of seconds).
-u	Unlinks the file after it has been successfully sent.
-v	Sends verbose output to stderr.

sxpm
Show X Pixmap
(X Window System
Command)

sxpm *option(s) filename*

Purpose

The sxpm command displays an X pixmap (graphics) file and can convert files formatted with the XPM 1 or XPM 2 format to the newer XPM 3 format.

Options

-closecolors	Uses "close colors" before reverting to other visuals.
-color	Displays the *colors* specified for a color visual.
-cp *colorname pixelvalue*	Overrides *colorname* color to *pixelvalue*.
-d *display*	Specifies the *display* to connect to.
-g *geom*	Sets the window geometry (the default is the pixmap size).
-grey	Displays the colors specified for a greyscale visual.
-grey4	Displays the colors specified for a four-color greyscale visual.
-hints	Sets *ResizeInc* hints for the window.
-icon *filename*	Creates an icon from the pixmap created from the file *filename*.
-mono	Displays a monochrome visual.
-nod	Does not display the pixmap in a window; use this option when converting between formats.
-nom	Ignores a clipmask.
-o *filename*	Write to *filename*.

`-pcmap`	Uses a private colormap.
`-plaid`	Shows a plaid pixmap stored as data.
`-sc symbol` *`colorname`*	Overrides symbol color to *colorname*.
`-sp symbol` *`pixelvalue`*	Overrides symbol color to *pixelvalue*.
`-rgb` *`filename`*	Searches the RGB database in *filename* and writes them out instead of the default RGB values.
`-v`	Prints extensions in verbose mode.

sz
Send Zmodem

sz option(s) command

Purpose

The `sz` command sends a file to another system using the Zmodem protocol. This command has a long list of available options.

● CROSS-REFERENCE

See the online manual page for more information.

tcsh
C Shell

tcsh

Purpose

The `tcsh` command launches a freely available version of the C shell, one of the many Linux command-line shells.

● CROSS-REFERENCE

See Chapter 12 for more information on shells.

tee
Send Information
to Two Files

tee *option filenames*

Purpose

The tee command sends the output of a command to two separate files. If the files already exist, the tee command will overwrite the contents of the files. If you specify only one file, the
output is directed to stdout instead of the second file. Likewise,
tee takes information from stdin for the information it redirects.
So, often you will use tee by running a command and piping the
output to tee.

Options

-a   Appends routed information to filenames, but does not over-
     write existing files.

-i   Ignores interrupt signals.

Example

```
$ tee output.kr output.pv
```

tload
Total System Load

tload *option(s) tty*

Purpose

The tload command displays the system load in a graph. By
default, information is displayed on the current terminal.
However, you can replace *tty* with a different terminal device
name to have output sent there instead.

Options

-d *delay*   Sets the delay between graph updates, in seconds.

-s *scale*   Specifies a vertical scale.

Related Commands

ps
top

top **Top Processes**	**top** *option(s)*

Purpose

The top command lists the top processes on the system — that is, those processes that are using the most CPU time.

5

Options

d   Specifies the delay between screen updates.

i   Ignores zombie or idle processes.

q   Refreshes without any delay.

S   Lists CPU time of dead children, as well.

s   Runs in secure mode.

Example

    $ top

Related Commands

ps
tload

true **Returns True** **(GNU Command)**	**true**

Purpose

The true command does nothing except return an exit status of 0, which means success. This is useful in shell scripts.

ul
Underline Text

ul option(s) terminals

Purpose

The ul command changes all underscored text to underlined text. This is an issue for terminal users hooked to a Linux system, not to most Linux users.

Options

-i   Uses a separate line containing appropriate dashes for underlining.

-t *terminal*   Specifies a new *terminal* type.

Related Commands

    colcrt
    nroff

unshar
Unpack Shar File

unshar option(s)
filename

Purpose

The unshar command unpacks a shar file.

Options

-c   Overwrites existing files.

-d *directory* Changes the directory to *directory* before unpacking files.

Related Command

    shar

uptime
System Information

uptime

Purpose

The uptime command tells how long the system has been running, how many users are currently logged on, and the system-load averages for the past 1, 5, and 15 minutes. This is useful when pointing out the superiority of the Linux operating system to bean counters or advocates of lesser operating systems.

Related Commands

```
users
w
who
```

users
User Information
(GNU Command)

users *filename*

Purpose

The users command lists information about the users currently logged in to the Linux system, based on information found in the /var/run/utmp file. If you want information from another system file, you must specify it on the command line.

Related Command

```
who
```

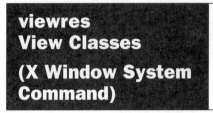

viewres *option(s)*

viewres
View Classes
(X Window System Command)

Purpose

The viewres command displays the widget class hierarchy of the Athena Widget Set.

Options

-top *name*   Specifies the *name* of the highest widget in the hierarchy to display.

-variable   Displays the widget variable names in nodes instead of displaying the widget class name.

-vertical   Displays output top to bottom rather than left to right.

w
System Information

w *option(s) usernames*

Purpose

The w command returns information about the system: users currently logged in to the system, usage statistics, and tasks that the users are performing. This is a combination of the who, ps -a, and uptime commands.

System information is returned in a header that includes the following: the current time, how long the system has been running, how many users are currently logged on, and the system-load averages for the past 1, 5, and 15 minutes.

User information includes the following: login name, tty name, the remote host, login time, idle, JCPU, PCPU, and the command line of their current process.

Options

-f   Prints the from (remote host name) field.

-h   Suppresses printing of the header.

-s   Suppresses printing of the login time, JCPU, or PCPU times.

-u   Ignores the current user while figuring out the current
      process and CPU times.

Related Commands

```
ps
top
uptime
who
```

whatis Command Information	whatis *keyword*

Purpose

The whatis command invokes a miniature help system, but the
topics are listed by keyword (which covers concepts) and not necessarily by commands. Because the help information is returned
as one line, it doesn't offer much depth concerning the keywords.

●—CROSS-REFERENCE

See the online manual pages for a list of the available options.

Example

```
$ whatis cat
```

Related Commands

```
apropos
man
```

who
User Information

who *option(s) filename*

Purpose

The who command displays information about the system or a specific user. By itself, the who command lists the names of users currently logged in to the system. As the command line who am i, the who command lists information about you.

●—CROSS-REFERENCE

See the online manual pages for a list of the available options.

Related Commands

w
whoami

whoami
Who Am I

whoami

Purpose

The whoami command is a one-word shortcut to the "who am I" variation of the who command. It's also the same as running the id -un command.

Example

```
$ whoami
kevin
```

Related Command

who

wish
Tcl Window Shell

wish *filename arg*

Purpose

The wish command is a shell window encompassing the Tcl command language, the Tk toolkit, and a main program that reads commands from standard input or from a file. It creates a main window and then processes Tcl commands. It will continue processing commands until all windows have been deleted or until the end of the file is reached on standard input.

Options

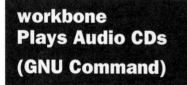

`-colormap` *new*	Creates a *new* private colormap instead of using the default colormap.
`-sync`	Executes X server commands synchronously, so errors are reported immediately.
`-visual` *visual*	Specifies the *visual* for the window.

workbone
Plays Audio CDs
(GNU Command)

workbone *option(s)*

Purpose

The workbone command plays an audio CD while you're working with Linux in text mode. It's a minimal program (as opposed to the flashier X-based workman) with limited feedback, displaying only the current track number and elapsed time. Use your numeric keyboard to control track-to-track playing, pausing, stopping, and resumption of CD playing.

Numeric Keyboard Commands

9   Plays CD.

8   Pauses and resumes.

7   Stops the CD.

6   Plays the next track.

5   Replays the previous track.

4   Goes to the previous track.

3   Goes forward 15 seconds.

2   Stops music and ends program.

1   Goes backward 15 seconds.

0   Exits the program, but the current track continues.

.   Displays the Help menu.

Options

-q   Launches in quick-start mode.

-a   Uses 7-bit ASCII for display.

Related Command

workman

workman **Plays Audio CDs** **(X Window System Command)**	**workman** *option(s)*

Purpose

The workman command plays an audio CD while you're working with Linux under X. It combines the features of a standard CD player — shuffle mode, programmable play lists, elapsed/remaining timers — and adds the ability to store information about a CD in a database, including track data, the disk's title, names of individual tracks, and the artist's name. (Because this is an XView program, it can use standard xview options.)

Options

-c *device*   Specifies a device other than the default.

-d   Doesn't display title information in the main window.

-D *filename*	Sets the location of the CD database file.
-e	Checks for the presence of a CD at startup.
-h	Displays all options.
-l *num*	Reserves *num* number of lines for track information.
-s *cmd*	Sends a command to a running process: stop, play, pause, back, forward, and eject.
-V *num*	Sets the minimum volume.

Related Command

workbone

---

x11perf
X Server Performance
(X Window System
Command)

x11perf *options*

Purpose

The x11perf command runs a set of tests on an X server and reports on the speed performance. These tests are specific to the X Window System, using benchmarks to determine the time it takes to create and map windows, map a preexisting set of windows onto the screen, and move windows around the screen. It also measures graphics performance for frequently used X applications, including mapping bitmaps into pixels, scrolling, and various stipples and tiles.

● **TIP**

The information actually is not as useful as you might think—you can't make any changes to the server (unless you're an experienced programmer and want to work with the X server source code), and you probably won't be changing your X server based on these numbers.

Options

-display *host:dpy*   Specifies the display.

-pack	Runs rectangle tests so that rectangles are packed next to each other.
-sync	Runs the tests in synchronous mode. This is a fairly worthless option.
-repeat *n*	Repeats each test *n* times. The default is five times.
-time *s*	Sets the time length of each test. The default is five seconds.
-all	Performs all the tests. Go out for a latte; this is a lengthy test.
-range *test1*,[*test2*]	Runs all the tests starting from the specified *test1* until the name *test2*, including the two specified tests. The test names should be one of the options starting from -dot.
-labels	Generates just the descriptive labels for each test specified.
-fg *color/pixel*	Sets the foreground color or pixel value.
-bg *color/pixel*	Sets the background color or pixel value.
-clips *default_num*	Sets the default number of clip windows.
-ddbg *color/pixel*	Sets the color or pixel value to use for drawing the odd segments of a DoubleDashed line or arc. The default is the background color.
-rop *rop0 rop1 ...*	Uses the specified raster ops (the default is *GXcopy*).
-pm *pm0 pm1 ...*	Uses the specified planemasks (the default is ∼*0*).
-depth *depth*	Uses a visual with *depth* planes per pixel. (The default is the default visual.)
-vclass *vclass*	Uses a visual of *vclass*. It can be StaticGray, GrayScale, StaticColor, PseudoColor, TrueColor, or DirectColor. (The default is the default visual.)

-reps *n*	Sets the repetition count (the default is five seconds).
-subs *s0 s1* ...	Sets the number of subwindows to use in the window tests. The default sequence is 4, 16, 25, 50, 75, 100, and 200.
-v1.2	Performs Version 1.2 tests using Version 1.2 semantics.
-v1.3	Performs Version 1.3 tests using Version 1.3 semantics.
-su	Sets the *save_under* window attribute to True on all windows. The default is False.
-bs *backing_store_hint*	Sets the *backing_store* window attribute to the given value on all windows created by x11perf. This can be WhenMapped or Always. The default is NotUseful.

Several other options are available that specify the exact tests to be performed. See the online manual pages for specifics.

Related Commands

    X
    xbench
    x11perfcomp

x11perfcomp **Compare Performance** **(X Window System Command)**	**x11perfcomp** *option(s) filenames*

Purpose

The x11perfcomp command merges the information returned by several x11perf tests in tabular format.

Options

-1 *label_file*   Specifies a label file to use.

-r	Specifies that output should include relative server performance.
-ro	Specifies that output should include only relative server performance.

Related Commands

X

x11perf

xargs Build Command Lines (GNU Command)	xargs *option(s)* *command*

Purpose

The xargs command reads arguments from standard input, delimited by blanks (protected with double or single quotes or a backslash) or newlines, and executes the command (if none is specified, /bin/echo will be run) one or more times with any initial arguments followed by arguments read from standard input. Blank lines on the standard input are ignored. The xargs command exits with the following status:

0	Successful.
123 through 125.	The command exits with a status of 1
124	The command exits with a status of 255.
125	The command is killed by a signal.
126	The command cannot be run.
127	The command is not found.
1	Another error occurred.

Options

-0, --null	Filenames are terminated by null characters instead of whitespace,

	and the quotes and backslash characters are not special characters.
-e[*eof-str*], --eof[=*eof-str*]	Sets the end-of-file string to eof-str.
-i[*replace-str*], --replace[=*replace-str*]	Replaces occurrences of *replace-str* in the initial arguments with names read from standard input.
-l[*max-lines*], --max-lines[=*max-lines*]	Uses *max-lines* nonblank input lines per command line; the default is one.
-n *max-args*, --max-args=*max-args*	Use *max-args* arguments per command line.
-p, --interactive	Prompts the user before each command is run.
-P *max-procs*, --max-procs=*max-procs*	Runs up to *max-procs* processes at a time; the default is one.
-r, --no-run-if-empty	Commands without nonblanks are not run.
-s *max-chars*, --max-chars=*max-chars*	Uses *max-chars* characters per command line, including the command and initial arguments and the terminating nulls at the ends of the argument strings.
-x, --exit	Exits if the size (as set by -s) is exceeded.

xauth
X User Authorization
(X Window System Command)

xauth *option(s)*
command arg...

Purpose

The xauth command displays and edits the authorization information used in connecting to the X server. This program doesn't actually contact the X server or create the authority information itself.

●—**CROSS-REFERENCE**———————————————————

A long list of commands exists for manipulating authority files; see the online manual pages for details.

Options

-b   Breaks authority file locks before proceeding. This
                option is used to clean up stale locks.
-f *authfile*   Sets the authority file to use. The default is the file
                listed with the XAUTHORITY environment vari-
                able or the .Xauthority file in the user's home
                directory.
-i   Overrides authority file locks.
-q   Works in quiet mode and doesn't print unsolicited
                status messages.
-v   Works in verbose mode, printing status messages
                indicating the results of various operations.

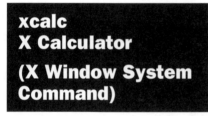

xcalc **X Calculator** **(X Window System Command)**	**xcalc** *option(s)*

Purpose

The xcalc command launches a scientific calculator. It emulates a TI-30 or an HP-10C.

●—**CROSS-REFERENCE**———————————————————

Numerous user commands are available after this program is launched; see the online manual pages for details.

Options

-rpn   Uses Reverse Polish Notation, which emulates an
            HP-10C; if this is not set, the emulation is TI-30.
-stipple   Uses a stipple of the foreground and background
            colors for the background of the calculator; useful
            for monochrome displays.

xclipboard
Display X Clipboard

xclipboard *option(s)*

Purpose

The xclipboard command displays the contents of the X clipboard, which contains text selections typically copied there by other applications. A clipboard is how applications can cut and paste within the application and with other applications; text is copied first to the clipboard and then copied from there.

Options

-w   Wraps lines that are too long to be displayed in one line in the clipboard.

-nw   Does not wrap lines that are too long to be displayed in one line in the clipboard.

Related Commands

X

xcutsel

xclock
X Clock
(X Window System
Command)

xclock *option(s)*

Purpose

The xclock command launches an analog or digital clock.

Options

-analog   Displays the time with a standard 12-hour analog clock face, with tick marks and hands. (This is the default.)

-d, -digital   Displays the time with 24-hour digits.

-chime	Sets a chime for once on the half hour and twice on the hour.
-hd *color*	Sets the color of the hands on an analog clock.
-hl *color*	Sets the color of the edges of the hands on an analog clock.
-update *seconds*	Sets how often the clock should be updated, in seconds. When a clock is obscured by another window, it is not updated. If seconds is 30 or less, a second hand will be displayed on an analog clock. The default is 60 seconds.
-padding *number*	Sets the width (in pixels) of the padding between the window border and the clock text or picture. The default is 10 pixels on a digital clock and 8 pixels on an analog clock.

Related Commands

```
date
oclock
rclock
```

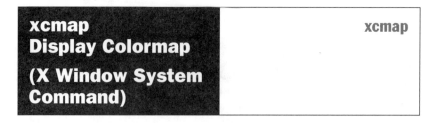

xcmap
Display Colormap
(X Window System Command)

xcmap

Purpose

The xcmap command displays the contents of the X color in a grid of squares corresponding to entries in the colormap. The xcmap command works on 4, 6, or 8-bit PseudoColor mapped displays, but not on higher resolutions.

xcmsdb **Device Color Management** **(X Window System** **Command)**	xcmsdb *option(s)*

Purpose

The xcmsdb command loads, queries, or removes Device Color
Characterization data stored in properties on the root window of
the screen as specified in Section 7 of the Inter-Client
Communication Conventions Manual (ICCCM). This information
is necessary for proper conversion of color specification between
device-independent and device-dependent forms.

Options

-query	Reads the XDCCC properties from the screen's root window.
-remove	Removes the XDCCC properties from the screen's root window.
-format 32|16|8	Specifies the property format in bits per entry: 32, 16, or 8.

Related Command

xprop

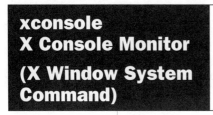

xconsole **X Console Monitor** **(X Window System** **Command)**	xconsole *option(s)*

Purpose

The xconsole command displays messages that are usually sent to
/dev/console.

Options

-daemon	Runs the command in the background.
-file *filename*	Specifies another device to monitor.
-notify	Displays applications that send new data to the console, even if the application is iconified. This is the default.
-nonotify	Toggles the -notify option.
-verbose	Adds an informative first line to the text buffer.
-exitOnFail	Exits when it is unable to redirect the console output.

xcutsel
X Cut Selection
(X Window System Command)

xcutsel *option(s)*

Purpose

The xcutsel command copies the current selection into a cut buffer and makes a selection that contains the current contents of a cut buffer. The command is used as a bridge between applications that don't support selections and those that do, although most newer applications do support selections.

Options

-selection *name*	Sets the *name* of the function to use; the default is primary. The only supported abbreviations are -select, -sel, and -s.
-cutbuffer *number*	Sets the *number* of the cut buffer to use; the default is 0.

Related Commands

xclipboard
xterm

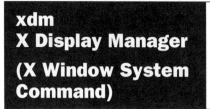

xdm
X Display Manager
(X Window System Command)

xdm *option(s)*

Purpose

The xdm command (X Display Manager) oversees X displays, whether they are on the local host or on remote servers. It oversees the session, prompting for a login name and password, authenticating the user, and running the actual session (which begins and ends with the session manager). When a session is ended, xdm resets the X server and restarts the whole process. It can also coordinate between sessions via the X Display Manager Control Protocol Description (XDMCP), offering host menus to other terminals.

> ●─**NOTE**──────────────────────────────
>
> The xdm command is a complex command that can't be covered in any depth here. Check out the online manual page or a good X Window System reference before tackling this command.

Options

-config *configuration_file*	Specifies the configuration file; the default is *XRoot*/lib/X11/xdm/xdm-config.
-debug *debug_level*	Sets the debugging level value, needed by the DisplayManager.debugLevel resource. However, this debugging information is worthless unless you want to work with the xdm source code.
-error *error_logfile*	Sets the value for the DisplayManager.errorLogFile resource.
-nodaemon	Uses false as the value for the DisplayManager.daemonMode resource.

`-resources resource_file`	Sets the value for the DisplayManger*resources resource. It contains configuration parameters for the authentication widget.
`-server server_entry`	Sets the value for the DisplayManager.servers resource.
`-session session_program`	Sets the value for the DisplayManager*session resource. This sets the program to run as the session after the user has logged in.
`-udpPort port_number`	Sets the value for the DisplayManager.requestPort resource, which controls the port number for XDMCP requests. Because XDMCP uses the registered UDP port 177, this is a setting you shouldn't change.
`-xrm resource_specification`	Sets an arbitrary resource.

Related Commands

```
xauth
xinit
```

xdpyinfo **X Display Info** **(X Window System** **Command)**	**xdpyinfo** *option(s)*

Purpose

The xdpyinfo command displays information regarding a specific X server. It's most useful when looking for graphics information.

Options

-ext *extension*   Displays information about a specific extension. If no extension is named, then information about all the extensions is named.

-queryExtensions   Also displays numeric information (opcode, base event, and base error) about protocol extensions.

Related Commands

xprop
xrdb
xwininfo

---

xev **X Event Display** **(X Window System** **Command)**	**xev** *option(s)*

Purpose

The xev command opens a window and then prints the event information about anything performed on or above the window (mouse movements, window resizing and moving, keyboard input, and so forth).

Options

-id *windowid*   Monitors existing *windowid*, not a new window.

-name *string*   Specifies that *string* be assigned to the new window.

-rv   Displays the window in reverse video.

-s   Enables save-unders on the new window.

Related Commands

xdpyinfo
xwininfo

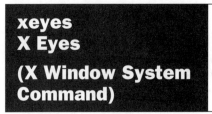

xeyes **X Eyes** **(X Window System** **Command)**	**xeyes** *option(s)*

Purpose

The xeyes command creates a window with a set of eyes that follows the movement of the cursor. An excellent way to waste X
resources.

Options

-fg *foregroundcolor*	Sets the color for the pupils of the eyes.
-bg *backgroundcolor*	Sets the background color.
-outline *outlinecolor*	Sets the color for the eye outlines.
-center *centercolor*	Sets the color for the center of the eyes.

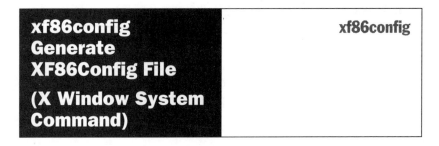

xf86config **Generate** **XF86Config File** **(X Window System** **Command)**	**xf86config**

Purpose

The xf86config command generates an XF86Config file, needed
before the X Window System can be run.

xfd
Display Font Information
(X Window System
Command)

xfd *option(s)*

Purpose

The xfd command displays all the characters in an X font in a window containing the name of the font being displayed, a row of command buttons, several lines of text for displaying character metrics, and a grid containing one glyph per cell.

Options

-fn *font*   Specifies the font to be displayed.

-center   Centers each glyph in its grid.

xfontsel
X Font Selector
(X Window System
Command)

xfontsel

Purpose

The xfontsel command provides a point-and-click interface for displaying X Window System font names and samples of the fonts, and for retrieving the full X Logical Font Description (XLFD) name for a font. You can choose to see all the fonts — which results in a voluminous output — or you can whittle down the list of files by combining a wildcard with the -pattern option.

Related Command

xfd

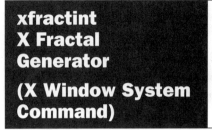

xfractint
X Fractal
Generator
(X Window System
Command)

xfractint *option(s)*

Purpose

The xfractint command is an X fractal generator and a port of the MS-DOS fractint program.

Options

-disk	Saves images to a file instead of to the screen.
-fast	Updates images frequently (every five seconds), if you're using a fast display.
-fixcolors *num*	Sets the number of colors, as a power of 2.
-onroot	Displays images on the root window. You probably won't want to do this, because rubberband zoom boxes don't work on the root window.
-private	Grabs as many colors as possible in a private colormap.
-share	Shares the current colormap.
-simple	Specifies simpler keyboard handling.
-slowdisplay	Updates images infrequently, if you're using a slow display.
@filename	Loads parameters from *filename*.

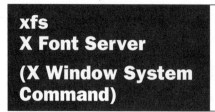

xfs
X Font Server
(X Window System
Command)

xfs *option(s)*

Purpose

The xfs command launches the X Window System font server.
It works exactly as the name implies: It serves rendered fonts to
requesting applications. This command is configured by a system
administrator. The system administrator sets it up to launch every
time X is launched.

Options

-config *configuration_file*   Sets the font-server config-
                                uration file.

-port *tcp_port*   Specifies the TCP port number.

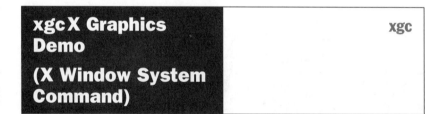

xgc X Graphics
Demo
(X Window System
Command)

xgc

Purpose

The xgc command launches a demo of X graphics capabilities.

xhost
X Server Access
(X Window System Command)

xhost +/- *hostname*

Purpose

The xhost command sets the names of hosts or users authorized to make connections to the X server. This isn't a particularly sophisticated method of access control. A host name preceded by a plus sign (+) is added to the access list, while a host name preceded by a minus sign (-) is deleted from the access list. Two plus signs (+ +) allows everyone access, while two minus signs (--) restricts access to those on the access list. With no options, xhost will return the current status. A plus sign alone allows access to all hosts; a minus sign denies access to all hosts.

Related Command

xdm

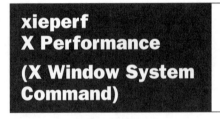

xieperf
X Performance
(X Window System Command)

xieperf *options*

Purpose

The xieperf command evaluates the X Image Extension (XIE) server extension.

●─CROSS-REFERENCE

A complete set of the extension tests can be found in the online manual pages.

Options

-all   Runs all tests. This may take a while.

-cache *n*	Sets a photomap cache of *n* entries.
-depth *depth*	Specifies *depth* planes per pixel.
-DirectColor	Uses a DirectColor visual.
-DIS	Runs tests covering only the protocol requests found in the DIS subset of XIE.
-display *host:dpy*	Sets the display.
-errors	Tests error-event generation.
-events	Tests event generation.
-GrayScale	Uses a GrayScale visual for testing.
-images *path*	Sets the path for loading images.
-labels	Generates the labels for all the scripts, but does not run the tests.
-loCal	Skips test calibration.
-mkscript	Generates a script file suitable for use with the script option.
-PseudoColor	Uses a PseudoColor visual for testing.
-range *test1 test2*	Runs tests beginning with *test1* and ending with *test2*, including the two specified tests.
-repeat *n*	Repeats each test *n* times (the default is two times).
-reps *n*	Sets the inner-loop repetitions to *n*.
-sync	Runs the tests in synchronous mode.
-script *file*	Runs the tests specified in a script file named *file*.
-showlabels	Prints a test label on the screen, indicating the test to be run. This is useful to figure out if any tests are crashing the system.
-showevents	Prints information about event and error tests.
-showtechs	Provides a long lists of techniques used by the XIE server.
-StaticColor	Uses a StaticColor visual.
-StaticGray	Uses a StaticGray visual.
-tests	Shows available tests.

−time *s*	Sets the time each test should run, in *s* seconds (the default is five seconds).
−timeout *s*	Sets the time that the test will wait for an event that may never arrive.
−TrueColor	Uses a TrueColor visual.
−WMSafe	Provides more accurate results by informing xieperf that it is running in a window-manager environment.

Related Commands

x11perf
x11perfcomp

---

xinit °	**xinit** *client*
X Initializer	
(X Window System	
Command)	

Purpose

The xinit command launches the X Window System (as called from startx) and can also launch a first client in situations where a system cannot start X directly from /etc/init.

In most situations, however, you won't be launching an application from the command line. In these situations, xinit uses the following sequence of steps when starting X:

1. It looks for a file called .xinitrc, which runs as a shell script to start client programs.
2. If .xinitrc does not exist, xinit uses xterm −geometry +1+1 −n login −display :0 as a command line.
3. If no server program exists on the command line, xinit looks for an .xserverrc script in the user's home directory.
4. If this file does not exist, xinit uses the X command and the display :0 as a default server.

When you set up an .xserverrc script, you must be sure to launch the read X server.

● **CAUTION** ────────────────────────────────────

There's a science to writing an `.xinitrc` script, if you choose not to use the mechanized tools for configuring X Window System. You must be sure that the applications launched in this file are run in the background, except for the last program (usually a window manager), which should run in the foreground to ensure that the script doesn't fail.

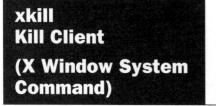

xkill
Kill Client
(X Window System
Command)

xkill *option(s)*

5

Purpose

The xkill command forces an X server to sever connections to clients. You can specify a program by a resource identifier. If you do not do this, xkill will display a little skull-and-crossbones cursor, and the window underneath this cursor of death will be killed when you click it.

● **CAUTION** ────────────────────────────────────

This is not the best way to go about closing programs, so use this command with caution.

Options

-all	Kills all clients with top-level windows on the screen. Use this only as a last resource.
-button *number*	Specifies the mouse button to use with the cursor of death. The default is the left mouse button. You can use *all* instead of a number to specify that any button can be used with the cursor of death.
-display *displayname*	Specifies the server to contact.
-id *resource*	Specifies the client to be killed.

-frame   Tells xkill that you want to kill direct
                                children of the root.

Related Command

xwininfo

xload **Display System** **Load** **(X Window System** **Command)**	**xload** *option(s)*

Purpose

The xload command periodically polls for the system-load average and relays the information in a histogram.

Options

-hl *color*   Sets the color of the scale lines in the
                                histogram.

-jumpscroll *pixels*   Sets the number of pixels to offset when
                                the graph reaches the right edge of the
                                window. The default is half the width of
                                the current window.

-label *string*   Specifies the string to put as the label
                                above the load average.

-lights *n*   Displays the load average with keyboard
                                LEDs. When the load level reaches *n*,
                                xload lights the first *n* keyboard LEDs, but
                                displays nothing on the screen.

-nolabel   Displays no label above the load graph.

-scale *integer*   Sets the minimum number of tick marks
                                in the display histogram.

-update *seconds*   Returns new information every *seconds*
                                number of seconds. The default is 10, and
                                the minimum is 1.

xlock **Lock Display** **(X Window System** **Command)**	**xlock** *option(s)*

Purpose

The xlock command locks an X display until a password is entered. When this happens, all new server connections are refused, the screen saver is disabled, the mouse cursor is turned off, and the screen is blanked.

Options

-cycles *num*	Sets the number of cycles until a pattern times out.
-display *dsp*	Sets the display to lock.
-font *fontname*	Sets the font name to be used on the login prompt screen.
-forceLogout *minutes*	Sets the number of minutes before auto-logout.
-info *textstring*	Displays informational text on the login screen; the default is *Enter password* to unlock, and *Select icon* to lock.
-invalid *textstring*	Sets *textstring* to display when a password is deemed invalid; the default is *Invalid login*.
-lockdelay *seconds*	Sets the number of seconds before a screen needs a password to be unlocked.
-logoutButtonHelp *textstring*	Sets *textstring* as the message shown outside the logout button.
-logoutButtonLabel *textstring*	Sets *textstring* as a messages shown inside the logout button when the logout button is displayed; the default is *Logout*.

-logoutFailedString textstring	Sets the *textstring* to be displayed when a text-string logout fails. The default is *Logout attempt FAILED.\n Current user could not be automatically logged out.*
-message textstring	Specifies a message, not a fortune.
-messagefile filename	Specifies a file where the contents are the message.
-messagesfile formatted-filename	Specifies a file containing a fortune message. The first entry is the number of fortunes, and the next line contains the first fortune.
-mfont mode-fontname	Specifies the font to be used with the marquee and nose modes.
-mode modename	Sets a display mode.
-mono	Displays in monochrome.
-name resource	Uses *resource* instead of the Xlock resource when configuring xlock. There are 45 resources; check out the online manual pages for a complete list. (Hint: we like the nose mode.)
-nice nicelevel	Sets the nice level.
-password textstring	Shows *textstring* in front of the password prompt; the default is Password:.
-program programname	Specifies a program to be used to generate a fortune message.
-resources	Displays the default resource file.
-saturation value	Sets the saturation of the color ramp.
-timeout seconds	Sets the number of *seconds* before the password screen times out.
-username textstring	Shows *textstring* in front of the username prompt; the default is Name:.
-validate textstring	Sets *textstring* to display when validating a password; the default is Validating login.
-/+allowroot	Allows the root user to log in to the system.

-/+echokeys	Displays ? for each key entered. The default is to display nothing.
-/+enablesaver	Keeps the screen saver running.
-/+grabmouse	Grabs the mouse and keyboard (the default).
-/+inroot	Runs xlock in a root window. This doesn't actually lock the system.
-/+install	Allows xlock to use its own colormap. This will not work with the fvwm window manager.
-/+inwindow	Runs xlock in a window.
+/-nolock	Works as a screen saver.
-/+remote	Allows you to lock remote X terminals. You should not be locking someone else's X terminal.
-/+timeelapsed	Tells you how long a machine has been locked.
-/+usefirst	Uses the first key pressed as the first key of the password. The default is to ignore the first key, because it's used to get the attention of the system.

xlogo
Show X Logo
(X Window System Command)

xlogo *option*

Purpose

The xlogo command displays the X logo. This is useful at trade shows, when gawkers want to know what operating system is running.

Option

-shape   Displays the logo window as a shape instead of a rectangle.

xlsatoms
List Atoms
(X Window System Command)

xlsatoms *option(s)*

Purpose

The xlsatoms command lists interned atoms from the server. All atoms starting from 1 (the lowest atom value defined by the protocol) are listed.

Options

-format *string*	Specifies the printf-style *string* used to list each atom. The default is %ld\t%s.
-name *string*	Specifies a single atom to list.
-range [*low*]-[*high*]	Specifies the range of atom values to check.

xlsclients
List Clients
(X Window System Command)

xlsclients *option(s)*

Purpose

The xlsclients command lists the client applications running on a display.

Options

-a	Lists clients on all screens, not just those on the default screen.
-l	Returns information in the long format, giving the window name, icon name, and class hints in addition to the machine name and command string shown in the default format.

-m *maxcmdlen*   Specifies the maximum number of characters in a command to print out. The default is 10,000.

Related Commands

    xprop
    xwininfo

xlsfonts List Fonts (X Window System Command)	xlsfonts *option(s)*

Purpose

The xlsfonts command lists the fonts installed on an X Window System. You can choose to see all the fonts — which results in a voluminous output — or you can whittle down the list of files by combining a wildcard with the -fn *pattern* option.

Options

-1	Prints information in a single column.
-C	Returns information in multiple columns.
-fn *pattern*	Specifies the font pattern to search for.
-l	Lists font attributes on one line, along with the font name.
-ll	Lists font properties in addition to -l output.
-lll	Lists character metrics in addition to -ll output.
-m	Lists minimum and maximum bounds of each font.
-n *columns*	Sets the number of columns.
-o	Performs OpenFont (and QueryFont, if appropriate) instead of ListFonts.
-u	Leaves output unsorted.
-w *width*	Sets the width in characters of the returned information; the default is 79.

Related Command

xfd

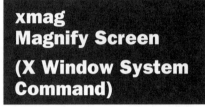

xmag
Magnify Screen
(X Window System
Command)

xmag *option(s)*

Purpose

The xmag command displays a portion of the screen. You can either specify a region on the command line or use a square with a pointer that you can drag over an area to be enlarged. After you decide on an area, a new window will appear, with the area magnified. Typing Q or C will end the program.

Options

-source *geom*	Sets the size and location of the area to be magnified.
-mag *integer*	Sets the level of magnification; 5 is the default.

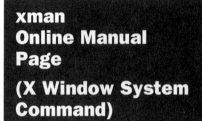

xman
Online Manual
Page
(X Window System
Command)

xman *option(s)*

Purpose

The xman command displays online manual pages. It's really an X Window System version of the man command, albeit with a prettier interface.

⦁—CROSS-REFERENCE—————————————————————————

See the entry for man earlier in this chapter for more information about Linux online help.

Options

-bothshown	Shows both a manual page and the manual directory.
-helpfile *helpfilename*	Specifies a *helpfilename* other than the default.
-notopbox	Starts without an opening menu.
-pagesize *WxH+X+Y*	Sets the size and location of all the manual pages.

Related Commands

apropos
man
whatis

xmessage	xmessage *option(s)*
Display X Message	
(X Window System	
Command)	

Purpose

The xmessage command displays a message or query in a window. It's basically an X-based /bin/echo file.

Options

-buttons *button*	Creates one button for each comma-separated button argument.
-default *label*	Defines the button with a matching label to be the default.
-file *filename*	Displays *filename*.
-print	Prints the label of the button pressed to standard output.

Related Commands

```
cat
echo
```

xmodmap **Modify Keymaps** **(X Window System** **Command)**	*xmodmap option(s)* *filename*

Purpose

The xmodmap command modifies keymaps under the X Window System. These are used to convert event keystrokes into keysyms.

Options

-e expression	Executes expression.
-n	Lists potential changes without actually making the changes.
-pk	Displays the current keymap table on standard output.
-pke	Displays the current keymap table on standard output in the form of expressions that can be fed back to xmodmap.
-pm	Displays the current modifier map on standard output.
-pp	Displays the current pointer map on standard output.

Related Command

```
xev
```

xonRemote Program (X Window System Command)	xon *option(s) command*

Purpose

The xon command runs an X program on a remote machine. The default is xterm -ls.

Options

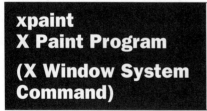

-access	Runs xhost locally to add the remote host to the host access list in the X server. xhost needs permission to modify the access list if this is to work.
-debug	Works in debugging mode, leaving stdin, stdout, and stderr intact.
-name *windowname*	Specifies an application name and window title for the default xterm command.
-nols	Doesn't pass along the -ls option to xterm.
-screen *screennum*	Sets the screen number of the DISPLAY variable passed to the remote command.
-user *username*	Passes along a username other than your own to the remote machine.

xpaint X Paint Program (X Window System Command)	xpaint *option(s) filename*

Purpose

The xpaint command launches a paint program. It allows for the editing of multiple images simultaneously and supports various formats, including PPM, XBM, TIFF, and more.

Options

-size   Sets the default width and height for new images.

-12   Uses a 12-bit PseudoColor visual.

-24   Uses a 24-bit TrueColor visual.

xpmroot   **xpmroot** *filename*
Set Root Image
(X Window System
Command)

5

Purpose

The xpmroot sets the root window of the current X display to an XPM pixmap, as specified by *filename* on the command line.

xprop   **xprop** *option(s)*
Displays X
Properties
(X Window System
Command)

Purpose

The xprop command displays window and font properties in an X server. You can choose a window or a font on the command line, or you can click a window to display its properties.

Options

-f name format [dformat]   Specifies the *format* and *dformat*
                            for *name*.

-font font   Returns the properties of font *font*.

-frame   Returns information about the win-
                            dow-manager frame instead.

-fs *file*	Uses *file* as the source of more formats for properties.
-grammar	Prints a detailed grammar for all command-line options.
-id *id*	Selects window *id* on the command line as the window to be examined.
-name *name*	Specifies that a window named window is the window to be examined.
-len *n*	Returns *n* bytes of any property (or less).
-notype	Ignores the type of each property.
-remove *property-name*	Removes the name of a property from a window.
-root	Uses the root window as the window of the client to be examined.
-spy	Examines window properties indefinitely, looking for property change events.

Related Command

xwininfo

xrdb **X Resource** **Database** **(X Window System** **Command)**	**xrdb** *option(s) filename*

Purpose

The xrdb command returns or sets the RESOURCE_MANAGER property on the root window of screen 0, or the SCREEN_RESOURCES property on the root window of any or all screens, or everything combined. You normally run this program from your X startup file.

The sort of information covered here includes color settings, font management, and more. The RESOURCE_MANAGER property is used for resources that apply to all screens of the display. The SCREEN_RESOURCES property on each screen specifies additional (or overriding) resources to be used for that screen.

Options

-all	Performs operations on the RESOURCE_MANAGER and the SCREEN_RESOURCES properties on every screen of the display.
-backup *string*	Appends *string* to backup files.
-cpp *filename*	Specifies the filename of the C preprocessor program to be used.
-edit *filename*	Places the contents of the specified properties into *filename*.
-global	Performs operations only on the RESOURCE_MANAGER property.
-load	Loads input as the new value of the specified properties, replacing the old contents.
-merge	Merges input with the current contents of the specified properties, instead of replacing them.
-n	Changes to the specified properties (when used with -load, -override, and -merge) or to the resource file (when used with -edit) should be shown on the standard output, but should not be performed.
-nocpp	Does not run the input file through a pre-processor before loading it into properties.
-override	Adds input to, instead of replacing, the current contents of the specified properties, as new entries override previous entries.
-query	Prints the current contents of the specified properties to standard output.
-quiet	Suppresses information about duplicate entries.
-remove	Removes specified properties from the server.

-retain	Does not reset the server if xrdb is the first client. The usefulness of this option is highly debatable, because very little chance exists that xrdb will ever be the first client of any X server.
-screen	Performs operations only on the SCREEN_RESOURCES property of the default screen of the display.
-screens	Performs operations only on the SCREEN_RESOURCES property of the default screen of the display. For -load, -override, and -merge, the input file is processed for each screen.
-symbols	Symbols defined for the preprocessor are printed to standard output.
-Dname[=value]	Defines symbols to use with the following conditions:
-Idirectory	Specifies a directory to look to for include files.
-Uname	Removes any definitions of this symbol.

xrefresh
Refresh Screen
(X Window System Command)

xrefresh *option(s)*

Purpose

The xrefresh command repaints all or part of your screen. It maps a window on top of the desired area of the screen and then immediately unmaps it, causing refresh events to be sent to all applications.

Options

-black	Shuts down the monitor for a second before repainting the screen.

-none	Repaints all windows without any gimmicks. This is the default, as well it should be.
-root	Uses the root window background.
-solid *color*	Uses a solid background of the specified color.
-white	Uses a white background, which causes the screen to appear to flash brightly before repainting.

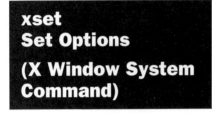

5

xset
Set Options
(X Window System
Command)

xset *option(s)*

Purpose

The xset command is used to set various aspects of X Window System. These settings will be reset to default values when you log out.

Options

b	Sets bell volume, pitch, and duration. You can set this with three numerical parameters, a preceding dash (-), or an on/off flag. If no parameters are given, the system defaults are restored.
bc	Controls bug-compatibility mode. Ancient X Window System clients (those created before Release 4) sent illegal requests to the server, and old servers would ignore the illegal requests.
c	Specifies the key click. You can set this with an optional value, a preceding dash (-), or an on/off flag. If no parameters are given, the system defaults will be used. If the dash or off flag is used, keyclick will be disabled. A value between 0 and 100 indicates volume as a percentage of the maximum.

fp=*path*	Sets the font path.
fp default	Resets the font path to the default.
fp rehash	Resets the font path to its current value, telling the server to reread the font databases in the current font path.
-fp *entries*	Removes *entries* from the font path. Entries must be a comma-separated list.
+fp *entries*	Prepends *entries* to the font path. Entries must be placed in a comma-separated list.
fp+ *entries*	Appends *entries* to the font path. Entries must be a comma-separated list.
led	Sets the keyboard LEDs. It accepts an optional integer, a preceding dash (-), or an on/off flag. With no parameters, all LEDs are turned on. With a preceding dash or the off flag, all LEDs are turned off. A value between 1 and 32 indicates that LEDs will be turned on or off depending on the existence of a preceding dash.
m	Controls the mouse parameters, one of acceleration or threshold. Acceleration is an integer or a simple fraction, while threshold is an integer. The mouse will go acceleration times as fast when it travels more than threshold pixels in a short time. If neither parameters nor the default flag is used, the system defaults will be used.
p	Sets pixel color values. The parameters are the colormap entry numbers in decimal and a color specification. The root background colors may be changed on some servers by altering the entries for BlackPixel and WhitePixel. A server may choose to allocate those colors privately, in which case an error will be generated.
r	Sets the autorepeat rate. A preceding dash or the off flag disables autorepeat. With neither parameters nor the on flag, autorepeat will be enabled.
s *flag*	Sets the screen-saver parameters. Flags can be blank/noblank, expose/noexpose, on/off, and activate/reset.
q	Returns the current settings.

Related Commands

xmodmap
xrdb
xsetroot

<table>
<tr><td>

**xsetroot
Set Root
Parameters

(X Window System
Command)**

</td><td>

xsetroot *option(s)*

</td></tr>
</table>

Purpose

The xsetroot command controls the settings for the background
(root) window on an X display. You really shouldn't be passing
along these parameters a lot; typically, you'll experiment with the
command line and then send the results in your X startup file.
With no options, the system restores to its default state.

● NOTE

Only one of the background color/tiling changing options (-solid, -
gray, -grey, –bitmap, and –mod) may be specified at a time.

Options

-bg *color*	Sets *color* as the background color.
-bitmap *filename*	Sets the bitmap in *filename* to the window pattern.
-cursor *cursorfile* *maskfile*	Specifies a new *cursorfile*.
-cursorname *cursorname*	Specifies a new cursor from the standard cursor set.
-def	Resets unspecified attributes to the default values.
-fg *color*	Specifies *color* as the foreground color.
-gray	Makes the background gray.

-grey	Makes the background gray.
-mod *x_y*	Implements a plaid-like grid pattern on your screen. The *x* and *y* values are integers ranging from 1 to 16.
-rv	Reverses the foreground and background colors.
-solid *color*	Sets *color* as the background of the root window.
-name *string*	Sets *string* as the name of the root window.

Related Commands
xrdb
xset

xsm **X Session Manager** **(X Window System** **Command)**	**xsm** *option*

Purpose
The xsm command launches the X Session Manager. A *session* is a group of applications in various states. You can set up various sessions for various purposes. After you exit the session, the application states are saved as part of the session.

When you run the xsm command, a session menu is loaded, allowing you to choose between sessions.

Option
-session *sessionName*	Loads *sessionName* without the session menu appearing.

Related Commands
smproxy
rstart

xsmclient **Tests Session** **Manager** **(X Window System** **Command)**	xsmclient

Purpose

The xsmclient tests the X Session Manager.

Related Command

xsm

xspread **X Spreadsheet** **(X Window System** **Command)**	xspread *option(s)* *filename*

Purpose

The xspread command is a very sophisticated spreadsheet running under the X Window System.

●—CROSS-REFERENCE

Check the online documentation (specifically, the Xspread Reference Manual in the file xspread.tex) to get an overview of its many capabilities.

Options

-c   Recalculates in column order. The default is row order.

-m   Works with manual recalculation; only values beginning with @ are recalculated. Otherwise, all cells are recalculated when a value changes (the default).

-n   Works in standard data-entry mode, in which a user must specify whether the data-entry item is numeric or a label.

-r   Recalculates in row order (the default).

-x   Encrypts files.

Related Commands

bc

dc

sc

xstdcmap X Colormap Utility (X Window System Command)	xstdcmap *option(s)*

5

Purpose

The xstdcmap command defines standard colormap properties.
You usually don't use this command from the command line,
but rather as part of your X startup script.

Options

-all	Defines all six standard colormap properties.
-best	Indicates that RGB_BEST_MAP should be defined.
-blue	Indicates that RGB_BLUE_MAP should be defined.
-default	Indicates that RGB_DEFAULT_MAP should be defined.
-delete *map*	Deletes a specified standard colormap property, one of default, best, red, green, blue, gray, or all.
-gray	Indicates that RGB_GRAY_MAP should be defined.
-green	Indicates that RGB_GREEN_MAP should be defined.
-red	Indicates that RGB_RED_MAP should be defined.

xterm X Terminal Emulator (X Window System Command)	xterm *option(s)*

Purpose

The xterm command launches a terminal-emulation window under X. It essentially gives you access to a shell command line via a window and, as such, is probably the most-used X command in Linux.

The xterm command has many available options, including one that controls columns in obscure terminal emulations. Here, we'll cover the major options.

●─CROSS-REFERENCE───────────────

Check the online manual pages for a more detailed listing of options.

Options

-ah	Always highlights the text cursor.
+ah	Highlights the text cursor if it's over the window with focus.
-aw	Turns on auto-wraparound.
-b *number*	Sets the size of the inner border (the distance between the outer edge of characters and the window border) in pixels. The default is 2.
-cr *colorb*	Sets the color for the text cursor.
-e *program args*	Runs *program* in the xterm window. This option must appear last in the command line.
-fb *font*	Sets the font for the bold text.
-j	Sets jump scrolling, where multiple lines can be scrolled at a time.
-ls	Sets the shell started in the xterm window as a login shell.

-mc *milliseconds*	Sets the maximum time between multiclick selections.
-ms *color*	Sets the color for the pointer cursor.
-rw	Turns on reverse wraparound.
-s	Sets scrolling asynchronously, so that the screen does not need to be kept up to date while scrolling.
-sb	Saves scrolled lines and displays a scroll bar.
-sl *number*	Sets the number of lines to save that have been scrolled off the top of the screen. The default is 64.
-tm *string*	Sets terminal setting keywords and the characters bound to those functions. Keywords are intr, quit, erase, kill, eof, eol, swtch, start, stop, brk, susp, dsusp, rprnt, flush, weras, and lnext.
-tn *name*	Sets the terminal type in the TERM environment variable.
-vb	Flashes the window — that is, a visual bell — instead of ringing a system bell.

Related Commands

```
getty
tty
```

xv **X Image Editor** **(X Window System** **Command)**	*xv option(s) filename*

Purpose

The xv command is an image editor that displays images in GIF, JPEG, TIFF, PBM, PGM, PPM, X11 bitmap, Utah Raster Toolkit RLE, PDS/VICAR, Sun Rasterfile, BMP, PCX, IRIS RGB, XPM, Targa, XWD, PostScript, and PM formats. It can also be used to generate screen captures in any of these formats.

CROSS-REFERENCE

To use the xv command, you'll want to check out the documentation, which runs to over 100 pages. It's in PostScript format and can be found at /usr/doc/xv/xvdocs.ps.gz.

Related Commands

gimp
xpaint
xvpictoppm

5

xvidtune
Video Mode Tuner
(X Window System
Command)

xvidtune *option(s)*

Purpose

The xvidtune command allows you to fine-tune your video performance via the XFree86 X server video-mode extension. With options, xvidtune provides a command-line interface to either switch the video mode or get/set monitor power-saver timeouts. With no options, xvidtune presents various buttons and sliders that can interactively adjust existing video modes. The resulting output can be inserted into an XF86Config file.

Options

-next	Switches to the next video mode.
-prev	Switches to the previous video mode.
-unlock	Turns on mode-switching key combinations.
-saver suspendtime [*offtime*]	Sets the suspend and off screen-saver inactivity timeouts. The values are in seconds.
-query	Displays monitor parameters and extended screen-saver timeouts.

Related Command

XF86Config

xvpictoppm xv Conversion (X Window System Command)	xvpictoppm

Purpose

The xvpictoppm command converts thumbnail files (in the .xvpics subdirectories) created by xv to standard Portable PixMap format files. The converted file is sent to stdout.

Related Command

xv

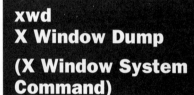

xwd X Window Dump (X Window System Command)	xwd *option(s)*

Purpose

The xwd command creates a screen capture of a screen or a portion of a screen to file. From there, it can be printed or converted to another file format. After running this command, the cursor changes to a small cross-hairs icon; place the cursor over the window to be captured and press the left mouse button. Placing the cursor over the screen background or the root window will capture the entire screen. System sounds indicate the beginning and end of the screen capture.

●—**TIP**——————————————————————————

The xv command also creates screen captures in a much easier fashion.

Options

-add *value*   Adds *value* to every pixel.

-frame	Specifically includes the window-manager frame with the screen capture.
-icmmap	Uses the first installed colormap of the entire screen to be used to obtain RGB values, not the colormap of the chosen window.
-id *id*	Specifies a window by specific *id* instead of with the pointer.
-name *name*	Specifies that a window with the WM_NAME property should be captured.
-nobdrrs	Doesn't capture the window border as part of a screen capture.
-out *file*	Specifies a file to store the captured image in.
-root	Automatically captures the root window for the screen capture. You don't need to specifically select a window for this to occur.
-screen	Captures the root window for the screen capture. This allows the selected window to be captured, along with any other windows or menus that overlap the selected window.
-xy	Specifies xy-format capturing.

Related Commands

```
gimp
xpr
xv
xwud
```

xwininfo **X Window** **Information** **(X Window System** **Command)**	**xwininfo** *option(s)*

Purpose

The xwininfo command displays system information about specific windows. You can select a target window with a mouse, specify the window by ID on the command line, or name a window on the command line.

Options

-all	Requests all information.
-bits	Returns information about the selected window's raw bits and how the selected window is to be stored, including the selected window's bit gravity, window gravity, backing-store hint, backing-planes value, backing pixel, and whether or not the window has save-under set.
-children	Returns information about the root, parent, and children of the selected window.
-english	Returns metric information about the selected window — individual height, width, and x and y positions are displayed in inches and the number of pixels.
-events	Displays the selected window's event masks.
-frame	Includes window-manager frames when manually selecting windows.
-id *id*	Specifies that window information be returned for the window by its *id*.
-int	Displays window IDs as integer values, not as the default hexadecimal values.
-metric	Returns metric information about the selected window — individual height, width, and x and y positions are displayed in millimeters and the number of pixels.
-name *name*	Specifies that window information be returned for the window by its name.
-root	Returns information for the root window.
-shape	Displays the selected window's border shape extents.
-size	Displays the selected window's sizing hints, including normal-size hints and zoom-size hints; user-supplied location and program-supplied location; user-supplied size, program-supplied size, minimum size, and maximum size; resize increments; and minimum and maximum aspect ratios, if any.

-stats	Returns a lot of information about the specified window, including its location, width and height, depth, border width, class, colormap ID (if any), map state, backing-store hint, and corner locations.
-tree	Returns information about the root, parent, and children of the selected window, and displays all children recursively.
-wm	Returns information about the selected window's window-manager hints, including whether or not the application accepts input, the window's icon window number and name, where the window's icon should go, and what the window's initial state should be.

Related Command

xprop

xwud **Display xwd** **Captures** **(X Window System Command)**	xwud *option(s)*

Purpose

The xwud command displays a window saved by the xwd command.

Options

-in *file*	Specifies the file to display.
-new	Creates a new colormap for displaying the image.
-noclick	Doesn't allow any button presses in the window to terminate the program.
-plane *number*	Specifies a single bit plane of the image to display.

-raw	Uses existing color values to display the image.
-rv	Reverses the video.
-std *maptype*	Displays the image using a specified Standard Colormap.
-vis *vis-type-or-id*	Specifies a visual or visual class.

Related Command

xwd

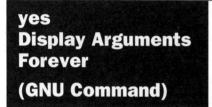

yes
Display Arguments
Forever
(GNU Command)

yes *string*

5

Purpose

The yes command prints the command-line arguments, separated by spaces and followed by a newline, forever, until it is killed. If you run yes with no arguments, yes displays the letter y as the string that it repeats.

zsh
Z Shell

zsh

Purpose

The zsh command launches the Z shell, one of the many Linux command-line shells.

●—**CROSS-REFERENCE**————————————————————
    See Chapter 12 for more details on shells.

in plain english in p
sh in plain english i
glish in plain english
in plain english in p
sh in plain english i
glish in plain english
in plain english in p
glish in plain english
in plain english in p
sh in plain english i
glish in plain english
in plain english in p
sh in plain english i
glish in plain english
in plain english in p
lish in plain english
in plain english in p
sh in plain english i
glish in plain english
in plain english in p
sh in plain english i
lish in plain english
in plain english in p
glish in plain english

File-Management Commands

File-management commands are used to manage your files and directories — move them, copy them, delete them, compress them, and more. Although the move in Linux is toward window managers and desktop environments such as KDE and GNOME, you'll still find that these window commands are handy when you want to work directly and quickly with files and directories.

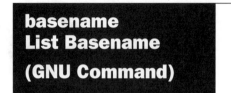

basename **List Basename** **(GNU Command)**	**basename** *filename* *[.suffix]*

Purpose

The basename command (if specified on the command line) strips leading directories and (optionally) the suffix.

Example

```
$ basename changes.txt .txt
changes
```

bzip2 **Compress Files**	**bzip2** *option(s) file(s)*

Purpose

The bzip2 command compresses files using the Burrows-Wheeler block-sorting text-compression algorithm. It works similarly to gzip, except that it creates smaller archives, with filenames ending in .bz2.

●—TIP

To uncompress files, use the bunzip2 command. To recover corrupted files, use the bzip2recover command.

Options

-d, --decompress   Forces decompression. The bzip2 and bunzip2 commands are actually the same, and the decision to compress or uncompress a file depends on the command you present. This option forces bzip2 to uncompress a file.

-z, --compress	Forces compression. The bzip2 and bunzip2 commands are actually the same, and the decision to compress or uncompress a file depends on the command you present. This option forces bunzip2 to compress a file.
-t, --test	Performs a trial compression without actually creating a compressed file.
-k, --keep	Keeps input files during compression, instead of deleting them.
-s, --small	Reduces memory usage, with a hit in compression performance.

Related Commands

gzip
gunzip

cd
Change Directory

cd *directory*

Purpose

The cd command changes the current directory. Although this is actually a shell command, it's normally treated as a standard Linux command.

Examples

This changes the current directory to your home directory:

    $ cd

This changes your current directory to the directory named /usr/kevin:

    $ cd /usr/kevin

This changes your directory to the subdirectory named kevin:

    $ cd kevin

This changes the current directory to your home directory:

    $ cd ~

This changes the current directory to the root directory:

```
$ cd /
```

Related Command

pwd

---

chgrp **Change Group**	*chgrp option(s) newgroup* *file(s)/directory*

Purpose

The chgrp command changes the group assignments associated with a file or directory. Group IDs or group names can be assigned to a file or a directory (the information is stored in /etc/groups). You must own a file or be the root user to change the groups.

Options

-c   Prints information about the changes made.

-f   Ignores information about files that can't be changed.

-v   Returns all information about the changes in verbose form.

-R   Changes recursively, which means that subdirectories are also changed.

Examples

This changes the group for kevin.memo to the restricted group:

```
$ chgrp management kevin.memo
```

This changes the group for the directory /home/kevin/memos, its contents, and all subdirectories within it to the restricted group:

```
$ chgrp -R restricted /home/kevin/memos
```

Related Commands

chown
chmod

chmod Change Mode	chmod *option(s) mode* *file(s)*

Purpose

The chmod command changes the permissions associated with a file or directory. Permissions are set for the owner of a file, a group owner of the file, and the world at large. Permissions are stored in one of two ways: numeric or symbolic form. The *symbolic* form is used to set values relative to the current permissions, whereas the *numeric* method is used to set absolute permissions. These values are in modes, which can be an octal number (when using the numeric form) or a symbol (when using the symbolic method). You can combine modes if you separate them with a comma.

You must own a file or be the root user to change the permissions.

The current permissions for a file can be displayed with the ls command, which is covered later in this section. The ls command lists the permissions in the following manner:

```
rwxr--w--
```

Permissions are set in trios: owner, group, and world. Any of the three can read (r), write (w), and execute (x). If permission is denied to one of the three, the letter is replaced with a hyphen (-). The root user has full permissions for every file.

● **TIP**

Assignment of permissions is one of the more important things to watch when using the Linux operating system. Many beginners get tripped up because they want to run or access a file, only to find out that they don't have permission to do so.

Examples Using Symbolic Form

This command line adds the permission to execute a file (x) to the group (g). In symbolic form, permissions are added or subtracted to existing permissions.

```
$ chmod g+x pat.memo
```

This command line removes the write permissions from the group and the world:

```
$ chmod go-w pat.memo
```

This command line adds the permission to execute a file to the group, while removing the write permissions from the group and the world:

```
$ chmod g+x,go-w pat.memo
```

Mode Symbols

The following symbols are used to set the mode:

u   User (the current owner of the file).

g   Group.

o   Other (world).

all   All (user, group and world, which is the default).

+   Adds a permission to the current permissions.

-      Deletes a permission from the current permissions.

=   Assigns a permission while deleting the other permissions from unspecified fields.

r   Read.

w   Write.

e   Execute.

s   Sets user ID.

t   Sets sticky bit, which is used for additional security both on a Linux system and the Internet.

Example Using Numeric Form

This command line combines chmod with a mode of 764, applied to the file pat.memo. This means that the owner can read, write, and execute the file (that's what the 7 designates), the group can read the file and write to it, but not execute it, and the world can read the file but not execute it or write to it.

```
$ chmod 764 pat.memo
```

How do we arrive at 764? We add the numerical value of modes, which we'll cover next in this section. A mode number can range between 000 and 777; 000 means that no one has any access to a file, while 777 means that everyone has full access to a file. Here's the exact math used to arrive at 764:

400	Owner has read permission.
200	Owner has write permission.
100	Owner has execute permission.
040	Group has read permission.
020	Group has write permission.
004	World has read permission.
764	(Total)

Using the ls command on the file in question, you'd see that it has the following permissions:

```
rwxrw-r--
```

Numeric Modes

The mode is a combination of the following:

400	Owner has read permission.
200	Owner has write permission.
100	Owner has execute permission.
040	Group has read permission.
020	Group has write permission.
010	Group has execute permission.
004	World has read permission.
002	World has write permission.
001	World has execute permission.

Options

-c	Prints information about the changes made.
-f	Ignores information about files that can't be changed.
-v	Verbose mode, where changes and failed changes are listed.
-R	Changes recursively, which means that subdirectories are also changed.

Four-Digit Modes

Occasionally, there will be four-digit modes. In these cases, the extra digit is actually at the beginning of the mode and adds the following permissions:

4   Sets user ID upon execution.

2   Sets group ID upon execution.

1   Sets the sticky bit.

Related Commands

chgrp
chown

6

chown
Change Owner

chown *option(s)*
newowner file(s)

Purpose

The chown command changes the ownership of a file or directory. The new owner is either a username or a user ID number (which are stored in /etc/passwd). You must be the owner of this file or a privileged user (in other words, root user) to change the ownership.

Options

-c   Prints information about the changes made.

-f   Ignores information about files that can't be changed.

-v   Verbose mode, where changes and failed changes are listed.

-R   Change recursively, which means that subdirectories are also changed.

Example

This changes the ownership of report to the user kevin:

```
$ chown kevin report
```

Related Commands

chmod
chgrp

chroot
Change Root
Directory

chroot *path command*

Purpose

The chroot command changes the root directory of a Linux system to that specified in *path*. This is typically done to run a command that you want to have a restricted view of the file system. Only the root user may change the root directory.

Example

The following example changes the root directory to /home/ftp and lists the contents of the new root directory:

```
# chroot /home/ftp ls /
bin   etc   lib   pub
```

compress
Compress Files

compress *option(s) file*

Purpose

The compress command compresses a file using adaptive Lempel-Ziv coding. This command works on one file at a time, although directories can also be compressed. Compressed files replace the original and end in .Z, retaining the same ownership modes, access, and modification times as the original file.

●—TIP

To uncompress a file compressed with the compress command, use the uncompress command.

Options

-c   Writes to standard output without changing files.

-f *file*   Forces compression of the specified file. This is used mainly when you want to compress an entire directory.

-v   Shows the percentage of reduction for each file
            compressed.

Related Commands

bzip2
gzip
gunzip
zcat

cp
Copy Files

cp option(s) *file1 file2*

cp option(s) *file1*
directory

cp option(s) *directory1*
directory2

Purpose

The cp command copies files — the contents of one file into another file, the contents of a file into a new directory, or the contents
of one directory into another. The existing file isn't changed.

Options

-a   Retains archival attributes.

-b   Creates a backup instead of overwriting an existing file.

-d   Maintains symbolic links between files.

-f   Forces copying.

-i   Turns on interactive mode, in which you are prompted
       before existing files are overwritten.

-l   Creates hard links between files copied to directories,
       instead of actually copying the files.

-p   Preserves existing permissions, including the ownership
       and time stamp.

-r   Copies entire directory and any subdirectories.

-R   Copies entire directory and any subdirectories.

-s   Creates symbolic links between files copied to directories, instead of actually copying the files.

-S   Sets a suffix to all new files; the default is ~ and is stored in the SIMPLE_BACKUP_SUFFIX environment variable. Don't change this variable, because other applications (notably emacs) also use it.

-u   Doesn't copy to new files that are newer than the existing file.

-v   Turns on verbose mode, in which all transactions are printed to the screen.

-V   Uses the version-control numbering set with the VERSION_CONTROL environment variable.

-x   Ignores subdirectories on remote file systems when copying.

Examples

This copies the file pat.letter into a new file called pat.old:

```
$ cp pat.letter pat.old
```

This copies the file kevin.letter, contained in the current directory, to the file kevin.letter, stored in the /home/Kevin directory:

```
$ cp kevin.letter /home/Kevin/kevin.letter
```

This copies the entire contents of /home/Kevin into the directory /home/Kevin/letters:

```
$ cp -r /home/Kevin /home/Kevin/letters
```

dd
Copy/Convert File
(GNU Command)

dd option(s)

Purpose

The dd command copies a file and performs a file conversion, if specified.

Options

if=*file*	Reads from *file* instead of standard input.
of=*file*	Writes to *file* instead of standard output.
ibs=*bytes*	Reads *bytes* bytes at a time.
obs=*bytes*	Writes *bytes* bytes at a time.
bs=*bytes*	Reads and writes *bytes* bytes at a time.
cbs=*bytes*	Converts *bytes* bytes at a time.
skip=*blocks*	Skips *blocks* ibs-sized blocks at the start of input.
seek=*blocks*	Skips *blocks* obs-sized blocks at the start of output.
count=*blocks*	Copies *blocks* ibs-sized input blocks.
conv=*conversion*	Converts the file into *conversion* format. The formats are as follows:

ascii	Converts EBCDIC to ASCII.
ebcdic	Converts ASCII to EBCDIC.
ibm	Converts ASCII to IBM's version of EBCDIC.
block	Pads newline-terminated records to size of cbs, replacing newline with trailing spaces.
unblock	Replaces trailing spaces in cbs-sized block with newline.
lcase	Converts uppercase characters to lowercase.
ucase	Converts lowercase characters to uppercase.
swab	Swaps every pair of input bytes.
noerror	Continues processing after receiving an error.
notrunc	Avoids truncating the output file.
sync	Pads every input block to the size of ibs with trailing NULs.

| dir
List Directory | dir *option(s) directory* |

Purpose

The dir command lists the content of a directory (for bash shells only). It's basically the same as the ls command, but it's included because MS-DOS uses dir and not ls to list directories.

Options

-A	Lists all hidden files beginning with a dot (.), except for the current (.) and parent (..) directories.
-a	Lists all hidden files beginning with a dot (.).
-B	Ignores backup files, which begin with a tilde (~).
-b	Prints octal escapes for nongraphic characters.
-C	Lists entries by column.
-c	Sorts by change time; displays the change time when combined with -1.
-D	Generates output suited to the emacs dired mode.
-d	Lists directory entries instead of contents.
-e	Lists both the date and the full time.
-F	Appends a character for typing each entry.
-f	Does not sort, enabling -aU and disabling -lsto.
-G	Inhibits display of group information.
-g	Ignored by dir; included for compatibility reasons.
-I*pattern*	Ignores entries matching *pattern*.
-I	Prints the index number of each file.
-k	Uses 1024 blocks, not 512.
-L	Lists entries pointed to by symbolic links.
-l	Uses a long listing format.
-m	Fills the width with a comma-separated list of entries.
-N	Does not quote entry names.
-n	Lists numeric UIDs and GIDs instead of names.

-o	Displays files in color according to type.
-p	Appends a character for typing each entry.
-Q	Encloses entry names in double quotes.
-q	Prints a question mark (?) instead of nongraphic characters.
-R	Lists subdirectories recursively.
-r	Lists files in reverse order while sorting.
-S	Sorts by file size.
-s	Prints the block size of each file.
-T*cols*	Sets tab stops at each *cols* instead of 8 characters.
-t	Sorts by modification time; displays the modification time when used with -1.
-U	List entries in directory order, without any sorting performed.
-u	Sorts by last access time; displays this time when used with -1.
-w*cols*	Assumes a screen width of *cols* (representing the number of characters) instead of current value.
-X	Sorts alphabetically by extension.
-x	Lists entries by lines instead of by columns.
-1	Lists one file per line.

**file
Display File Type**   **file** *option(s) filename*

Purpose

The file command returns the file type of a given file. Sometimes, the magic file (/etc/magic) must be consulted. Don't put a lot of stock into the information returned — the information returned by this command is not always correct, and it works best when detecting text-based or text-oriented file types, such as ASCII files, shell scripts, PostScript files, and commands.

Options

-c	Checks the magic file automatically.
-f *list*	Runs the file command on the files in *list*.
-L	Follows symbolic links.
-m *file*	Checks *file* for file types instead of the magic file.
-z	Checks compressed files.

find
Find File
(GNU Command)

find *pathname(s)*
condition(s)

Purpose

The find command finds a file. It can be just that simple, or it can be as complex as you'd like. You can enter any number of conditions — wildcards relating to the filename, when the file was created or last accessed, what links are present, and so on. It descends the directory tree, beginning with the root directory or another directory that you name.

You can use the find command to learn if someone really knows Linux. If they use the find command and always place -print at the end of a command line, that means they know UNIX, not Linux. In standard UNIX, the find command requires -print at the end of the command line, to tell the command to print output to the screen. However, the Linux version of find doesn't require -print, but instead assumes that you always want to print to the screen. So, any book or magazine article that includes -print as part of the example command lines shows that the author doesn't really know Linux.

Options

-amin *min*	Replace *min* with any of the following to find files that were accessed:
	+*m* more than *m* minutes ago.
	m exactly *m* minutes ago.
	-*m* less than *m* minutes ago.

-anewer *file*	Finds files that were accessed after they were modified.
-atime *days*	Finds files that were accessed:
	+d more than *d* days ago.
	d exactly *d* days ago.
	-d less than *d* days ago.
-cmin *min*	Finds files that were changed:
	+m more than *m* minutes ago.
	m exactly *m* minutes ago.
	-m less than *m* minutes ago.
-cnewer *file*	Finds files that were changed after they were modified.
-ctime *days*	Finds files that were changed:
	+d more than *d* days ago.
	d exactly *d* days ago.
	-d less than *d* days ago.
-daystart	Assumes that times are calculated from the beginning of the day, not from now.
-empty	Continues the search even if a file is empty.
-exec *command* {}\;	Runs the Linux command after a file is found.
-false	Returns a false value if a match is made.
-follow	Follows symbolic links and the associated directories.
-fstype *type*	Finds files stored on specific file system *type*: ufs, 4.2, 4.3, nfs, tmp, mfs, S51K, and S52K.
-gid *num*	Finds files belonging to a specific group *num*.
-group *group*	Finds files belonging to a specific group, which can be an ID or a name.
-ilname *file*	Searches for symbolic links pointing to file, which can include metacharacters and wildcards. The case doesn't matter.
-iname *file*	Finds a file named *file*. The case doesn't matter.

6

-inum *num*	Finds files with a specific inode number of *num*.
-ipath *name*	Finds files that match *name*, which is an absolute path name. The case doesn't matter.
-links *num*	Finds files with *num* number of links.
-lname *file*	Searches for symbolic links pointing to *file*, which can include metacharacters and wildcards. The case must match.
-maxdepth *num*	Stops search after descending *num* levels of directories.
-mindepth *num*	Begins search at *num* levels of directories and lower.
-mmin *min*	Finds files that were modified:
	+*m* more than *m* minutes ago.
	m exactly *m* minutes ago.
	-*m* less than *m* minutes ago.
-mtime *days*	Finds files that were modified:
	+*d* more than *d* days ago.
	d exactly *d* days ago.
	-*d* less than *d* days ago.
-name *file*	Finds a file named *file*. The case must match.
-newer *file*	Finds files that have been modified more recently than *file*.
-nogroup	Finds files whose group owner isn't listed in /etc/group.
-nouser	Finds files whose owner isn't listed in /etc/passwd.
-ok *command* {}\;	Runs the Linux command after a file is found, verifying that you do indeed want to run the command.
-path *name*	Finds files that match *name*, which is an absolute path name. The case matters.
-perm *nnn*	Finds files that have permissions matching specified file permissions (such as *rwx*).

`-size num[c]`	Finds a file containing *num* blocks or *num* characters if *c* is added.
`-type t`	Returns names of file whose type is *t*, which can be b (block special file), c (character special file), d (directory), f (plain file), l (symbolic link), p (pipe), or s (socket).
`-user user`	Finds files belonging to specified *user*.

Examples

The following finds all the files on the entire file system that have been changed less than two days ago:

```
$ find / -ctime -2
```

This lists all the files and directories in your home directory:

```
$ find $HOME
```

fromdos
Convert from DOS

> **fromdos < *dosfile.txt* >**
> ***unixfile.txt***

Purpose

The `fromdos` command takes a DOS text file and converts it to a UNIX file, replacing the carriage-return/linefeed (CR LF) sequence at the end of DOS text files to the UNIX linefeed (LF) usage.

funzip
Extract Content
from Zip File

> **funzip *password***
> ***input_file***

Purpose

The `funzip` command is a filter for extracting from a Zip archive in a pipe.

Related Commands

`gzip`

```
unzip
zip
```

| **getfilename Rename File in New Format** | getfilename *format-name* *filename* |

Purpose

The getfilename command asks a user to name a file in a given format. It's not useful on its own, but becomes useful when combined with a mailcap-oriented command, such as mailto.

Related Commands

```
mailto
metamail
```

| **gunzip Unzip Archive (GNU Command)** | gunzip *option(s) file(s)* |

Purpose

The gunzip command is used to unzip files compressed with the gzip command or the UNIX compress and pack commands.

Options

-c   Uses standard output without changing the original files.

-N   Keeps the original name and time stamp.

-q   Works in quiet mode, without returning status information.

-t   Tests the new file for data integrity.

-v   Works in verbose mode, with all changes noted to the screen, including the name of the new file.

Related Commands

```
compress
gzip
pack
```

**gzexe
Compress
Executable
(GNU Command)**   *gzexe option file(s)*

Purpose

The gzexe command compresses executable files. When you go to run the compressed executable file, it automatically uncompresses and is run. It takes a little longer to run compressed commands, but you can save on precious disk space.

Option

-d   Decompresses compressed executable command.

**gzip
Compress File
(GNU Command)**   *gzip option(s) file(s)*

Purpose

The gzip command compresses a file using Lempel-Ziv coding. A compressed file is renamed *file*.gz and the original is deleted. The access permissions and time stamps associated with the original file are maintained by the new compressed file.

Options

-c   Uses standard output without changing the original files.

-d   Decompresses files (the same as gunzip).

-f	Forces compression in cases where a compressed file already exists, has multiple links, or is already compressed.
-l	Creates compressed files out of files that are already compressed by deflate, compress, gzip, lzh, or pack.
-N	Keeps the original name and time stamp.
-q	Works in quiet mode, without returning status information.
-r	Works in recursive mode, in which subdirectories are also compressed.
-S *suffix*	Adds specified *suffix* to the new filename, instead of the default .gz.
-t	Tests the new file for data integrity.
-v	Works in verbose mode, with all changes noted to the screen, including the name of the new file.

Related Command

gunzip

hattrib **Change File** **Attributes**	**hattrib** *option(s)* *hfs_path*

Purpose

The hattrib command alters HFS (Macintosh) file attributes.

Options

-c	Sets the creator attributes.
-t	Sets the type attributes.
+i	Sets the invisible flag.
-i	Clears the invisible flag.
+l	Sets the locked flag.
-l	Clears the locked flag.

Related Commands

hcopy
hls

hcd Change Working Directory	hcd *hfs_path*

Purpose

The hcd command changes the "current working directory" for the current HFS volume. All subsequent HFS commands interpret file-names relative to this directory.

Option

hfs_path   Sets path to the new working directory.

Related Commands

hls
hpwd

hcopy Copy Files	hcopy *mode source_path* *target_path*

Purpose

The hcopy command transfers files between an HFS volume to a Linux file system. The target path must be a directory if multiple files are copied.

Modes

-m   MacBinary II, recommended for copying binary files.

-b   BinHex, recommended for ASCII files; both forks of the Macintosh file are preserved.

-t   Text, copying only the data fork of the Macintosh file and performing end-of-line translation.

-r   Raw data, performing no translation and copying only the data fork.

-s   Automatic, where hcopy determines what mode would
      work best.

Related Commands

hattrib
hls

| **hdel**
Delete File | **hdel** *hfs_path* |

Purpose
The hdel command deletes both forks of a Macintosh data file.

Related Command
hrmdir

| **hdir**
Display Directory | **hdir** *hfs_path* |

Purpose
The hdir command displays the contents of an HFS directory in
long format. It's the same as hls −1.

Related Command
hls

| **hformat**
Create HFS
File System | **hformat** *option(s)*
destination partition |

Purpose
The hformat command creates a new HFS file system to a volume.
The key is that a Linux path name to the volume's destination
must be specified (either as a block device or as a regular file)
and already exist.

Options

-f	Formats an entire partition as a single file system, erasing all existing data.
-l *label*	Specifies a label for the new HFS file system.

---

hfs
Run HFS Shell   **hfs *hfs_path partition***

Purpose

The hfs command launches a Tcl-based shell for manipulating
HFS volumes. Within hfc, you can run a variety of commands
to mount volumes, change directories, and do other operations.

Commands

mount *path*	Mounts the *path* as an HFS volume.
umount *path*	Unmounts the previously mounted *path*.
vol *path*	Makes current the previously mounted *path*.
info	Returns information about the currently mounted volume.
pwd	Prints the full path to the HFS directory.
cd *directory*	Changes the current working directory to *path*.
dir *directory*	Returns the contents of the specified *directory*.
mkdir *directory*	Creates a new, empty directory at *directory*.
rmdir *directory*	Removes the specified *directory*.
create *path*	Creates a new file at *path*.
del *file*	Deletes both forks of the specified *file*.
stat *path*	Returns status information about the specified HFS *path*.
cat *file*	Displays the data fork of the specified HFS *file*.
copyin *unixfile* *hfsfile*	Copies the UNIX file to the HFS volume.
copyout *hfsfile* *unixfile*	Copies the HFS file to the UNIX volume.
format *path*	Formats the specified UNIX *path*.

Related Command

xhfs

hls **List Contents**	**hls** *option(s) hfs_path*

Purpose

The hls command lists the files and directories in an HFS volume.

Options

-1	Lists one file per line.
-a	Lists all files in a directory, including hidden files.
-b	Displays nongraphic characters, using alphabetic and octal backslash sequences similar to those used in C.
-c	Sorts contents according to status change time.
-d	Lists directory names , without their contents.
-f	Displays contents as found in disk, and not sorted in any way.
-i	Displays catalog IDs for each file.
-l	Lists files in long format, including the file type, permissions, number of hard links, owner name, group name, size in bytes, and time stamp (the modification time, unless other times are selected).
-m	Lists files horizontally, separated by commas.
-q	Prints question marks in the place of nongraphic characters in filenames.
-r	Sorts filenames in reverse order.
-s	Prints the size of the file (in 1K blocks) to the left of the filename.
-t	Sorts files by time stamp (newest first) instead of alphabetically.
-x	Prints listings in columns, sorted horizontally.
-w cols	Sets the screen as *cols* characters wide. The default is 80.

-C	Lists files in columns, sorted vertically.
-F	Lists the file types by character: / for directories, @ for symbolic links, | for FIFOs, = for sockets, * for Macintosh executables, and nothing for regular files.
-N	Lists files verbatim without any escaping or question mark substitution.
-Q	Encloses filenames in double quotes ("") and displays nongraphic characters as they would be displayed in the C programming language.
-R	Lists contents of directories recursively.
-S	Sorts files by file size, not alphabetically, with the largest files first.
-U	Displays contents as found in disk, and not sorted in any way.

Related Commands

hcd
hcopy
hdir
hpwd

hmount **Mount HFS Volume**	**hmount** *path partition*

Purpose

The hmount command mounts a new HFS volume and makes it current.

Related Commands

hformat
humount
hvol

hpwd **Print Working** **Directory**	**hpwd**

Purpose

The hpwd command displays the full path name of the current working directory.

Related Command

hcd

hrename **Rename HFS File**	hrename *source_path* *target_path*

Purpose

The hrename command changes the name and/or location of a specified file or directory.

hrmdir **Remove HFS** **Directory**	hrmdir *directory*

Purpose

The hrmdir command removes an empty HFS directory from the current volume.

humount **Unmount HFS** **Volume**	humount *volume*

Purpose

The humount command unmounts a current HFS volume.

Related Command

hmount

hvol
Display Current
Volume

hvol *path*

Purpose

The hvol command displays the name and path to the current HFS volume.

Related Commands

hmount
humount

6

ln
Link Files

ln *option(s) originalfile*
linkfile

ln *option(s) file(s)*
directory

Purpose

The ln command links two or more files. As a result, only one copy of a file exists though it can be accessed by multiple names and from different directories. The purpose is to cut down on disk space used by files. Although you may not feel the need to link files on your single-user Linux system, you may feel the need if you're overseeing a network installation. And Linux itself uses links in a standard installation; some Linux files are stored in nonstandard locations, but links make it appear that the standard locations are valid.

The two types of links are hard links and symbolic links. For the most part, you'll want to stick with symbolic links, because they're easier to keep track of with the ls command.

●—**TIP**

You can either keep the same name for both files or have a new name for the link file. Always remember that the first name is the original file, and the second name is the new, link file; if you reverse the order, you'll trash your original file.

Options

-b	Backs up the original file before removing it.
-d	Creates hard links to directories (available only to privileged users).
-f	Forces the link, without asking for permission to overwrite existing files.
-F	Creates hard links to directories (available only to privileged users).
-i	Confirms before overwriting existing files.
-n	Replaces symbolic links before dereferencing them.
-s	Creates a symbolic link.
-S *suffix*	Adds *suffix* to the end of a backed-up file, instead of the standard tilde (~).

Example

This links the file kevin to the pat file:
$ ln pat kevin

Related Commands

chmod
chown
cp
ls
mv

locate	locate *option(s)*
Locate Pattern	*pattern(s)*

Purpose

The locate command locates a pattern in a database of filenames and returns the filenames that match. A pattern can contain shell-style metacharacters (*, ?, and []), but / and . are treated as part of the filename. If there are no metacharacters, then all filenames that contain the string are returned from the database. (The string doesn't have to match the whole file name.) If metacharacters are included, the locate command displays filenames that contain the exact pattern, so use * at the beginning or end of a pattern with metacharacters.

Options

-d *path*   Searches the filename database in *path*, a colon-separated list of database filenames.

--help   Prints a list of options and exits.

--version   Returns the version number of the locate command.

Related Commands

```
find
locatedb
lockfile
updatedb
xargs
```

6

locatedb
Locate File
(GNU Command)

locatedb *option(s)*
pattern(s)

Purpose

The locatedb command locates a pattern in a database of filenames and returns the filenames that match. A pattern can contain shell-style metacharacters (*, ?, and []), but / and . are treated as part of the filename. If there are no metacharacters, then all filenames that contain the string are returned from the database. (The string doesn't have to match the whole file name.) If metacharacters are included, the locatedb command displays filenames that contain the exact pattern, so use * at the beginning or end of a pattern with metacharacters.

Related Commands

```
find
locate
lockfile
updatedb
xargs
```

lockfile Lock File	lockfile *option filename*

Purpose

The lockfile command creates one or more semaphore files, which
limit access to a file. If lockfile can't create the semaphore files in
order, it waits for eight seconds and tries again; you can use the -r
option to specify the number of times it will retry. The resulting
files will have an access permission of 0 and need to be removed
with rm -f.

Option

-r *num*   Retries *num* number of times before giving up.

Related Command

rm

ls List Files (GNU Command)	ls *option(s) name(s)*

Purpose

The ls command lists the contents of a specified directory
or extended information about a specified file. If no name is
given, then it's assumed that you want the contents of the
current directory. By default, files are listed in columns, sorted
vertically. Although this can be a complex command, especially
in the option-laden GNU version (with 38 options), chances
are good that you'll use the -F and -l options the most and
use the -u and -c options the least.

Options

-1   Lists one file per line.

-A   Lists all the contents of a directory, except for the
            current directory (.) and the parent directory (..).
            All other hidden files are shown, however.

-b	Displays nongraphic characters using alphabetic and octal backslash sequences that are the same as sequences used in the C programming language.
-B	Ignores backups (files ending with ~).
-c	Sorts contents according to status change time.
-C	Lists files in columns, sorted vertically.
-d	Lists all file and directory names, without listing the contents of the directories.
-e	Lists all times in full.
-f	Displays contents as found in disk, and not sorted in any way.
-F	Lists the file types by character: / for directories, @ for symbolic links, | for FIFOs, = for sockets, and nothing for regular files.
-G	Omits group ownership when listing files in long format.
-i	Displays an inode number of each file.
-I pattern	Ignores files that match pattern.
-k	Lists file sizes in kilobytes.
-l	Lists files in long format, including the file type, permissions, number of hard links, owner name, group name, size in bytes, and time stamp (the modification time, unless other times are selected).
-L	Displays files by symbolic links instead of listing the contents of the links.
-m	Lists files horizontally, separated by commas.
-n	Lists the numeric UID and GID instead of the filenames.
-N	Omits filenames from the listings.
-o	Toggles the display of the files by colors.
-p	Appends a character to each filename, indicating the type.
-q	Prints question marks in the place of nongraphic characters in filenames.
-Q	Encloses filenames in double quotes ("") and displays nongraphic characters as they are displayed in the C programming language.

-r	Sorts filenames in reverse order.
-R	Lists contents of directories recursively.
-s	Prints the size of the file (in 1K blocks) to the left of the filename.
-S	Sorts files by file size, not alphabetically, with the largest files first.
-t	Sorts files by time stamp (newest first) instead of alphabetically.
-T*cols*	Sets the tab stops at *cols* columns. The default is 8. Setting 0 disables tabs.
-u	Sorts files by the last time they were accessed, not modified.
-U	Displays contents as found in disk, and not sorted in any way.
-w *cols*	Sets the screen as *cols* characters wide. The default is 80.
-x	Prints listings in columns, sorted horizontally.
-X	Sorts files alphabetically by file extensions.

Related Command

dircolors

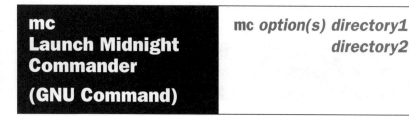

mc Launch Midnight Commander (GNU Command)	mc *option(s) directory1* *directory2*

Purpose

The mc command launches the Midnight Commander, a directory browser and file manager for Linux that doesn't require the X Window System. It allows you to move, copy, and delete files and directories, either with mouse actions and pull-down menus or with commands entered on a command line, such as with the vi command.

● **CROSS-REFERENCE**

An extensive set of commands is associated with the Midnight Commander; see the online man pages for more details.

Options

-b	Works in black and white.
-c	Works in color.
-C arg	Uses arg color set instead of the default.
-d	Turns off mouse support.
-f	Displays compiled-in search paths for Midnight Commander files.
-l file	Saves the ftpfs dialog with the server in file.
-P	Prints the last working directory after Midnight Commander exits. (See the online man pages for shell scripts that make this option very useful.)
-s	Works in slow mode, in which line drawings are suppressed and verbose mode is turned off.
-t	Uses TERMCAP (/etc/termcap) for terminal information.
-u	Disables a concurrent shell.
-U	Enables a concurrent shell.
-v file	Launches the internal viewer to view file.
-x	Works under xterm.

---

merge
Merge Three Files

merge *option(s) file1*
file2 file3

Purpose

The merge command merges three files, incorporating all changes that lead from *file2* to *file3* into *file1*. The command warns you if a conflict exists between the files. The merge command works similarly to the diff3 command, and many of the options associated with diff3 are supported in merge.

Related Commands

```
diff
diff3
```

mkdir Make Directory (GNU Command)	mkdir *option(s)* *directories*

Purpose

The mkdir command is used to create directories. It can also be used to create a directory hierarchy. The default mode of new directories is 0777.

Options

-m *mode*   Sets the mode of the new directories to *mode*.

-p   Creates new parent directories, as needed.

mkdirhier Make Directory Hierarchy	mkdirhier *directory*

Purpose

The mkdirhier command creates a directory hierarchy. This command is made redundant by the GNU version of the mkdir command, which will create a directory hierarchy.

Related Command

mkdir

mkdosfs Make DOS FAT File System	mkdosfs *option(s)*

Purpose

The mkdosfs command creates an MS-DOS FAT file system under Linux on a device (usually a disk partition).

Options

-c	Checks the partition for bad blocks.
-f *fats*	Specifies the number of File Allocation Tables (*fats*) in the file system. The default — and limit — is 2.
-F *fatsize*	Specifies the type of File Allocation Tables (*fats*) used: 12-, 16-, or 32-bit. This is the option to use when creating a FAT32 file system.
-i *volume*	Sets the volume ID of the new file system.
-l *filename*	Reads the bad blocks list from *filename*.
-m *message_file*	Sets the message a user receives when booting the file system without having properly installed an operating system.
-n *volume*	Sets the volume name of the file system.
-r *dir_entries*	Sets the number of entries available in the root directory.
-s *sectors*	Sets the number of disk sectors per cluster.

Related Command
mkfs

mkfifo
Make FIFO
(GNU Command)

mkfifo *option(s)*
filename

Purpose
The mkfifo command creates a FIFO, or a named pipe. The mode of the new FIFO is 0666.

Option
-m *mode*   Sets the mode of new FIFOs to *mode*.

mkfontdir
Make Font
Directory
(X Winow System
Command)

mkfontdir *directory*

Purpose

The mkfontdir command creates an index of X font files, fonts.
dir, in the specified directory. You have no option to change this
filename, and you wouldn't want to — this is the name that the X
font server and the X server look to for font information.

Related Commands

xfs
xset

mkfs
Build a File System

mkfs *option(s)*
filesystem blocks

Purpose

The mkfs command builds a Linux file system on a specified device,
usually a hard-disk partition. The *filesystem* can be a device name or
a mount point, while *blocks* refers to the number of blocks used for
the file system.

●—NOTE

This command is actually a front end to the many commands needed to
build a file system.

Options

-l *filename*	Read the bad blocks list from *filename*.
-v	Verbose output.
-c	Checks for bad blocks before building the file system.
-t *fstype*	Specifies the type of file system to build.
-V	Provides information about each of the steps needed to produce a file system.

mkmanifest
Restore Linux
Filenames

mkmanifest *file(s)*

Purpose

The mkmanifest command creates a shell script to restore
Linux filenames that have been truncated by the MS-DOS
filename restrictions.

Related Command

mtools

mknod
Make Special Files
(GNU Command)

mknod *option(s)*
filename filetype
major_dev minor_dev

Purpose

The mknod command creates special files (FIFOs, character
special files, or block special files) with the given filename.
The default mode of these files is 0666. The file type can be
one of the following:

p   FIFO.

b   Block (buffered) special file.

c   Character (buffered) special file.

u   Character (unbuffered) special file.

●—NOTE

Major_dev and *minor_dev* refer to major and minor device numbers.

Option

-m *mode*   Sets the mode of the new file to *mode*. This is a symbolic value.

mv **Move Files**	**mv** *option(s) sources* *target*

Purpose

The mv command moves files — or, more accurately, gives them a
new name and a new location on the file hierarchy. If the target
names a directory, mv moves the sources into files with the same
names in that directory. Otherwise, if two files are given as source
and target, it moves the first file onto the second. If the new file is
unwritable, mv will ask you to confirm that you want to overwrite
a file.

Options

-b   Creates backups before removing files.

-f   Removes existing destination files without prompting you.

-i   Prompts you before overwriting destination files.

-S   Sets a new suffix for backups; the system default is ~.
Other commands assume that the suffix is ~, so don't
change this unless you have a good reason.

-u   Declines moving a file to a new destination with the same
or a newer modification time.

-v   Verbose mode; prints the name of each file before moving it.

Related Command

cp

newgrp **Change Group** **Permissions**	**newgrp** *groupname*

Purpose

The newgrp command changes your group permissions after
you've already logged in to the system. If you don't specify
a new *groupname*, your login groupname is used.

Related Commands

```
login
```

**od
Print Octal File
Offsets
(GNU Command)**

od *option(s) file*

Purpose

The od command prints file offsets in octal and the file data as 2-byte octal numbers. A host of options is available.

●—**CROSS-REFERENCE**

To see the other available options, check out the online manual pages for more information.

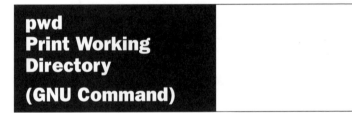

**pwd
Print Working
Directory
(GNU Command)**

pwd

Purpose

The pwd command prints the name of the current (working) directory.

●—**CAUTION**

Don't confuse this command with this `passwd` command (covered in Chapter 5), which changes passwords.

rm **Remove Files** **(GNU Command)**	rm *option(s) filename*

Purpose

The rm command removes files from the Linux file system. You are prompted before the file is actually removed (if rm is run with the -i option).

Options

-d   Removes linked directories with the unink command instead of the rmdir command. (Only root users have access to the -d option.)

-f   Ignores nonexistent files.

-i   Explicitly sets prompting before removing files.

-r   Removes the contents of directories recursively.

-v   Works in verbose mode, printing the name of each file before removing it.

rmdir **Remove Empty** **Directory** **(GNU Command)**	rmdir *option(s)* *directory*

Purpose

The rmdir command removes empty directories. Directories with contents will not be deleted.

Option

-p   Removes parent directories if they're mentioned as part of the command line.

size List Sizes (GNU Command)	size *option(s) object-* *file(s)*

Purpose

The size command lists the section sizes and the total size for the *object-file(s)* listed on the command line. One line of output is generated for each file.

Options

-A	Output resembles System V size output.
-B	Output resembles Berkeley size format.
-d	Sizes are listed in decimals.
-o	Sizes are listed in octals.
-x	Sizes are listed in hexadecimal.
--target bfdname	Specifies object-code format as *bfdname*.

sq Squeeze Word List	sq *inputfile outputfile*

Purpose

The sq command squeezes a sorted word list. It's generally used for large text files, such as dictionaries. The squeezing is achieved by eliminating common prefixes and replacing them with a single character, which encodes the number of characters shared with the preceding word.

Related Command

unsq

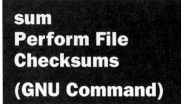

sum
Perform File
Checksums
(GNU Command)

sum option(s)
filename(s)

Purpose

The sum command performs a checksum on a file and counts the blocks. It computes a 16-bit checksum for each named file. It prints the checksum for each file along with the number of blocks in the file. The GNU version of sum computes checksums using an algorithm that is compatible with the BSD sum command, and prints file sizes in units of 1K blocks.

Options

-r   Uses the BSD-compatible algorithm, which is the default.

-s   Uses a System V-compatible algorithm and prints out file sizes in 512-byte blocks.

test
Check File Type
(GNU Command)

test *expression*

Purpose

The test command returns a status of 0 (true) or 1 (false) depending on the evaluation of the conditional expression, which can be unary or binary. A long list of expressions is available.

●—**CROSS-REFERENCE**——————————————————————

For more information about the available expressions, check the online manual or info pages.

unsq Unsqueeze Word List	unsq *inputfile outputfile*

Purpose

The unsq command unsqueezes a sorted word list that's been squeezed by the sq command.

Related Command

sq

unzip Unzip File	unzip *option(s)*

Purpose

The unzip command unzips a file that's been compressed using the PKZip or WinZip Zip format found on MS-DOS/Windows systems.

●—CROSS-REFERENCE

See the online manual pages for more information on the many options available.

Related Command

unzipsfx

unzipsfx Create Self- Extracting Zip	unzipsfx *option(s)*

Purpose

The unzipsfx command creates a new archive file with unzip prepended to existing Zip archives, forming self-extracting archives.

● CROSS-REFERENCE

See the online manual pages for more information on the many options available.

Related Command

unzip

updatedb
Update Filename
Database
(GNU Command)

updatedb *option(s)*

Purpose

The updatedb command updates a filename database used by the locate command. This database contains lists of files that were in particular directory trees when the databases were last updated.

Options

--localpaths=*path1* *path2*	Specifies nonnetwork directories to put in the database.
--netpaths=*path1* *path2*	Specifies network directories to put in the database.
--netuser=*user*	Specifies the user to search network directories as.
--old-format	Creates the database in the old format instead of the new one.
--output=*dbfile*	Specifies the database file to build.
--prunepaths=*path1* *path2*	Specifies directories not to put in the database.

Related Command

locate

xfilemanager Launch X-Based File Manager (X Window System Command)	xfilemanager *option(s)*

Purpose

The xfilemanager command launches an X-based file manager with drag-and-drop capabilities. It can be used to perform all the usual file-manager tasks, such as moving and copying files, launching applications, and managing directories.

Options

-doubleClickTime *time*	Sets the interval within mouse clicks before they are treated as double-clicks; the default is 300 milliseconds.
-iconDir *path*	Sets the file-icons directory.
-iconFont *fontname*	Sets the font to be used with the icons.
-multiWindow	Displays directories in separate windows.
-noDragCopyAsk	Doesn't ask for confirmation before copying a file by dragging it.
-noDragDeleteAsk	Doesn't ask for confirmation before deleting a file by dragging it.
-NoDragExecAsk	Doesn't ask for confirmation before executing a file by dragging it.
-noDragMoveAsk	Doesn't ask for confirmation before moving a file by dragging it.
-rootDir *path*	Sets the opening directory. The default is the user's home directory.
-saveWS	Saves workspace settings before exiting.
-selectColor *colorname*	Sets the color used to mark selected files.

-singleWindow	Displays everything in one big window.
-trashcan *directory*	Turns on the trashcan option; deleted files are sent to the trashcan directory, instead of being deleted from the system.

Related Commands

mc
xfm

xfm
Launch X-Based
File Manager
(X Window System
Command)

xfm *option(s)*

Purpose

The xfm command launches an X-based file manager with drag-and-drop capabilities. It can be used to perform all the usual file-manager tasks, such as moving and copying files, launching applications, and managing directories. It actually has two different components that work together: an application manager and a file manager.

●─NOTE─────────────────────────────

Before running this command on a new system, use the xfm.install script to create new configuration files.

Options

-appmgr	Launches only the application manager.
-filemgr	Launches only the file manager.

Related Commands

mc
xfilemanager

xhfs
Open HFS File Manager
(X Window System Command)

xhfs *left_path*
right_path

Purpose

The xhfs command opens a graphical application for copying and browsing files. The display has two sides: one with an HFS volume and one with a Linux file system. You can view text files by double-clicking them, or you can copy a file by selecting it and pressing the Copy button. After you press the Copy button, you can select from the following modes:

-m   MacBinary II, recommended for copying binary files.

-b   BinHex, recommended for ASCII files; both forks of the Macintosh file are preserved.

-t   Text, copying only the data fork of the Macintosh file and performing end-of-line translation.

-r   Raw data, performing no translation and copying only the data fork.

-s   Automatic, where hcopy determines what mode would work best.

Related Commands

hcopy
hfs

zcat
Uncompress Gzip File

zcat *file*

Purpose

The zcat command uncompresses a gzip-compressed file and writes it to standard output, usually the screen (in the same manner that the cat command works).

Related Commands

cat
gzip

zforce Force New Filename	zforce *filename(s)*

Purpose

The zforce command forces files compressed with the gzip command to have a file extension of .gz.

Related Command

gzip

znew Recompressed File (GNU Command)	znew *option(s)* *filename.Z filename.gz*

Purpose

The znew command takes existing compressed .Z files and recompresses them in the gzip (.gz) format. The old .Z file will then be deleted.

Options

-9	Optimal compression method; also the slowest.
-f *filename*.gz	Compresses new *filename*.gz, even if *filename*.gz already exists.
-K	Checks whether the new *filename*.gz file is smaller than the old *filename*.Z file; if not, then no recompression work is done.
-P	Pipes to conversion program, conserving disk space.

-t	Tests new *filename*.gz before deleting old *filename*.Z file.
-v	Verbose mode.

Related Command

gzip

---

zoo
Manipulate
Compressed
Archives

zoo *option(s) archivefile*

Purpose

The zoo command uses the Lempel-Ziv compression algorithm to create file archives. It can work with multiple generations of the same file and store each generation. To see a summary of zoo options, type zoo -h.

●—CROSS-REFERENCE

See the voluminous online zoo manual page for more information.

in plain english in p
sh in plain english in
glish in plain english
in plain english in p
sh in plain english in
glish in plain english
in plain english in p
glish in plain english
in plain english in p
sh in plain english in
glish in plain english
in plain english in p
sh in plain english in
glish in plain english
in plain english in p
lish in plain english
in plain english in p
sh in plain english in
glish in plain english
in plain english in p
sh in plain english in
lish in plain english
in plain english in p
glish in plain english

Text-Processing Commands

These commands are designed to work directly with text files. With Linux, this can mean any number of things: end users can use these commands to edit or create letters and memos, programmers can use these commands to edit source code, and system administrators can use these commands to create and edit configuration files.

bpe bpe Edit Binary Files	bpe filename

Purpose

The bpe command is used to modify or edit binary files, either in hexadecimal or ASCII. Several commands are available as the binary file is displayed; to go into editing mode, select e for ASCII edit, or E for hex edit.

Commands

D   Dumps one page from the current file position.

e   Edits the ASCII part of the file.

E   Edits the hex part of the file.

F   Finds a string in the file, after the current file position.

H   Locates hex bytes in the file, after the current file position.

N   Displays the next sector.

P   Displays the previous sector.

Q   Quits the program.

S   Sets the current file pointer.

W   Writes the modified sector to disk.

+   Scrolls forward two lines.

-    Scrolls backward two lines.

/   Finds a string in the file, after the current file position.

?   Displays help information.

Related Commands

hd
od

cat Read and Print Files	cat *option(s) files*

Purpose

The cat command is the most useful command in the Linux operating system, thanks to the many (mostly) mundane functions that it performs. On a basic level, it reads a file and prints it to standard output (usually the screen, unless standard output has been piped to another command or file). The cat command can also be combined with the > operator to combine files into a single file, as well as the > operator to append files to an existing file. Finally, the cat command can create a new text file when combined with the name of a new file.

Options

-A or --show-all	Prints nonprinting and control characters, except for linefeeds and tabs; places a dollar sign at the end of each line; and prints tabs as ^I. (The same as -vET.)
-e, -E, or --show-ends	Prints a dollar sign ($) at the end of each line.
-n	Numbers the lines, beginning with 1 at the beginning of the first line.
-s	Squeezes out blank lines.
-t ^L.	Prints each tab as ^I and form feeds as
-T or --show-tabs	Prints each tab as ^I.
-u	Doesn't do anything; exists for compatibility with other UNIX scripts.
-v	Shows nonprinting and control characters, except for linefeeds and tabs.

Examples

This displays the file named report:

```
$ cat report
```

This displays the file report, followed immediately by the file report2:

```
$ cat report report2
```

This combines report and report2 into a new file called report3. The combination occurs in the order that the files are specified on the command line.

```
$ cat report report2 > report3
```

This copies the contents of the file report into a new file named report2. The old file report remains unchanged.

```
$ cat report > report2
```

This creates a new file named report and sends your subsequent keyboard input into the file. You can end the input by pressing Ctrl + D.

```
$ cat > report
```

This places the contents of the file report at the end of the existing file report2:

```
$ cat report > report2
```

This places keyboard input at the end of the existing file report2. You can end the input by pressing Ctrl + D.

```
$ cat - > report
```

Related Commands

```
cp
more
page
```

cmp
Compare Contents
of Two Files

cmp option(s)
filename1 filename2

Purpose

The cmp command compares the contents of two files. If no difference exists between the files, cmp returns nothing. If the files are different, then cmp returns the line number and byte position of the first difference. This command can be used with binary files as well as text files, as opposed to text-only tools, such as the diff command.

Options

-c   Prints the differing bytes as characters.

-i *num*   Ignores the first *num* of bytes in the files.

-l   Displays the byte position and differing characters for all differences within the files.

-s   Works in silent mode, returning only the exit codes and
            not any instances of differences. The exit code is one of
            the following:

            0   Files are identical.

            1   Files are different.

            2   One of the files cannot be read.

Example

```
$ cmp report memo
report memo differ: char 12, line 1
```

Related Commands

```
comm
diff
sdiff
```

colrm
Remove Columns

colrm *start stop*

Purpose

The colrm command takes text from standard input, removes the
specified columns, then sends the results to standard output. To
specify which columns to cut, replace *start* with the column number to start with and *stop* with the column number to end with.

Example

In the following example, there is a long listing of a directory
that is piped to the colrm command. The numbers 1 and 15 tell
colrm to strip out the first 15 characters of each line and print the
rest of the output. Try changing the numbers to have different
columns of characters stripped out.

```
$ ls -l | colrm 1 15
```

column
Format Input
Into Columns

column *option(s) file*

Purpose

The column command formats input into columns, whether from a file or from standard input.

Options

-c *num*   Sets the number of columns as *num*.

-s *char*   Sets *char* as the column delimiter. Must be used in conjunction with -t.

-t   Formats input as a table and not as a column. The default is to format with spaces, unless an alternative has been set with -s.

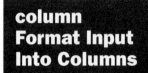

-x   Fills characters before filling the rows.

comm
Compare Contents
of Two Files

comm *option(s) file1*
file2

Purpose

The comm command compares the contents of two files that have already been sorted with the sort command. The output is sorted into three columns:

    Lines in *file1*   Lines in *file2*   Lines in both files

●—NOTE

This command is similar to the diff and uniq commands, except that comm can be used with two sorted files to seek out duplicate or unique lines.

Options

-1   Suppresses the printing of the first column.

-2   Suppresses the printing of the second column.

-3   Suppresses the printing of the third column.

-12   Suppresses the printing of the first and second columns.

-13   Suppresses the printing of the first and third columns.

-23   Suppresses the printing of the second and third columns.

Related Commands

```
cmp
diff
sdiff
sort
uniq
```

csplit	csplit *option(s)*
Split a Long File	*file arguments*

Purpose

The csplit command splits a long file into two or more smaller files. You can tell csplit to split files based on size or by content, using specific expressions as markers for splitting. The original file will be unchanged.

The new files will begin with *xx*. The first file is *xx*00 (remember, Linux likes to begin everything with 0), the next file is *xx*01, and so on. The limit is 100 files, so the highest filename numerically is *xx*99.

Options

-f *txt*   Uses *txt* instead of *xx* to begin the new filenames.

-k   Keeps files even if the command line fails.

-n *num*   Uses numbers that are *num* characters long in filenames, instead of two, the default.

-q   Suppresses character counts.

-s   Suppresses character counts.

-z   Doesn't create empty files, but does maintain numbering.

Arguments

/expr/	Creates a file that begins with a current line to the line containing *expr*. You can add a suffix that ends a file *num* lines before or after *expr* — either +*num* or -*num*.
%expr%	Causes the section from the current line up to the first line containing *expr* to be ignored.
line	Creates a file at the current line and ends one line before *line*.
{n}	Repeats an argument *n* number of lines. The default is to repeat an argument once.

Example

This splits a file named bonfire into 20 chapters, each beginning with *Chapter*.

```
$ csplit -k bonfire '/Chapter/' {20}
```

cut	**cut** *option(s) files*
Cut File Columns	
or Fields	

Purpose

The cut command cuts columns or fields from a file or set of files and displays them. You can use the information to view parts of a file, or else you can take the information and send it to another new file.

Options

-c *list*	Cuts columns specified in *list*.
-d *character*	Specifies a delimiter for determining columns or fields; the default is a tab. If a non-alphanumeric character is used (such as a space), then it must be enclosed in single quote marks. This option must be used with the -f option.
-f *list*	Cuts fields specified in *list*.

-s   Suppresses lines without a delimiter; used with
                 the -f option.

Examples

This cuts the first and fourth fields from the file payroll and
displays them on the screen:

```
$ cut -f1,4 payroll
```

This cuts the first and fourth columns from the file payroll
and places them in a new file entitled payroll.old:

```
$ cut -c1,4 payroll > payroll.old
```

Related Commands

```
grep
join
paste
```

diff	diff *option(s) diroptions*
Compare Two Files	*file1 file2*

Purpose

The diff command compares two files and returns the lines that
differ. The line numbers of the differing files are marked with the
< and > symbols. The differing line from file1 is marked with <
and the differing line from file2 is marked with >. Three hyphens
(---) separate the contents of the files.

The diff command can also be used to compare files in
different directories. In this situation, use diroptions.

●─TIP────────────────────────────────────

This command works best with smaller text files.

Options

-a   Compares all files, including binary files.
-b   Ignores differences in white space.
-B   Ignores blank lines within the files.

-c	Prints three lines of context for each difference.
-d	Attempts to find more specific differences, resulting in increased processing time.
-e	Returns commands to re-create file2 from file1 using the ed text editor.
-H	Scans for scattered small changes; will miss out on many other changes.
-i	Ignores the case when comparing files.
-I *expr*	Ignores file lines that match *expr*.
-n	Returns information in RCS diff format.
-N	Treats nonexistent files as empty.
-t	Expands tabs to spaces in output.
-T	Inserts tabs at the beginning of lines.
-u	Prints old and new versions of a file as a single line.
-w	Ignores tabs and spaces (white space).
-y	Returns information in two columns.

Diroptions

-l	Paginates the output to pr.
-r	Recursively runs diff to look at files in common subdirectories.
-s	Returns identical files.
-S*file*	Begins with *file* when comparing directories, ignoring files alphabetically listed before *file*.
-x *expr*	Ignores files that match *expr*; wildcards cannot be used.
-X *filename*	Ignores files that match *filename*; wildcards can be used.

Example

```
$ diff letter.1212 letter 1213
1c1
< December 12, 1997
- - -
```

> December 13, 1997

...

Related Commands

```
cmp
diff3
sdiff
```

diff3 Compare Multiple Files	diff3 *option(s) file1 file2 file3*

Purpose

The diff3 command compares three files and returns the differences between them, as with diff, but does not automatically return the differences. Instead, one of the following codes is returned:

= = = =	All three files differ.
= = = = 1	*file1* is different.
= = = = 2	*file2* is different.
= = = = 3	*file3* is different.

Options

-a	Treats all files as text; useful for determining if there are differences between binary files.
-A	Creates an ed script that shows all differences between the files in brackets.
-e	Creates an ed script that places differences between *file2* and *file3* into *file1*.
-E	Creates an ed script that incorporates unmerged changes, delineated by brackets.
-i	Adds the w (save) and q (quit) commands to the end of ed scripts.
-L *name*	Uses *name* instead of the filename in the output.

-m   Creates a new file with the changes merged; this is
            done directly and not with an ed script.

-T   Inserts a tab at the beginning of each line of
            differences, instead of the default two spaces.

-x   Creates an ed script that places all differences in the
            files in *file1*.

-X   Creates an ed script that places all differences in
            the files in *file1*. This is same as -x, except that the
            differences are surrounded by brackets.

-3   Creates an ed script that places differences between
            file1 and *file3* into *file1*.

Related Commands

    cmp
    diff
    sdiff

egrep
Search Files
for Text

egrep option(s)
pattern file(s)

Purpose

The egrep command searches files for text (referred to as *patterns*
or *expressions*) in multiple files or a single file. It is a cousin to the
fgrep and grep commands and usually is considered the most
powerful and fastest of the three. However, it doesn't support all
ASCII characters — it will search for +, |, (,), and ? as long as they
are surrounded by quotation marks, but it will not search for
patterns beginning with \.

Options

-A *num*   Displays *num* of lines after the matched pattern.

-B *num*   Displays *num* of lines before the matched pattern.

-b   Returns the block number of the matched line.

-c   Returns the number of matches without listing the
               actual matches.

-c	Displays two lines before and after the matched pattern.
-e *pattern*	Searches for *pattern* when *pattern* begins with a hyphen (-).
-f *file*	Uses a pattern from *file*.
-h	Lists lines with matches without listing the files that contain them.
-i	Ignores case when matching.
-l	Lists files with matches without listing the actual matches.
-L	Lists files that don't contain matching lines.
-n	Lists matched lines and their line numbers.
-s	Suppresses error messages about files that can't be read or accessed.
-v	Lists lines that do not match the pattern.
-w	Lists only whole words that are matched.
-x	Lists only whole lines that are matched.

Example

This searches the current directory — as noted with * — for the strings *Cogswell Cogs* and *Spacely Sprockets*:

```
$ egrep "Cogswell Cogs|Spacely Sprockets" *
```

Related Commands

```
grep
fgrep
```

elvis **Launch a** **Text Editor**	**elvis** *option(s) filename*

Purpose

The elvis command launches a text editor. It's a clone of the popular vi text editor; on Linux systems, if you use vi on a command line, you'll really be invoking the elvis text editor. It responds to all the standard vi commands.

Options

-e	Starts in colon command mode, similar to the UNIX ex command.
-m *file*	Searches through *file* for an error message from a compiler.
-r	Invokes the elvrec command to recover files.
-R	Opens a file in read-only status.
-s	Works in safe mode, so neophytes can't do too much damage to files or a system.
-t *tag*	Opens the file with *tag* as the first line.
-v	Starts in visual command mode, similar to the UNIX vi command.

Related Commands

```
elvrec
emacs
joe
jove
vi
```

emacs
Launch a
Text Editor

(GNU Command)
(X Window System
Command)

emacs *option(s)*
filename(s)

Purpose

The emacs command launches a text editor. Most Linux distributions install emacs to work under the X Window System, but it can be installed and configured to work under a terminal interface.

● **NOTE** ──────────────────────────────

The full documentation to emacs can be found online using the info
command. (Type info emacs.)

Options

+number	Opens the file on line *number*.
-font *font*	Specifies a fixed-width font for the window. (Used with X Window.)
-i	Uses the kitchen sink bitmap icon when iconifying the emacs window. (Used with X.)
-name *name*	Specifies a name for the initial X window.
-nw	Works with a terminal interface under X.
-q	Doesn't load an init file.
-r	Displays in reverse video. (Used with X.)
-t *file*	Uses *file* as the terminal instead of standard input/output.
-title *title*	Specifies a title for the initial X window.
-u *user*	Loads user's init file.

Related Commands

```
elvis
joe
jove
vi
```

expand **Convert Tabs** **to Spaces**	**expand** *option file(s)*

Purpose

The expand command converts tabs to spaces.

Option

-i   Converts only tabs at the beginning of lines.

fgrep
Search for
Patterns or
Expressions

fgrep *string file(s)*

Purpose

The fgrep command searches files for a text string that you enter and outputs lines that contain that text. You can enter multiple file names or pipe text from standard input.

●─NOTE────────────────────────────────

fgrep is a cousin to the egrep and grep commands and usually is considered the simplest of the three. Running fgrep is the same as running grep -F *string*.

Options

−A *num*	Displays *num* lines after the matched pattern.
−B *num*	Displays *num* lines before the matched pattern.
−b	Returns the block number of the matched line.
−c	Returns the number of matches without listing the actual matches.
−C	Displays two lines before and after the matched pattern.
−e *pattern*	Searches for *pattern* when *pattern* begins with a hyphen (-).
−f *file*	Uses a pattern from *file*.
−h	Lists lines with matches without listing the files that contain them.
−i	Ignores case when matching.
−l	Lists files with matches without listing the actual matches.
−L	Lists files that don't contain matching lines.
−n	Lists matched lines and their line numbers.
−v	Lists lines that do not match the pattern.

-w	Lists only whole words that are matched.
-x	Lists only whole lines that are matched.
-*num*	Displays *num* lines before and after the matched pattern.

Related Commands

```
egrep
grep
```

fmt
Format Files

fmt *option(s) files*

Purpose

The fmt command formats files by justifying the text to the right margin and eliminating newlines. However, the fmt command does preserve spacing, indentations, and blank lines from the original file.

● NOTE

Because this function is not performed by text editors, it's usually invoked within the text editor (elvis has a mechanism for doing this) or piped from a text editor. In addition, because it's often used to format a file and then sent directly to a printer, it usually exists as one step in a pipeline.

Options

-c	Overrides formatting of the first two lines.
-p *prefix*	Formats lines beginning with *prefix*.
-s	Overrides joining lines.
-t	Tags paragraphs.
-u	Applies uniform spacing of one space between words and two spaces between sentences.
-w *num*	Sets the line width to *num* characters; the default is 72.

fold **Format Text to** **Specific Width**	**fold** *option(s) file(s)*

Purpose

The fold command formats text to a specific width, breaking words in the middle to achieve that width. The default is 80 characters.

Options

-b   Counts bytes instead of characters. Here, tabs and formatting commands (such as backspace commands and carriage returns) are considered countable.

-s   Breaks only on spaces.

-w *num*   Sets the line width to *num* characters; the default is 80.

7

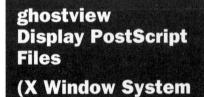

ghostview **Display PostScript** **Files** **(X Window System** **Command)**	**ghostview** *option(s)* *filename*

Purpose

The ghostview command displays PostScript files, using the ghostscript interpreter. A large number of options are associated with this command, but generally it is invoked only with a filename. (Often the gv command is used instead of ghostview.)

● CROSS-REFERENCE

See the online manual pages for more information on the many options. (Type man gv to see the description.)

grep **Search Files** **for Text Strings**	*grep option(s) pattern* *file(s)*

Purpose

The grep command searches a file or multiple files for text strings (referred to as *patterns* or *expressions*), and displays the results of the search onscreen.

●—NOTE

The grep command is a relative of the fgrep and egrep commands.

Options

-A *num*	Displays *num* lines after the matched pattern.
-b	Returns the block number of the matched line.
-B *num*	Displays *num* lines before the matched pattern.
-c	Returns the number of matches without listing the actual matches.
-C	Displays two lines before and after the matched pattern.
-e *pattern*	Searches for *pattern* when *pattern* begins with a hyphen (-).
-f *file*	Uses a pattern from *file*.
-h	Lists lines with matches without listing the files that contain them.
-i	Ignores case when matching.
-l	Lists files with matches without listing the actual matches.
-L	Lists files that don't contain matching lines.
-n	Lists matched lines and their line numbers.
-s	Suppresses error messages.
-v	Lists lines that do not match the pattern.
-w	Lists only whole words that are matched.
-x	Lists only whole lines that are matched.

7

-num	Displays *num* lines before and after the matched pattern.

Example

This searches the current directory — as noted with * — for the string *mail pixmap*:

```
$ grep "mail pixmap" *
```

Related Commands

egrep
fgrep

grodvi **Convert Groff** **Output**	grodvi *option(s)* *filename(s)*

Purpose

The grodvi command converts groff output to the TeX DVI format.

Options

-d	Does not use tpic specials to implement drawing commands.
-F*dir*	Searches the directory *dir* for font and device description files.
-w*n*	Sets the default line thickness to *n* thousandths of an em.

Related Commands

eqn
groff
tfmtodit
troff

| groff
Format Groff
Documents | groff *option(s)*
filename(s) |

Purpose

The groff command is a front end to the groff document-formatting commands. It typically runs the troff program and a postprocessor to prepare documents for a specific device.

The postprocessor is specified by the postpro command in the device-description file.

Devices

ps	PostScript printers and previewers (default).
dvi	TeX DVI format.
X75	X Window 75-dpi previewer.
X100	X Window 100-dpi previewer.
ascii	Line printers with no formatting.
latin1	Line printers with the ISO Latin-1 character set.

Options

-e	Preprocesses with eqn.
-p	Preprocesses with pic.
-R	Preprocesses with refer.
-s	Preprocess with soelim.
-t	Preprocesses with tbl.
-V	Prints a pipeline without executing it.
-z	Suppresses output from troff; prints error messages.
-Z	Overrides postprocessing output from troff.
-P*arg*	Passes *arg* to the postprocessor.
-l	Sends output to a printer.
-L*arg*	Passes *arg* to the spooler.
-T*dev*	Prepares output for *dev*. The default is ps.

-X   Previews with gxditview instead of using the usual postprocessor.

-N   Doesn't allow newlines with eqn delimiters.

-S   Runs in safer mode.

Related Commands

```
eqn
postpro
troff
tbl
```

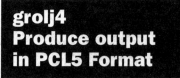

**grolj4
Produce output
in PCL5 Format**

grolj4 *option(s)*
filename(s)

Purpose

The grolj4 command is a groff driver for the HP Laserjet 4 family, producing output in PCL5 format.

Options

-c*n*   Prints *n* copies of each page.

-F*dir*   Searches directory dir/devlj4 for font and device-description files.

-l   Prints the document with a landscape orientation.

-p *size* Sets the paper size to *size*: letter, legal, executive, a4, com10, monarch, c5, b5, or dl.

-w*n*   Sets the default line thickness to *n* thousandths of an em.

Related Commands

```
eqn
groff
tfmtodit
troff
```

grops Drive PostScript for Groff	grops *option(s)* *filename(s)*

Purpose

The grops command is a PostScript driver for groff. It's now a somewhat redundant command, because the default output for groff is PostScript.

Options

-b*n*   Works with previewers and spoolers that don't conform to the Document Structuring Conventions 3.0. *n* specifies how grops deals with this; see the online manual pages for the specific values.

-c*n*   Prints *n* copies of each page.

-F*dir*   Searches directory dir/devname for font and device-description files.

-g   Guesses the page length.

-l   Prints the document with a landscape orientation.

-m   Turns on manual feed.

-w*n*   Sets the default line thickness to *n* thousandths of an em.

Related Commands

```
eqn
groff
tfmtodit
troff
```

grotty Format Output for Typewriter	grotty *option(s)* *filename(s)*

Purpose

The grotty command formats output for a typewriter-type device.

Options

-b	Suppresses overstriking for bold characters.
-B	Uses overstriking for bold-italic characters.
-d	Ignores all \D commands.
-f	Uses form feeds.
-F*dir*	Searches directory dir/devname for font and device-description files.
-h	Imposes horizontal tabs.
-o	Suppresses overstriking, other than for bold or underlined characters.
-u	Suppresses underlining for italic characters.
-U	Uses underlining for bold-italic characters.

Related Commands

```
eqn
groff
tfmtodit
troff
```

gs
Ghostscript
Previewer

gs *option(s) file(s)*

Purpose

The gs command reads a file or files and executes them as Ghostscript programs. After doing this, it reads further input from the standard input stream (normally the keyboard). Each line is interpreted separately. To exit from the interpreter, enter quit or Ctrl-C.

Options

-h	Prints help information, including available devices.

-?	Prints help information, including available devices.
--filename *arg1* ...	Takes the next argument as a filename, but takes all remaining arguments (even if they have the syntactic form of switches) and defines the name ARGUMENTS in userdict (not systemdict) as an array of those strings, before running the file. When Ghostscript finishes executing the file, it exits back to the shell.
-dname=*token*	Defines a name in systemdict with the given definition. The token must be exactly one token (as defined by the token operator) and must not contain any white space.
-dname	Defines a name in systemdict with value = null.
-sname=*string*	Defines a name in systemdict with a given string as value.
-q	Launches gs without normal startup messages.
-g*number1*x*number2*	Specifies the width and height.
-r*number1*x*number2*	Specifies X and Y resolutions.
-I*directories*	Adds the designated list of directories at the head of the search path for library files.
--	Tells Ghostscript that the standard input is coming from a file or a pipe.

head **Display Beginning** **of File**	**head** *options file(s)*

Purpose

The head command displays the beginning of a file. The default is ten lines. If you specify more than one file, a header will be placed at the beginning of each file.

Options

-c *num*	Prints the first *num* bytes of the file.
-c *numk*	Prints the first *num* kilobytes of the file.
-c *numm*	Prints the first *num* megabytes of the file.
-n *num*	Prints the first *num* lines of the file.
-v	Prints a header at the beginning of each file.

---

ispell **Check Spelling** **of Words** **(GNU Command)**	**ispell** *option(s) file(s)*

Purpose

The ispell command checks the spellings of words in a file or files against the system dictionary. If ispell runs across a word not in the dictionary, it asks you what to do with the word and displays correctly spelled words, at which point you enter a command. The ispell command also creates a personal dictionary file that's also checked, allowing you to place frequently used words there. (You cannot change the system dictionary file.) If you override the ispell suggestion, the word is then added to a personal dictionary.

●—TIP———————————————

The ispell command is used as the spelling checker in the emacs text editor.

Options

-b	Creates a backup file, adding .bak to the original filename.
-B	Searches for missing blank spaces, where words are jammed together (concatenated).
-C	Ignores concatenated strings.
-d *file*	Uses *file* as the dictionary file, instead of the standard ispell dictionary.

-L num	Shows *num* lines around the misspelled word.
-M	Displays interactive commands at the bottom of the screen.
-N	Suppresses display of interactive commands.
-n	Checks the spelling of nroff or troff files.
-p file	Uses *file* as the personal dictionary file, instead of your standard ispell personal dictionary.
-P	Suppresses suggestion of root/affix combinations.
-S	Sorts replacement words by level of likelihood of correctness.
-t	Checks the spelling of TeX or LaTeX files.
-T type	Assumes that files are formatted by *type*.
-w chars	Exempts *chars* from the spelling check.
-W num	Skips words that are *num* characters or less.
-V	Displays control characters in hat notation (^C, for example) and - to denote high bits.

7

Commands

a	Designates the word as spelled correctly, but doesn't add it to the personal dictionary.
i	Adds the word to your personal dictionary.
l	Searches the system dictionary.
q	Quits ispell without saving the spelling changes.
r	Replaces the word with the suggestion.
u	Adds a lowercase version of the word to your personal dictionary.
x	Skips to the next file when multiple files are designated.
number	Replaces misspelled word with *number* word.
!command	Runs *command* after launching a shell.

Related Command

wc

joe
Joe's Own Editor
(GNU Command)

joe *global_option(s)*
local_option(s) file(s)

Purpose

The joe command is an ASCII-text screen editor. It has a "mode-less" user interface similar to many user-friendly PC editors — users who can remember WordStar or the editors employed in the Borland Turbo series of programming languages will feel at home.

The joe command also emulates several other editors: you can run it in WordStar, pico, or emacs imitation modes.

● **NOTE**

The mode is controlled by the command line used to launch the editor, even though only one executable file controls all five.

After you are in the editor, you can type text and use special control-character sequences to perform other editing tasks.

● **CROSS-REFERENCE**

See the online manual pages for a complete list of the voluminous possibilities. (Type man joe to see the information.)

Emulation Command Lines

joe   Launches generic joe.

jstar Launches joe in WordStar mode. Beware of control keys in this mode.

jmacs Launches joe in emacs mode.

rjoe   Launches joe in restricted mode, where the user can edit only the files specifically listed on the command line.

jpico Launches joe in pico mode.

Global Command-Line Options

-asis   Sends characters with codes above 127 to the terminal as-is, instead of inverse to the corresponding character below 128.

-backpath *path*	Stores backup files in the specified directory instead of in each file's original directory.
-baud *nnn*	Sets the baud rate for purposes of terminal screen optimization to *nnn*. joe inserts delays for baud rates below 19,200, which bypasses tty buffering so that typeahead will interrupt the screen output. Scrolling commands will not be used for 38,400 baud. This is useful for xterms and other console ttys that really aren't going over a serial line.
-beep	Beeps on command errors and when the cursor goes past extremes.
-columns *nnn*	Sets the number of screen columns to *nnn*.
-csmode	Launches continued search mode: a search immediately following a search will repeat the previous search instead of prompting for new string. This is useful for the ^[S and ^[R commands and for when joe is trying to be emacs.
-dopadding	Begins flow control between joe and the tty, outputting extra ^@s to the tty as specified by the termcap entry. The extra ^@s allow the terminal to catch up after long terminal commands.
-exask	Requires the ^KX command to verify the filename that it's about to write.
-force	Forces a file to have a linefeed as the last line of the file.
-help	Shows help screen.
-keepup	Updates the column number and control-key prefix fields of the status lines after each keystroke, instead of after every other keystroke.
-lightoff	Turns off block highlighting.
-lines *nnn*	Sets the number of screen lines to *nnn*.
-marking	Highlights text between ^KB and the cursor.
-mid	Scrolls the window so that the cursor is in the center of the window. This option is forced on slow terminals that don't have scrolling commands.
-nobackups	Prevents backup files.

-nonotice	Prevents the copyright notice from being displayed when the editor starts.
-nosta	Eliminates the topmost status line.
-noxon	Turns off ^S/^Q processing, which is useful in WordStar or emacs modes.
-orphan	Places extra files on the command line in orphaned buffers instead of in extra windows. Useful for when joe is trying to be emacs.
-pg *nnn*	Specifies the number of lines to keep after PgUp/PgDn (^U/^V). If -1 is given, half the window is kept.
-skiptop *nnn*	Skips the top *nnn* lines of the screen.

Local Options

+*nnn*	The cursor starts on the specified line *nnn*.
-crlf	joe uses CR-LF as the end-of-line sequence instead of just LF. This is for editing MS-DOS or VMS files.
-wordwrap	joe wraps the previous word when you type past the right margin.
-autoindent	When you hit Return on an indented line, the indentation is duplicated onto the new line.
-overwrite	Typing overwrites existing characters instead of inserting before them.
-lmargin *nnn*	Sets the left margin to *nnn*.
-rmargin *nnn*	Sets the right margin to *nnn*.
-tab *nnn*	Sets the tab width to *nnn*.
-indentc *nnn*	Sets the indentation character for ^K, and ^K. (32 for space, 9 for tab).
-istep *nnn*	Sets the indentation step for ^K, and ^K..
-linums	Displays line numbers before each line.
-rdonly	Loads a file as read-only.
-keymap *name*	Uses an alternate section of the joerc file for the key sequence bindings.

Related Commands

```
elvis
emacs
jove
pico
vi
vim
```

join Join Lines of Two Files (GNU Command)	join *option(s) file1 file2*

Purpose

The join command joins lines of two files (*file1* and *file2*) on a common join field.

Options

-1 *field*	Joins on *field* field of *file1*.
-2 *field*	Joins on *field* field of *file2*.
-a *file-number*	Prints a line listing each unpairable line in *file1* or *file2*.
-e *string*	Replaces empty output fields with *string*.
-o *field-list*	Uses the format in *field-list* to construct the output lines.
-t *char*	Inserts *char* as the input and output field separator.
-v *file*	Prints a line for each unpairable line in *file* (either *file1* or *file2*), instead of the normal output.

jove Text Editor	jove *option(s) file(s)*

Purpose

The jove command launches Jonathan's Own Version of Emacs. It is based on the original emacs editor, but although jove is meant to be compatible with emacs, some major differences exist between the two editors, and you shouldn't rely on their behaving identically.

Options

-d   Specifies the current directory.

+*num*   Loads the file and places the cursor at line *num* instead of at the beginning of the file. If *num* is not specified, then the cursor is positioned at the end of the file.

-p *file*   Parses the error messages in the file designated by the following argument. The error messages are assumed to be in a format similar to the C compiler, lint, or grep output.

-t*tag*   Runs the g command on the string of characters immediately following the -t, if there is one (as in -t*Tagname*), or on the following argument (as in -t *Tagname*) otherwise.

-w   Divides the window in two. When this happens, either the same file is displayed in both windows or the second file in the list is read in and displayed in its own window.

-r   Runs the jove recover program. Use this when the system crashes, or jove crashes, or you accidentally get logged out while in jove. If there are any buffers to be recovered, this will find them.

Related Commands

    elvis
    emacs
    joe
    pico

```
vi
vim
```

less Display Portions of File Interactively (GNU Command) (X Window System Command)	less *option(s) file(s)*

Purpose

The less command displays portions of a file interactively. It's designed as a more-advanced version of the old UNIX more command — it allows you to move backward in the file as well as forward — and it reads in portions of files, not entire files, so it's quicker than text editors.

You may find that the less command is one of your most frequently used commands, because it's so flexible and provides the best aspects of the cat command and your text editors.

●─NOTE ──────────

An X Window version of this command, xless, also exists. It works identically to the less command, except that it runs in an X window.

Options

-?	Displays available commands, along with a summary of their functionality.
--help	Displays available commands, along with a summary of their functionality.
-a	Creates a new display after the last line displayed. (The default is two lines.)
-b*buffers*	Displays by *buffers* bytes of size. A buffer is 1K, and ten buffers are used for cach file.
-B	Allocates buffers automatically, as needed, if data is read through a pipe.

-c	Redraws the screen from the top, not the bottom.
-C	Redraws the screen from the top, not the bottom, and clears the screen before repainting.
-d	Suppresses error messages displayed on dumb terminals, such as noting that the terminal lacks the ability to clear the screen.
-e	Exits less the second time it reaches the end of the file.
-E	Exits less the first time it reaches the end of the file.
-f	Forces less to open nonregular files, such as directories or device drivers, and also suppresses error messages when binary files are opened.
-g	Highlights strings matching only the last search command, not all search commands.
-G	Suppresses highlighting of strings.
-hnum	Specifies the maximum num of lines to scroll backward.
-i	Disregards case when searching. If an uppercase letter is included in a search pattern, then case is taken into account.
-I	Disregards case when searching, even if an uppercase letter is included in a search pattern.
-jnum	Specifies a "target" line to be positioned at the top of the screen. This can be the object of a text search, tag search, line number, file percentage, or marked position. A negative number would position the "target" line relative to the bottom of the screen.
-kfilename	Opens a file as a file that is in lesskey format, not as a normal text file.
-m	Opens in verbose mode a la the more command, with percentages listed at the bottom of the screen.
-M	Opens in verbose mode a la the more command, with percentages, line numbers, and total lines listed at the bottom of the screen.
-n	Turns off listing line numbers.

7

-N	Lists line numbers at the beginning of each line in the display.
-o*filename*	Copies output to *filename* from a pipe. If *filename* exists, less asks for permission before overwriting it.
-O*filename*	Copies output to *filename* from a pipe. If *filename* exists, less will not ask for permission before overwriting it.
-p*pattern*	Starts less at the first occurrence of *pattern*.
-P*prompt*	Defines *prompt* in one of three ways:

	-P*string*	Prompt is *string*.
	-Pm*string*	Medium prompt is *string*.
	-Pl*string*	Long prompt is *string*.

-q	Works in quiet mode, where no sounds are made if an attempt is made to scroll past the end of the file or before the beginning of the file.
-Q	Works in totally quiet mode, where no system sounds are made.
-r	Displays "raw" characters instead of using carets. Can cause display errors.
-s	Squeezes consecutive blank lines into a single blank line. Usually used with nroff files.
-S	Chops off lines longer than the screen, discarding them instead of folding them into the next line.
-t*tag*	Edits a file containing *tag*, contained in ./tags and generated by the ctags command.
-T*tagfile*	Specifies a tags file to be used instead of ./tags.
-u	Treats backspaces and carriage returns as printable characters.
-U	Treats backspaces and carriage-returns as control characters.
-V	Displays the version number of less.
-w	Represents lines after the end of the file as blank lines instead of tilde (~) characters.
-x*num*	Sets the tab every *num* positions; the default is 8.
-X	Disables sending the termcap initialization and deinitialization strings to the terminal.

-y*num*	Specifies a maximum number of lines to scroll forward.
-[z]*num*	Changes the default scrolling window size to *num* lines; the default is one screen.

Commands

h	Displays help information.
Space, Ctrl-V, f, Ctrl-F	Scrolls forward the default number of lines (one window; this can be changed by the -z option).
z *num*	Scrolls forward the default number of lines; if *num* is specified, then it becomes the new window size.
Enter, Ctrl-N, e, Ctrl-E, j, Ctrl-J	Scrolls forward *n* lines (the default is 1). Scrolls forward one line.
d, Ctrl-D *num*	Scrolls forward one half of the screen; if *num* is specified, less scrolls forward that number of lines, and it becomes the default.
b, Ctrl-B, Esc-v	Scrolls backward the default number of lines (one window; this can be changed by the -z option or w command).
w *num*	Scrolls backward the default number of lines (one window; this can be changed by specifying *num*).
y, Ctrl-Y, Ctrl-P, k, Ctrl-K	Scrolls backward the default number of lines (one).
u, Ctrl-U *num*	Scrolls backward the default number of lines (one half of one screen). If *num* is specified, it becomes the default for the d and u commands.
r, Ctrl-R, Ctrl-L	Redraws the screen.
R	Redraws the screen and discards the input in the buffer.
F	Scrolls forward, even when the end of the file is reached (similar to tail -f).
g, <, Esc-<	Scrolls to the beginning of the file.
G, >, Esc->	Scrolls to the end of the file.

p, % *num*	Scrolls to a position *num* percent into the file. Num must be between 0 and 100.
{	Scrolls to the matching } if { appears in the top line of the screen.
}	Scrolls back to the matching { if } appears in the top line of the screen.
(	Scrolls to the matching) if (appears in the top line of the screen.
)	Scrolls back to the matching (if) appears in the top line of the screen.
[	Scrolls to the matching] if [appears in the top line of the screen.
]	Scrolls back to the matching [if] appears in the top line of the screen.
Esc-Ctrl-F *char1 char2*	Scrolls to the matching *char2* if *char1* appears in the top line of the screen.
Esc-Ctrl-B *char1 char2*	Scrolls back to the matching *char1* if *char2* appears in the top line of the screen.
m *letter*	Marks the current position with lowercase *letter*.
' *letter*	Returns to the position marked with lowercase *letter*.
Ctrl-X Ctrl-X	Returns to the position marked with lowercase letter.
/*pattern*	Searches for next occurrence of *pattern*, starting at the second displayed line.
/!*pattern*	Searches for lines that do not contain *pattern*.
/**pattern*	Searches for next occurrence of *pattern*, starting at the second displayed line, and extending the search through the next files in the command-line list.
/@*pattern*	Searches for next occurrence of *pattern*, starting at the first line of the first file listed on the command line.
?*pattern*	Searches backward in the file for the next occurrence of *pattern*, starting with the line immediately before the top line of the screen.

`?!pattern`	Searches backward for lines that do not contain *pattern*.
`?*pattern`	Searches backward for next occurrence of *pattern*, starting at the line immediately before the top line of the screen, and extending the search backward through the previous files in the command-line list.
`?@pattern`	Searches for next occurrence of *pattern*, starting at the last line of the last file listed on the command line.
`Esc-/pattern`	Searches for next occurrence of *pattern*, starting at the second displayed line, and extending the search through the following files in the command-line list.
`Esc-*pattern`	Searches backward for next occurrence of *pattern*, starting at the line immediately before the top line of the screen, and extending the search backward through the previous files in the command-line list.
`n`	Repeats the previous search.
`N`	Repeats the previous search, but in the reverse direction.
`Esc-n`	Repeats the previous search and extends the search to files specified on the command line.
`Esc-N`	Repeats the previous search, but in the reverse direction, and extends the search to files specified on the command line.
`Esc-u`	Turns off highlighting of patterns matched by the searches.
`:e filename`	Opens a new *filename*. If no new file is specified, the current file is reloaded.
`Ctrl-X, Ctrl-V, E filename`	Opens a new *filename*. If no new file is specified, the current file is reloaded.
`:n num`	Opens the next file that was entered on the less command line. If *num* is present, then the file indicated by that number will be opened.

`:p` *num*	Opens the previous file that was entered on the `less` command line. If *num* is present, then the file indicated by that number will be opened.
`:x` *num*	Opens the first file on the command line. If *num* is present, then the file indicated by that number on the command line will be opened.
`=, Ctrl-G, :f`	Returns information about the file being viewed: name, line number, byte offset of the bottom line being displayed, length of the file, number of lines in the file, and percent of the file above the last displayed line.
`-option`	Changes a command-line *option* while `less` is running. If a value is required, you are asked for it; if no new value is entered, the current value is displayed.
`-+option`	Resets a command-line *option* to the default value.
`--option`	Resets a command-line *option* to the opposite of the default value. Useless when working with options that require numerical or string-based input.
`_option`	Returns the current value of *option*.
`+command`	Runs *command* every time a new file is loaded.
`V`	Prints version number.
`q, :q, :Q, ZZ`	Quits `less`.
`v`	Launches an editor (defined by VISUAL or EDITOR shell environment variables) to edit the current file.
`! shell-command`	Runs the specified *shell-command*. To list the current file in the command, use the percent sign (%). To list the previously viewed command in the command line, use the pound sign (#). To repeat the previous shell command, use ! !. To launch a shell with no command, use !.

| `| mark_letter`
`shell-command` | Uses *mark_letter* to send a section of the file via pipe to the specified *shell-command*. (Use the m letter command to mark a file.) The beginning of the section is the top of the screen, while the end of the section is the mark_letter. |

Editing Commands

`Left arrow, Esc-h`	Moves the cursor one space to the left.
`Right arrow, Esc-1`	Moves the cursor one space to the right.

`Ctrl-left-arrow,`
`Esc-b,`
`Esc-left-arrow`
	Moves the cursor one word to the left.

`Ctrl-right-arrow,`
`Esc-w,`
`Esc-right-arrow`
	Moves the cursor one word to the right.

`Home, Esc-0`	Moves the cursor to the beginning of the line.
`End, Esc-$`	Moves the cursor to the end of the line.
`Backspace`	Deletes the character to the left of the cursor, or cancels a command.
`Delete, Esc-x`	Deletes the character under the cursor.
`Ctrl-Backspace,` `Esc-Backspace`	Deletes the word to the left of the cursor.
`Ctrl-Delete, Esc-X,` `Esc-Delete`	Deletes the word under the cursor.
`Up arrow, Esc-k`	Retrieves the previous command line.
`Down arrow, Esc-j`	Retrieves the next command line.
`Tab`	Completes a partial filename. If more than one filename matches, the potential filenames are cycled through every time Tab is used.
`Esc-Tab`	Completes a partial filename. If more than one filename matches, the potential filenames are cycled in reverse through every time Tab is used.
`Ctrl-L`	Completes a partial filename. If more than one filename matches, all the potential filenames are displayed.

7

Ctrl-U   Deletes a command line or cancels
                a command.

Related Commands

more
xless

look   look *option(s) string file*
Look for Lines

Purpose

The look command looks for lines beginning with a string. If file
isn't specified, then /usr/dict/words is used.

Options

-a   Uses the alternate dictionary /usr/dict/web2.

-d   Compares only alphanumeric characters.

-f   Ignores case.

-t   Sets a string termination character.

Related Commands

grep
sort

lpq   lpq *option(s) user*
**Check Print Spool
and Status**

Purpose

The lpq command checks the print spool (used by lpd) and also
reports on the status of specified jobs, either by job ID or user. By
itself on a command line, lpq returns information about all jobs in
the queue.

The lpq command reports the user's name, the current rank in the queue, the names of files comprising the job, the job identifier, and the total size in bytes.

Options

-l   Prints information about each of the files in a job entry; the default is to truncate information at a single line.

-Pprinter   Designates a specific printer; the default is the value of the PRINTER environment variable or the default line printer.

Related Commands

lpc
lpd
lpr
lprm

lpr	lpr option(s) file(s)

Purpose

The lpr command sends files to a print-spool daemon, which then sends files to the printer when it is available. The file options are used to designate specific types of files (the assumption is that a text file is on the way), so the printer can adjust accordingly.

File Options

-c   Assumes the files are produced by cifplot.

-d   Assumes the files are produced by TeX (DVI format).

-f   Uses a filter that interprets the first character of each line as a standard FORTRAN carriage-control character.

-g   Assumes the files are produced by plot routines.

-l   Filters control characters as printable characters and suppresses page breaks.

-n   Assumes the files are produced by `ditroff`.

-p   Uses the `pr` command to format the files (same as `print`).

-t   Assumes the files are produced by `troff`.

-v   Assumes the files contain a raster image for devices such as the Benson Varian.

General Options

-C *class*   Specifies a job classification on the burst page.

-h   Suppresses printing of the burst page.

-i [*col*]   Indents the output *col* number of columns. If no *col* is specified, then each line will be indented eight characters.

-m   Sends mail when print job is complete.

-P*printer*   Sends output to *printer*.

-r   Removes file upon completion of spooling or upon completion of printing (with the -s option).

-s   Uses symbolic links, instead of copying files to the spool directory. If you do this, do not change files until they have been printed.

-T *title*   Specifies a *title* name for pr, instead of the filename.

-U *user*   Specifies a username to print on the burst page.

-w*num*   Uses *num* as the page width for pr.

-#*num*   Prints *num* copies of each file.

-[*num*]*font* Specifies a *font* to be mounted on font position *num*.

Related Commands

```
lpc
lpd
lpq
lprm
pr
```

Purpose

The lprm command removes print jobs from the print spool. Use the lpq command to determine the job IDs. You must own the job or be the superuser to remove print jobs.

Options

-Pprinter   Specifies a *printer* queue instead of the default.

-user   Removes jobs owned by *user*.

Related Commands

    lpd
    lpq
    lpr

| more
Display All or
Part of File | more *option(s) file(s)* |

Purpose

The more command displays all or parts of a file, one screen at a time. It has largely been superseded by the less command in functionality.

●—NOTE—————————————————————

Type q to quit more. Press the spacebar to continue scrolling through a file.

Certain commands are used when more is displaying a file. They're entered at the bottom of the screen, as with the vi text editor. These commands are shown next in this section.

Commands

`Retrun`	Displays the next line of text. If an argument is provided, that becomes the new default.
`b or ^B`	Moves backward one screen of text. If an argument is provided, that becomes the new default.
`d or ^D`	Scrolls 11 lines of text. If an argument is provided, that becomes the new default.
`f`	Skips forward one screen of text. If an argument is provided, that becomes the new default.
`h or ?`	Displays a summary of commands.
`Ctrl-L`	Redraws the screen.
`n`	Repeats the last search.
`q or Q`	Exits more.
`s`	Skips forward one line of text. If an argument is provided, that becomes the new default.
`v`	Launches vi at the current line.
`z`	Displays the next screen of text. If an argument is provided, that becomes the new default.
`'`	Reverts to where the previous search started.
`=`	Displays the current line number.
`/pattern`	Searches for the next occurrence of *pattern*. If an argument is provided, that becomes the new default.
`!cmd or :!cmd`	Runs *cmd* in a subshell.
`:f`	Displays the current file and line number.
`:n`	Opens the next file.
`:p`	Opens the previous file.
`.`	Repeats the previous command.

Options

`+num`	Starts display at line number *num*.
`+/pattern`	Searches for *pattern* before the file is displayed.
`-num`	Sets the screen size to *num* of lines.

-c	Turns off scrolling; instead, the screen is cleared and the new text is painted from the top of the screen.
-d	Displays the following prompt at the bottom of the screen: *[Press space to continue, 'q' to quit.]*.
-f	Counts logical lines, not screen lines.
-l	Ignores the ^L (form feed) as a special character.
-p	Turns off scrolling; instead, the screen is cleared and the new text is displayed.
-s	Squeezes multiple blank lines into one.
-u	Suppresses underlining.

Related Command

```
less
```

nroff
Call on groff
Command

nroff *option(s) filename*

Purpose

The nroff command calls on the groff command to emulate the nroff command found on other UNIX systems.

●—CROSS-REFERENCE

See the groff command, earlier in this chapter, for details and command-line options.

Related Commands

```
groff
troff
```

paste
Merge Files
(GNU Command)

paste *option(s) file(s)*

Purpose

The paste command merges files and places the files side by side. The first line of *file1* will be followed by the first line of *file2*, separated by a tab and ending with a newline.

Options

-d*char*   Uses *char* instead of a tab to separate lines.

-s   Merges lines from files, instead of printing both on the same line.

Related Commands

cut
join

pico
Text Editor

pico *option(s) filename*

Purpose

The pico text editor is a slim tool based on the composing tools found in the pine mail manager. If you work a lot with pine and want to maintain some consistency in your tools, you might want to use pico for your basic editing needs.

Options

+*n*   Loads a file with the cursor *n* lines into the file.

-d   Rebinds the Del key so that the character the cursor is on is deleted rather than the character to its left.

-e	Enables filename completion.
-g	Shows cursor before the current selection, rather than the lower left corner of the display.
-k	Removes text from the cursor to the end of the line, instead of removing the entire line.
-m	Enables mouse functionality; available only when running under X Window.
-n*n*	Notifies you when new mail arrives; checks for mail every *n* seconds.
-o *dir*	Works in *dir* directory.
-r*n*	Sets *n* column used to limit the right margin.
-t	Enables tool mode, which provides neither prompting for a save on exit nor renaming of the buffer. Used when composing text in other tools, such as elm or Pnews.
-v	Views the file without editing.
-w	Disables word wrap.
-x	Disables the key menu at the bottom of the screen.
-z	Enables ^Z suspension.

Related Command

pine

pr **Prepare File** **for Printing** **(GNU Command)**	**pr** *options file*

Purpose

The pr command prepares a file for printing. It doesn't actually print the file — you need to send the file to the printer to do that — but it creates a paginated, columnar file that is suitable for printing.

Options

+page	Begins printing with page *page*.
-column	Prints *column* number of columns.
-a	Prints columns across rather than down.
-b	Evens columns on the last page.
-c	Prints control characters using carets (^G); prints other unprintable characters in octal backslash notation.
-d	Prints output double-spaced.
-e *width*	Expands tabs to spaces on input; if *width* is specified, exchange tab for width.
-F	Uses form feeds instead of newlines between pages.
-h *header*	Replaces the filename in the header with *header*.
-i[*out-tab-char*] [*out-tab-width*]	Replaces spaces with tabs. You can specify an output tab character (*out-tab-char*) or the output tab character's width (*out-tab-width*), which has a default of 8.
-l *page-length*	Sets the page length to *page-length* lines; the default is 66.
-m	Prints all files in parallel, one in each column.
-n[*number-separator* [*digits*]]	Precedes each column with a line number; with parallel files, precedes each line with a line number. The optional argument *number-separator* is the character to print after each number. The optional *digits* is the number of digits per line number; the default is 5.
-o *left-margin*	Offsets each line with a margin *left-margin* spaces wide.
-r	Ignores warnings when a file cannot be opened.
-s[*column-separator*]	Separates columns by the single character *column-separator*.

7

-t	Suppresses printing the header and trailer on all pages.
-v	Prints unprintable characters in octal backslash notation.
-w *page-width*	Sets the page width to *page-width* columns; the default is 72.

Related Commands

```
lpd
lpq
lpr
lprm
```

printf **Print String** **(GNU Command)**	**printf** *argument*

Purpose

The printf command prints a string, using % directives and \
escapes in the same manner as the C-language printf command.
(Type man 3 printf for descriptions of the directives and escapes.)

psbb **Return Dimensions** **of Bounding Box**	**psbb** *file*

Purpose

The psbb command returns the dimensions of a bounding box
from a PostScript document. If it finds one, it prints a line:

llx lly urx ury

It then exits. If it does not find one, it prints a message saying
so and exits.

| **refer**
Preprocess
Bibliographic
Reference
(GNU Command) | **refer** *option(s) filename* |

Purpose

The refer command preprocesses bibliographic references for the groff command. It copies the contents of *filename* to standard output, except that lines between .[and .] are interpreted as citations, and lines between .R1 and .R2 are interpreted as commands about how citations are to be processed.

●─CROSS-REFERENCE─────────────────────────

A longer description of citations and their significance, as well as references to obscure options, can be found in the man pages. (Type man refer to see the information.)

| **rev**
Reverse File Lines | **rev** *filename* |

Purpose

The rev command reverses the lines of a file. It copies the file to standard output, reversing the order of characters in every line. We have yet to see a practical application for this command, and we're not sure that there is one.

| **sdiff**
Merge Two Files
(GNU Command) | **sdiff** *option(s) file1 file2* |

Purpose

The sdiff command merges two files and prints the results to a third file.

Options

-a	Treats all files as text and compares them line by line, even if they do not appear to be text.
-b	Ignores changes in amount of white space.
-B	Ignores changes that only insert or delete blank lines.
-d	Changes the algorithm to find a smaller set of changes.
-H	Uses heuristics to speed handling of large files that have numerous scattered small changes.
--expand-tabs	Expands tabs to spaces in the final file.
-i	Ignores changes in case.
-I regexp	Ignores changes that only insert or delete lines that match regexp.
--ignore-all-space	Ignores white space when comparing lines.
--ignore-blank-lines	Ignores changes that only insert or delete blank lines.
--ignore-case	Ignores case.
--ignore-matching-lines=regexp	Ignores changes that insert or delete lines that match regexp.
--ignore-space-change	Ignores changes in the amount of white space.
-l	Prints only the left column of two common lines.
--minimal	Changes the algorithm to seek a smaller set of changes.
-o file	Saves the merged output to file.
-s	Doesn't print common lines.

`--speed-large-files`	Uses heuristics to speed handling of large files with numerous scattered small changes.
`-t`	Expands tabs to spaces.
`--text`	Treats all files as text.
`-w columns`	Sets an output width of *columns*.
`-W`	Ignores horizontal white space when comparing lines.

Related Commands

```
cmp
comm
diff
diff3
```

sed
Read Files and Modify Input

sed option(s)
filename(s)

Purpose

The sed command reads files and modifies the input as specified by a list of commands. The input is then written to the standard output.

Options

`-a`	Files listed as parameters for the w' functions are created (or truncated) before any processing begins.
`-e command`	Appends the editing commands specified by *command* to the list of commands.
`-f command_file`	Appends the commands from *command_file* to the list of commands.
`-n`	Suppresses echoing of each line of input.

selection
Transfer
Characters

selection *option(s)*

Purpose

The selection command takes characters from the current Linux console and pastes them into another section of the current console. The command is typically launched at boot time from the /etc/rc.local file and run as a background process.

Options

-a*accel*	Movements of more than *delta* pixels are multiplied by *accel* (the default is 2).
-b*baud-rate*	Sets the baud rate of the mouse. This is an option to be avoided, because setting the incorrect baud rate can cause your mouse to freeze, and other mechanisms for setting the baud rate are available elsewhere in Linux and XFree86.
-c*l|m|r*	Sets the copy button to left (l), middle(m), or right (r). (The default is left.)
-d*delta*	Movements of more than *delta* pixels are multiplied by *accel* (the default is 25).
-m*mouse-device*	Sets the mouse device (the default is /dev/mouse).
-p*l|m|r*	Sets the paste button to left (l), middle(m), or right (r). (The default is right.)
-s*sample-rate*	Sets the *sample rate* of the mouse (the default is 100).
-t*mouse-type*	Sets the mouse type: Microsoft is ms, Mouse Systems is msc, MM Series is mm, Logitech is logi, Bus Mouse is bm, MSC 3-bytes is sun, and PS/2 mouse is ps2. The default is ms. Despite the seeming usefulness of this feature, this is an option to be avoided, because setting the mouse type can cause your mouse to freeze, and other mechanisms for setting the mouse type are available elsewhere in Linux and XFree86.

| -wslack | Sets the amount of *slack* before the pointer reappears at the other side of the screen. |

Related Command

gpm

| **soelim**
Interpret Requests | soelim *option*
filename(s) |

Purpose

The soelim command interprets .so requests in groff input. It reads a specified filename and replaces lines of the form:

.so filename

It replaces them with the contents of *filename*.

Option

-C   Recognizes .so even when it is followed by a character other than space or newline.

Related Command

groff

| **sort**
Sort, Merge, or
Compare File Lines
(GNU Command) | sort *option(s)*
filename(s) |

Purpose

The sort command sorts, merges, or compares the lines of text files. The results are written to the screen.

You can change the mode with the available mode options. These are listed next.

Mode Options

-c   Checks whether files are sorted; if they are not, an error message is printed.

-m   Merges files by sorting them as a group, but the files must already be sorted.

General Options

+*POS1* [-*POS2*]	Within each line, sets the field to use as the sorting key.
-b	Ignores leading blanks in lines.
-d	Sorts in phone directory order, ignoring all characters except letters, digits, and blanks when sorting.
-f	Folds lowercase characters into the equivalent uppercase characters when sorting.
-i	Ignores non-ASCII characters.
-k *POS1*[,*POS2*]	Sets the field within each line to use as the sorting key.
-M	Month abbreviations are changed to uppercase and sorted in order.
-n	Compares using arithmetic value.
-o *file*	Writes output to *file*.
-r	Reverses the order.
-t *separator*	Specifies *separator* as the field separator.
-u	Displays only the first of a sequence of lines that compare equal when using the -m option, or checks that no pair of consecutive lines compares equal when using the -c option.

---

split **Split File** **(GNU Command)**	**split** *option(s) infile* *outfile*

Purpose

The split command splits a file into two or more output files. The default is to split a file after each 1,000 lines, but that can be changed with a command-line option.

Options

-*lines*	Uses *lines* as the number of lines in a file (the default is 1000).
-b *bytes*[*bkm*]	Separates files by *bytes* number of bytes. You can add a character to specify different units:

      b   512-byte blocks

      k   1K blocks

      m   1MB blocks

-C *bytes*[*bkm*]	Separates files by *bytes* number of bytes, but makes sure that the file ends on a complete line. You can add a character to specify different units:

      b   512-byte blocks

      k   1K blocks

      m   1MB blocks

7

tac **Display Files in Reverse Order (GNU Command)**	**tac** *option(s) filename*

Purpose

The tac command (opposite of cat) is used to display files in reverse order; that is, the ending line of a file is displayed first, followed by the second-to-last line, and so on.

Options

-b	Attaches the separator to the beginning of the record that precedes it.

-r   Sets the separator to a regular expression.

-s *string*   Sets *string* as the record separator.

Related Command

cat

| tail
Print Last Ten
File Lines
(GNU Command) | tail *option(s) filename* |

Purpose

The tail command prints the last ten lines of *filename* to the
screen. You can display more or less of the file using options.
The command is the opposite of the head command, used to
display the first ten lines of a file.

Options

-c *num*   Displays *num* number of bytes.

-f   Loops forever, trying to read more characters at the end
            of the file, on the assumption that the file is growing.

-l *num*   Displays *num* number of lines.

-q   Does not print filename headers.

-v   Prints filename headers.

Related Command

head

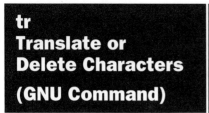

tr
Translate or
Delete Characters
(GNU Command)

tr *option(s)* [*string1*
[*string2*]]

Purpose

The tr command translates or deletes characters, replacing *string1* with *string2*.

● **CROSS-REFERENCE**

See the online manual pages for a list of available options.

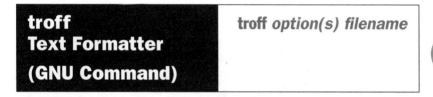

troff
Text Formatter
(GNU Command)

troff *option(s) filename*

7

Purpose

The troff command is a text formatter, part of the groff family of formatters. You usually don't use it on your own. Rather, it is invoked by the groff command on its own.

● **CROSS-REFERENCE**

Check out the groff command, earlier in this chapter, for the available options and more information.

Related Command

groff

unexpand
Convert Text
File Tabs
(GNU Command)

unexpand *option(s)*
filename

Purpose

The unexpand command converts spaces to tabs in a text file.

Options

-a   Converts all strings of two or more spaces or tabs, not just initial ones, to tabs.

-t *tab1*   Sets the tabs *tab1* spaces apart, instead of the default 8.

uniq
Strip Duplicate
File Lines
(GNU Command)

uniq *option(s)*
filename1 filename2

Purpose

The uniq command strips duplicate lines from a specified file (*filename1*) and then sends them either to another file (*filename2*) or to standard output if no other file is named.

Options

-c   Counts duplicate lines.

-d   Returns duplicate lines, but no unique lines.

-f*n*   Skips the first *n* fields of a line; fields are separated by spaces or tabs.

-s*n*   Skips the first *n* characters of a field; fields are separated by spaces or tabs.

-u   Returns unique lines, and duplicate lines are sent to the ether.

-w *n*	Compares the first *n* characters of a line.
-*n*	Skips the first *n* fields of a line; fields are separated by spaces or tabs.
+*n*	Skips the first *n* characters of a field; fields are separated by spaces or tabs.
--check-chars=*n*	Compares the first *n* characters of a line.
--skip-chars=*n*	Skips the first *n* characters of a field; fields are separated by spaces or tabs.
--skip-fields=*n*	Skips the first *n* fields of a line; fields are separated by spaces or tabs.

Related Commands

```
comm
sort
```

vi
Runs visual
text editor

vi *option(s) filename*

Purpose

The vi command starts a visual text editor. In some Linux systems, it is actually a shortcut to the elvis text editor. (Technically, the vi editor found on other UNIX systems is not the same vi as this one.)

●—CROSS-REFERENCE

See the discussion of the elvis command, earlier in this chapter, for the available options and more information.

vim
Text Editor

vim *option(s) filename*

Purpose

The vim text editor is a vi-compatible text editor that is useful for editing text files.

CROSS-REFERENCE
See the online manual pages for a list of the available options.

wc	**wc** *option(s) filename*
Count Words in Text File	

Purpose

The wc command counts the lines, words, and characters in a text file; if no filename is specified, then standard input is counted. This is a handy command when combined with other text-processing commands within a pipeline.

Options

-bytes	Prints the character count.
-c	Prints the character count.
--chars	Prints the character count.
-1	Prints the number of lines in the file.
--lines	Prints the number of lines in the file.
-w	Prints the number of words in the file; this is the default.
--words	Prints the number of words in the file; this is the default.

Example

```
$ wc /etc/passwd
21 26 750 /etc/passwd
```

| **xedit**
Launch Text Editor
(X Window System
Command) | **xedit** *filename(s)* |

Purpose

The xedit command launches a simple text editor running under the X Window System.

| **zcmp**
Compares and
Uncompresses
Compressed Files | **zcmp** *option(s) file(s)* |

Purpose

The zcmp command uncompresses a gzip-compressed file and calls on cmp. The options associated with this command are actually cmp options, which are passed along to cmp along with the compressed file.

●—CROSS-REFERENCE

See the cmp command, earlier in this chapter, for the available options and more information.

Related Commands

cmp
gzip
zcat
zegrep
zfgrep

zdiff
Uncompress a File

zdiff *option(s) file(s)*

Purpose

The zdiff command uncompresses a gzip-compressed file and calls on diff. The options associated with this command are actually diff options, which are passed along to diff along with the compressed file.

●─CROSS-REFERENCE───────────────

See the explanation of the diff command, earlier in this chapter, for the available options and more information.

Related Commands

    diff
    gzip

zegrep
Uncompress a File

zegrep *option(s) file(s)*

Purpose

The zegrep command uncompresses a gzip-compressed file and calls on egrep. The options associated with this command are actually egrep options, which are passed to egrep along with the compressed file.

●─CROSS-REFERENCE───────────────

See the explanation of the egrep command, earlier in this chapter, for the available options and other information.

Related Commands

    egrep
    gzip
    zgrep
    zfgrep

zfgrep
Uncompress a File

zfgrep option(s) file(s)

Purpose

The zfgrep command uncompresses a gzip-compressed file and calls on fgrep. The options associated with this command are actually fgrep options, which are passed to fgrep along with the compressed file.

●─CROSS-REFERENCE────────────────────────────────

See the explanation of the fgrep command, earlier in this chapter, for the available options and other information.

Related Commands

```
fgrep
gzip
zgrep
zegrep
```

zgrep
Uncompress a File

zgrep option(s) file(s)

Purpose

The zgrep command uncompresses a gzip-compressed file and calls on grep. The options associated with this command are actually grep options, which are passed to grep along with the compressed file.

●─CROSS-REFERENCE────────────────────────────────

Check out the description of the grep command, earlier in this chapter, for the available options and other information.

Related Commands

```
grep
gzip
zegrep
zfgrep
```

zmore **Print Compressed** **Files** **(GNU Command)**	**zmore** *file(s)*

Purpose

The zmore command is the GNU version of the venerable UNIX
more command. zmore prints files to the screen, one screen at a
time. The twist here is that zmore will display files compressed
with gzip. zmore has no command-line options, only commands
that can be invoked when zmore is running.

Commands

space	Prints the next screen of the file.
d or ^D	Prints the next 11 lines, or the *num* set with i[*num*].
i	Prints the next screen of the file.
i[*num*]	Sets the number of lines to be displayed as *num*, instead of a full screen.
Q	Quits reading the current file and moves to the next (if any).

Related Commands

less
more
zless

in plain english in p
sh in plain english in
glish in plain english
in plain english in p
sh in plain english in
glish in plain english
in plain english in p
glish in plain english
in plain english in p
sh in plain english in
glish in plain english
in plain english in p
sh in plain english in
glish in plain english
in plain english in p
lish in plain english
in plain english in p
sh in plain english in
glish in plain english
in plain english in p
sh in plain english in
lish in plain english
in plain english in p
glish in plain english

Internet/Electronic-Mail Commands

These commands are used to read and send electronic mail, read and send Usenet postings, download from FTP servers, and surf the World Wide Web. Most commands provide text-based interfaces for using the Internet, though some of these commands start graphical, X-based commands.

actsync Synchronize Newsgroups	actsync *option(s)* actsyncd *option(s)*

Purpose

The actsync command synchronizes, compares, or meges an "active" file containing newsgroup information. (The "active" file is usually /var/news/etc/active, and it contains the newsgroups received locally by the innd command.) The point is to make sure that multiple news servers support the same newsgroups as other news servers on a network; in addition, the command can be used to restore a backup configuration file. It's used mainly with the innd command.

The actsyncd daemon works similarly in that it can be used to try persistently to update newsgroup information, should an initial connection fail. This daemon, however, works in the foreground and sends output to standard input/output.

Options

-b hostid	Ignores newsgroups with the same three words in the name, such as alt.barney.die.die.die. (These are known as "bork style" names.)
-d hostid	Ignores newsgroups with numeric path components.
-g max	Ignores newsgroups with *max* levels.
-i ignore_file	Ignores specific newsgroups.
-I hostid	Applies the -i option to specific hosts.
-k	Overrides the practice in actsync to delete newsgroups that generate errors. Usually used with the -m option.
-l hostid	Flags problem newsgroups containing " = " characters, but does not delete them.
-m	Merges newsgroups instead of synchronizing them.
-n name	Changes the name of the creator of the newsgroup to *name*.
-o fmt	Sets the output/action format of the command. See the online manual pages for the long list of possible formats.
-p min_%_unchg	Ensures that massive changes don't wipe out a good configuration file.
-q hostid	Quiets errors from specified *hostid*.
-s size	Ignores newsgroups with names longer than *size*.
-S spool_dir	Checks *spool_dir* for new newsgroups.
-t hostid	Ignores improper newsgroups with only a top component in *hostid*.

8

-T	Ignores newsgroups from new hierarchies previously set to be ignored.
-v *level*	Sets verbosity level of actsync, ranging from 0 (no debug information) to 4 (full debug information).
-z *sec*	Pauses actsync for *sec* seconds before each command is executed.
-d *hostid*	Ignores newsgroups with numeric path components.

Related Commands

```
ctlinnd
getlist
innd
printmail
```

answer
Create Phone Messages

answer *option(s)*

8

Purpose

The answer command is a secretarial tool used to transcribe telephone messages to an electronic mail message in a form that can be used with the elm command. After launching, answer checks the .elm/aliases file for a list of users and then guides the user through a form designed to mimic phone-message slips (with fields such as Message-To and Please Call).

Options

-p	Prompts for message fields.
-u	Allows for names that aren't in the .elm/aliases file.

Related Commands

```
elm
mail
printmail
```

audiocompose **Compose Audio**	**audiocompose** *filename*

Purpose

The audiocompose command records audio. If you want to record
audio clips to attach to your outgoing mail messages, this is the
command to use. Run this command on the command line with
a filename; you'll be prompted to record a file, and then asked if
you want to listen to the file after recording it.

Then, you'll need to use the audiosend, mailto, or metamail
command to attach the file to an outgoing mail message. You must
have an audio device installed on your Linux system, usually as
/dev/audio.

If you want to make this format the default for your system,
you'll need to set up a RECORD_AUDIO environment variable to
audiocompose.

Example

```
$ audiosend hello
```

Related Commands

```
audiosend
mailto
metamail
showaudio
```

audiosend **Send Audio**	**audiosend** *e-mail_address*

Purpose

The audiosend command, unlike audiocompose, can be used to
both record the audio and e-mail it to another user. The audio seg-
ment makes up the entire e-mail message; you can't attach text or
other files to the mail message.

The command is simple: You use audiosend on a command
line, along with an e-mail address. (If you don't specify an
address, the command will prompt you for one.) The command

then prompts you for Subject and Cc fields, after which you record your message. Before sending the message, audiosend asks if you want to re-record the message or listen to it. You must have an audio device installed on your Linux system, usually as /dev/audio.

If you want to make this format the default for your system, you need to set up a RECORD_AUDIO environment variable to audiocompose.

Example

    $ audiosend hello

Related Commands

    audiocompose
    showaudio

---

biff
Check for Mail

biff *options*

8

Purpose

The biff command notifies you that new mail has been received, as long as your system uses sendmail or smail as a mail-transport agent. To see the current status of biff, type it alone on a command line. To enable biff, use the y option; to disable biff, use the n option.

Options

n	Turns biff off.
y	Turns biff on.

Related Command

    xbiff

checknews
Check New News
Messages

checknews

Purpose

The checknews command usually is used in a user profile (.profile)
or a shell script (.login) to call the readnews command in order to
check for unread Usenet news messages when a user logs in. The
readnews command is used with the -c option.

Related Command

readnews

chfn
Change Finger Info

chfn *option(s)*

Purpose

The chfn command changes the information stored in your finger profile. This information is returned over the network to anyone requesting information about you via the finger command.
This information includes your name, office number, office phone
number, and home phone number. The existing finger information is returned in brackets if you decide to enter the new finger
information interactively (the process that you use if you run chfn
on a command line by itself).

● **NOTE**
> By default, the information is not stored on a Linux system; you must
> enter it yourself.

Options

-f *name*	Enters your full name.
-h *number*	Enters your home phone number.
-o *office*	Enters your office number.
-p *number*	Enters your office phone number.

-u	Returns help information.
-v	Prints the version number.

Example

```
$ chfn
Changing finger information for Kevin.
Name [Kevin]:
Office [101]:
Office Phone [555-1212]:
Home Phone [555-1213]:
```

Related Commands

```
answer
finger
passwd
```

elm **Electronic Mail**	**elm** *option(s)*

Purpose

The elm command is an interactive mail system, more advanced in its capabilities than the mail command. You can use elm to send a message from a command line (with text input from the command line), send a file to a user from a command line, or specify nothing and use the elm interface to read and send mail.

Options

-a	Uses an arrow cursor.
-c	Expands an alias.
-d *level*	Sets the debugging *level*.
-f *folder*	Reads mail from *folder* rather than from the inbox.
-i *file*	Includes *file* in the outgoing mail message.

-m	Turns the menu off and uses the space to display more message headers.
-s *subj*	Specifies a subject.

Related Commands

```
fastmail
mail
metamail
pine
```

---

fastmail **Send Fast Mail**	**fastmail** *option(s)* *filename address-list*

Purpose

The fastmail command sends batch mail to a large group of people in staggered fashion so that the mail system is not overwhelmed. Basically, it's a simplified mail system for the general user.

Options

-b *bcc-list*	Sends blind carbon copies (BCC) to the e-mail addresses in *bcc-list*.
-c *cc-list*	Sends carbon copies (CC) to the e-mail addresses in *cc-list*.
-C *comments*	Adds *comments* as a Comments: line, added to the RFC 822 header.
-d	Lists errors in debugging mode.
-f *from*	Sets *from* as the username in the From: line.
-i *msg-id*	Adds a message ID to the mail message.
-r *replyto*	Sets Reply-to: field.
-R *references*	Sets descriptive/reference text for the message.
-s *subject*	Sets the Subject: line of the message with subject.

Related Commands

```
elm
rmail
sendmail
```

fetchmail *option(s)*
mailserver

Purpose

The fetchmail command retrieves mail from a remote mail server and forwards it to your local machine's delivery system, where it can be managed using commands such as elm or mail. Designed for use in dial-up situations, fetchmail can fetch mail from POP3, IMAP4, or ESMTP ETRN mail servers, as well as mail servers using the infrequently implemented POP2 or IMAPbis protocols.

The fetchmail command can be run in daemon mode to repeatedly fetch and forward mail. (We list the options for fetchmail running in standard mode.) The mail is delivered via SMTP to port 25 on the local machine, from where it will be delivered via a Mail Delivery Agent, such as sendmail.

● **NOTE**

See the online manual pages for the options available when running fetchmail in daemon mode.

If you don't specify a mail server on the command line, fetchmail will query the servers listed in your ~/.fetchmailrc file. This file also controls all aspects of fetchmail. Usually, using this file to configure fetchmail is better than passing along options on the command line. Options to fetchmail are divided into categories that relate to its different features (retrieval, relay, resource management, etc.).

General Options

-V, --version   Displays version information and verifies that fetchmail is working correctly.

-c, --check	Informs you that mail is waiting, without actually fetching or deleting mail from the server. It also turns off fetchmail running as a daemon.
-s, --silent	Works in silent mode, suppressing all progress/status messages that normally are echoed to standard error during a fetch.
-v, --verbose	Works in verbose mode, in which all control messages passed between fetchmail and the mail server are echoed to standard error.

Retrieval Options

-a, --all	Retrieves both old and new messages from the mail server.
-k, --keep	Leaves retrieved messages on the mail server, instead of deleting them after retrieval.
-K, --nokeep	Deletes retrieved messages from the remote mail server.
-F, --flush	Deletes previously retrieved messages from the mail server before retrieving new messages. This option works only with POP3 and IMAP servers.
-p, --protocol niproto	Specifies a protocol to use when communicating with the mail server. The options are as follows:

POP2	Uses Post Office Protocol 2.
POP3	Uses Post Office Protocol 3.
APOP	Use POP3 with MD5 authentication.
RPOP	Uses POP3 with RPOP authentication.
KPOP	Uses POP3 with Kerberos v4 authentication on port 1109.
IMAP	Uses IMAP2bis, IMAP4, or IMAP4rev1.
IMAP-K4	Uses IMAP4 or IMAP4rev1 with RFC 1731 Kerberos v4 authentication.

IMAP-GSS	Uses IMAP4 or IMAP4rev1 with RFC 1731 GSSAPI authentication.
ETRN	Uses ESMTP ETRN.
-U, --uidl	Forces UIDL use in POP3.
-P, --port	Specifies a TCP/IP port for connections.
-r folder, --folder folder	Retrieves an entire folder.

Relay Options

-D domain, --smtpaddress domain	Specifies the domain to be put in RCPT TO lines shipped to SMTP.
-m, --mda	Forces mail to be sent to an MDA directly, instead of through port 25.
-S host, --smtphost host	Specifies a hunt list of hosts to forward mail to.
-Z nnn, --antispam nnn	Specifies the numeric SMTP error that is to be interpreted as a spam-block response from the listener. A value of -1 disables this option.

Resource-Management Options

-b, --batchlimit num	Specifies the maximum number of messages that will be shipped to an SMTP listener before the connection is deliberately torn down and rebuilt.
-B, --fetchlimit	Limits the number of messages accepted from a given server in a single poll.
-e, --expunge num	Sets how often (in terms of messages) an EXPUNGE command will be issued to an IMAP server.
-l, --limit num	Specifies that messages larger than num bytes will not be fetched, will not be marked seen, and will be left on the server.

Authentication Options

-A, --auth	Specifies an authentication format. The possible values are password, kerberos_v5, or kerberos.
-I specification, -- interface specification	Requires that a specific interface device be up and have a specific local IP address (or range) before polling.
-M interface, -- monitor interface	Monitors an IP interface for inactivity.
-u name, -- username name	Specifies a username.

Miscellaneous Options

-E, --envelope	Specifies the header carrying a copy of the mail's envelope address.
-f path name, -- fetchmailrc path name	Specifies another location for the .fetch mailrc file.
-i path name, -- idfile path name	Specifies another location for the .fetchids file.
-n, --norewrite	Disables a rewrite of RFC 822 address headers.

Related Commands

```
elm
imapd
mail
sendmail
```

---

finger
Return User Information

finger *option(s)*
user

Purpose

The finger command returns information about a user, stored in their .plan and .project files. (Most users don't bother to set up these files, so don't be surprised if no information is returned.)

Also, many administrators turn of this feature for security reasons. You can specify *user* as a login name (which must be exact) or as a first or last name (where all matches are returned; this can be a long list in a networked environment).

Options

-l   Displays information in the long format. In addition to the information provided in the -s option (login name, real name, terminal name, write status, idle time, office location, and office phone number), this option adds the home directory, home phone number, login shell, mail status, and the contents of the .plan, .project, and .forward files.

-m   Overrides matching of first and last names.

-p   Cancels delivery of .plan and .project files.

-s   Displays information in the short format: login name, real name, terminal name, write status, idle time, office location, and office phone number.

Related Command
chfn

---

formail
Format Mail

formail *option(s)*

Purpose

The formail command formats standard input (usually a file, in this instance) into a mailbox format, which can then be manipulated by mail programs.

Options

+num   Skips the first *num* messages.

-num   Splits only *num* number of messages.

-a *headerfield*	Adds *headerfield* to messages lacking headers.
-b	Ignores bogus From fields.
-c	Concatenates header fields that are more than one line long.
-d	Allows loose formatting.
-e	Places messages immediately after one another, instead of inserting blank lines between them.
-f	Ignores nonmailbox-format lines.
-i *headerfield*	Adds new *headerfield* even if one already exists; the old *headerfield* is renamed *Old-headerfield*.

frm List **From/Subject Fields**	**frm** *option(s)* [*folder* | *username*]

Purpose

The frm command lists the From and Subject fields of selected messages in a mailbox or folder.

Options

-n	Uses the same numbering scheme as the readmsg command.
-q	Works in quiet mode, producing only a one-line summary for each mailbox or folder specified.
-Q	Works in very quiet mode, returning only error messages.
-s *status*	Uses *status* to specify messages; *status* can be new, unread, old, or read.
-S	Summarizes the number of messages.
-t	Displays full From field, even if it means displacing the Subject field.
-v	Prints a header before listing the contents.

Related Commands

```
elm
mail
mailx
readmsg
```

ftp *option(s) host name*

Purpose

The ftp command connects to a remote computer — either on your own network or on the wider Internet. After you're connected to the remote computer, you can copy files back and forth, delete files, and view directory contents, as long as you have the proper permissions on the remote computer to do so.

Two different levels of FTP access usually are found on the Internet:

- **Anonymous FTP:** Occurs when certain portions of a computer are opened to the Internet at large, and anyone can download files from the FTP server. In these cases, you pass along a username of **anonymous**, and your e-mail address as a password.

- **FTP servers are set up to allow access to specific people:** In these cases, you'll need an account on the FTP server, complete with username and password.

Using the ftp command is rather simple — you merely use it on a command line (with or without options; options are usually unnecessary) with or without a host name. A new FTP prompt replaces the system prompt (as you will see later in the example), and from there, you enter commands that are executed on the remote machine.

●—NOTE

Most Linux distributions, including Slackware Linux, come with the WU-FTP FTP server.

Commands

! command arg(s)	Runs a shell on the local machine, along with optional argument(s).
$ macro arg(s)	Runs a macro on the local machine.
? command	Displays help information for the specified ftp command.
account password	Specifies a *password* that will be required after you log in to a remote system. This is used with FTP servers that are not anonymous in nature.
append file1 file2	Appends the local *file1* to the remote *file2*.
ascii	Sets transfer mode to ASCII (text) format, which is the default. If you transfer binary files in ASCII format, you'll find that the binary files have been reduced to rubbish.
bell	Launches a system sound every time a file is transferred.
binary	Sets transfer mode to binary (file) format. This can be used to transfer any file; it's the opposite of the ascii setting.
bye	Ends the remote FTP session and the local ftp program.
case	Changes the case of all incoming files to lowercase.
cd directory	Changes the current directory on the remote machine to *directory*. This only works if you have access to the cd command on the remote FTP server.
cdup	Changes the current directory on the remote machine to one level up in the hierarchy.
chmod options file	Changes the permissions on the specified *file* on the remote machine. If you don't specify new permissions with options, the ftp command will prompt you for new permissions.
close	Ends the remote FTP sessions, but leaves the ftp program running locally.

8

cr	Changes carriage-return stripping to on.
delete *filename*	Deletes *filename* from the remote FTP server.
debug	Turns on debugging mode.
dir *directory filename*	Returns the contents of the specified *direc tory* (or the current working directory, if no directory is specified) on the remote machine, either to the screen or to a specified *filename* on the local machine.
disconnect	Ends the remote FTP sessions, but leaves the ftp program running locally.
get *file1 file2*	Downloads *file1* from the remote machine and stores it locally as *file2*. If *file2* is not specified, the file will be stored locally as *file1*.
glob	Turns on filename expansion for the mget, mdelete, and mput commands.
hash	Returns hash marks (#) for each block transferred.
help *command*	Returns help information for the specified *command*.
idle *seconds*	Sets the idle setting on the remote machine in *seconds*.
image	Sets transfer mode to binary (file) format. This can be used to transfer any file; it's the opposite of the ascii setting.
lcd *directory*	Changes the current local directory to *directory*. If a directory is not specified, the current local directory is changed to your home directory.
ls *directory filename*	Lists the contents of *directory* (or the cur rent working directory, if no directory is specified) on the remote machine, either to the screen or to a specified *filename* on the local machine.
macdef *macrofile*	Defines a macro, ending with a blank line; the result is stored in *macrofile*.
mdelete *filename(s)*	Deletes *filename(s)* on the remote machine.

mdir *filename(s)*	Returns directory information for multiple, specified *filename(s)*.
mget *filename(s)*	Gets the specified *filename(s)* from the remote machine.
mkdir *directory*	Creates a new directory on the remote machine.
mls *directory localfile*	Lists the contents of the remote directory into *localfile*.
mode *modename*	Changes the mode to the new *modename*. The default is streaming mode.
modtime *filename*	Displays the last modification time of the specified *filename*.
mput *filename(s)*	Uploads specified *filename(s)* from the local machine to the FTP server.
newer *remotefile*	Downloads *remotefile* if it is newer than the version on the local machine.
nlist *directory localfile*	Lists the contents of the remote directory into *localfile*.
open *host (port)*	Opens a connection to the specified *host* and optional *port*. If you don't specify a host, the command will prompt you for one.
prompt	Turns off (or on) interactive prompting.
proxy *command*	Runs *command* on another connection.
put *file1 file2*	Copies local file *file1* to the remote machine as *file2*. If *file2* is not specified, then the name *file1* will be used.
pwd	Prints the current (working) directory on the remote machine.
quit	Ends the remote FTP session and the local ftp program.
recv *file1 file2*	Downloads *file1* from the remote machine and stores it locally as *file2*. If *file2* is not specified, the file will be stored locally as *file1*.

reget *file1* *file2*	Downloads *file1* from the remote machine and stores it locally as *file2*. If there was an interruption in the transfer, the new transfer will start where the old one was interrupted.
remotehelp *command*	Returns help information about *command* from the remote machine.
remotestatus *file*	Returns the status of the remote machine or *file* on the remote machine.
rename *file1* *file2*	Renames *file1* on the remote system to *file2*.
reset	Resets the transfer queue.
restart *byte*	Restarts a transfer, beginning with a specific *byte* count.
mdir *directory*	Deletes *directory* on the remote machine.
runique	Turns on unique local file naming; if you're attempting to grab a file from a remote machine, and a file already exists with the same name locally, the remote filename will be grabbed and a number (.1, .2, and so on) will be added to the new file.
send *file1* *file2*	Copies local file *file1* to the remote machine as *file2*. If *file2* is not specified, then the name *file1* will be used.
site *command*	Returns information about the remote site.
size *file*	Returns the size of the remote *file*.
status	Returns information about the current session.
struct *name*	Changes the file-transfer structure to *name*. The default is streaming.
sunique	Turns on unique remote file naming; if you're attempting to upload a file to a remote machine, and a file already exists with the same name, the file will be uploaded and a number (.1, .2, and so forth) will be added to the new file.
system	Returns the name of the operating system running on the remote machine.

trace	Turns on packet tracing.
type *type*	Sets the file-transfer type to *type*; the default is ASCII. Without *type* specified, the current type is returned.
umask *mask*	Sets the mode mask on the remote machine. Without *mask* specified, the current mask is returned.
user *name password account*	Sends your name, password, and account number to the remote server. If you don't specify *password* and *account*, the remote server will prompt you for the information.
verbose	Turns on verbose mode.

Options

-d	Turns on debugging.
-g	Turns off filename globbing.
-i	Turns off interactive mode.
-n	Turns off autologin after connecting to a remote site.
-v	Turns on verbose mode, in which all information from the remote server is displayed.

Example

The following example shows the beginning of an ftp session to connect to the Red Hat FTP site (ftp.redhat.com). The user logs in as anonymous, then enters an e-mail address as the password. At that point, the user can do any FTP commands (ls, cd, get, etc.).

```
$ ftp ftp.redhat.com
Connected to ftp.redhat.com.
220 FTP server ready.
Name (ftp.redhat.com:jake): anonymous
331 Guest login ok, send your complete email address
as password.
Password: *********
```

Related Command

```
ftpd
ncftp
```

ftpcount
List FTP Users

ftpcount

Purpose

The ftpcount shows the current number of users for each class defined in the ftpaccess file.

Related Command

```
ftpwho
```

getlist
Get NNTP List

getlist *option list*

Purpose

The getlist command gets a list from an NNTP server. The list can take a value of active, active.times, distributions, or newsgroups. These values request the active, active.times, /usr/lib/news/distributions, or /usr/lib/news/newsgroups files, respectively.

Option

-h *host name*   Connects to specified *host name*.

Related Commands

```
active
nnrpd
```

lynx **Launch Text** **Web Browser**	**lynx** *option(s) URL*

Purpose

The lynx command launches a character-based Web browser.
It doesn't display images in a graphics-rich environment. As a
result, it's a fairly speedy Web browser, because you don't have
to wait for graphics to load.

Options

-anonymous	Specifies an anonymous account.
-ascii	Disables Kanji translation when Japanese mode is on.
-auth=*ID passwd*	Sets the ID and password for sites that require such authentication.
-book	Launches lynx with the bookmark pages as the initial document.
-cache=*number*	Sets the number of cached documents; the default is 10.
-case	Turns on case-sensitive string searching.
-cfg=*filename*	Specifies a new configuration file.
-crawl	Outputs each page to a file if used with -traversal; outputs each page to standard output if used with -dump.
-display=*display*	Sets the *display* variable for X rexeced programs.
-dump	Sends the formatted output of the default document to standard output.
-editor=*editor*	Launches edit mode with the specified *editor*.
-emacskeys	Uses emacs-like key movement.
-force_html	Interprets the first document as an HTML page, no matter what.
-ftp	Disables FTP access.

-get_data	Sends form data from standard input using the GET method and dump results.
-head	Sends a HEAD request for the MIME headers.
-homepage=URL	Sets a home page separate from the start page.
-image_links	Toggles inclusion of links for all images.
-index=URL	Set the default index file to the specified URL.
-localhost	Disables URLs that point to remote hosts.
-locexec	Enables local-program execution from local files only.
-mime_header	Displays a MIME header of a fetched document along with its source.
-nobrowse	Disables directory browsing.
-noexec	Disables local program execution.
-nolist	Disables the link-list feature in dumps.
-nolog	Disables mailing of error messages to document owners.
-noprint	Disables print functions.
-noredir	Prevents automatic redirection and prints a message with a link to the new URL.
-nostatus	Disables the retrieval status messages.
-number_links	Starts numbering of links.
-post_data	Sends form data from standard input using the POST method and dump results.
-realm	Restricts access to URLs in the starting realm.
-reload	Flushes the cache on a proxy server (only the first document is affected).
-restrictions option=	Disables services; option is one of the following:
	all Restricts all options.
	bookmark Disallows changing the location of the bookmark file.

`bookmark_exec`	Disallows execution links via the bookmark file.
`change_exec_perms`	Disallows changing the execute permission on files (but still allows it for directories).
`default`	Disables default services for anonymous users.
`dired_support`	Disallows local file management.
`disk_save`	Disallows saving binary files to disk.
`download`	Disables downloads.
`editor`	Disallows editing.
`exec`	Disables execution scripts.
`exec_frozen`	Disallows the changing of the local execution option.
`file_url`	Disables the opening of files via URLs.
`goto`	Disables the goto command.
`inside_ftp`	Disallows FTP connections for people from inside your domain.
`inside_news`	Disallows Usenet news posts from people from inside your domain.
`inside_rlogin`	Disallows rlogin for people from inside your domain.
`inside_telnet`	Disallows telnet for people from inside your domain.

	jump	Disables the jump command.
	mail	Disables outgoing mail.
	news_post	Disables news posting.
	options_save	Disallows saving options in .lynxrc.
	outside_ftp	Disallows FTPs for people coming from outside your domain.
	outside_news	Disallows news postings for people from outside your domain.
	outside_rlogin	Disallows rlogin for people from outside your domain.
	outside_telnet	Disallows telnet for people from outside your domain.
	print	Disallows most print options.
	shell	Disallows shell escapes.
	suspend	Disallows Linux Ctrl-Z suspends with escape to shell.
	telnet_port	Disallows specifying a port in telnet connections.
-rlogin		Disables recognition of rlogin commands.
-selective		Requires .www_browsable files to browse directories.
-show_cursor		Positions the cursor at the start of the currently selected link, not hidden in the right-hand corner.
-source		Sends the raw HTML code of the default document to standard output.
-telnet		Disables recognition of telnet commands.

-term=TERM	Sets terminal type.
-trace	Turns on WWW trace mode.
-traversal	Traverses all HTTP links derived from startfile.
-underscore	Toggles use of underline format in dumps.
-validate	Accepts only HTTP URLs for validation.
-vikeys	Enable vi-like key movement.

mail
Send and Receive Electronic Mail

mail *option(s) users*

Purpose

The mail command (also known in Linux as the mailx command) is used to send and receive e-mail, from either other users on the system or users from the Internet at large (if your system has Internet capabilities).

The mail command is only one of many e-mail options under Linux; virtually all distributions include the easier-to-use pine and elm programs, and other distributions include more advanced graphical mail tools.

●─TIP─

Netscape Communicator includes an excellent mail program. If you're connecting directly to a mail server and don't need any other transport mechanisms, you should consider using Netscape, which is now open-source software and part of every Linux distribution.

Commands

-num	Displays the preceding message; if *num* is specified, then the *num* number of previous messages is printed.
?	Displays a summary of commands.
!command	Executes shell *command*.

alias (a) *alias*	Prints all aliases if *alias* is not specified. If *alias* is specified, then information about that alias is listed. If multiple aliases are specified, a new one is created or an old one is changed.
alternates (alt)	Manages accounts on multiple machines, informing you about the status of listed addresses or alternates.
chdir *dir* (c)	Changes your current directory to *dir*. If no directory is specified, then the current directory changes to your home directory.
copy (co)	Copies a message, but does not delete the original.
delete (d)	Deletes messages.
dp, dt	Deletes the current message and displays the next message.
edit (e)	Launches text editor to edit message; after editing, the message is reentered into `mail`.
exit (ex or x)	Quits `mail` without saving changes to the mailbox.
file (fi)	Lists all folders in the folder directory.
folder (fo)	Opens a new mail file or folder. If you don't specify a new folder, the name of the current file is displayed. If you do switch to a new mail file or folder, the changes in the old mail file or folder will be written before switching. Shortcuts for the name of the new mail file or folder are as follows:

#	Previous file.
%	System mailbox.
%*user*	*user*'s system mailbox.
&	Your mbox file.
+*folder*	File in your *folder* directory.

folders	Lists all folders in the folder directory.
from (f)	Prints message headers of messages.
headers (h)	Lists the current range of headers, which is an 18-message group.

help	Displays a summary of commands.
hold (ho, preserve)	Marks messages that are to be stored in your system mailbox instead of in mbox.
ignore *header*	Adds a *header* field to a list of fields to be ignored. If *header* is not specified, then the current list of fields to be ignored is displayed.
mail (m) *user*	Sends mail to *user*; a list of users can also be specified.
mbox	Moves messages to mbox when exiting. (Default.)
next (n)	Displays next message in the sequence.
preserve (pre)	Marks messages that are to be stored in your system mailbox instead of in mbox.
print list (p)	Prints messages in list.
Print list (P)	Prints list of files, as well as ignored header fields.
quit (q)	Ends mail session, saving all undeleted, unsaved messages in the mbox file, preserving all messages marked with hold or preserve or never referenced in the system mailbox, and removing all other messages from the system mailbox.
reply (r)	Composes a reply to the originator of the message and the other recipients.
Reply (R)	Composes a reply to the originator of the message, but not to any of the other recipients.
respond	Composes a reply to the originator of the message and the other recipients.
retain *header*	Adds *header* to the list of fields named in retained_list, which are shown when you view a message.
save (s)	Saves a message to a specific folder.
set (se)	Displays all variables. If an argument is presented, it is used to set an option.
saveignore	Removes ignored fields when saving a message.

saveretain	Retains specified fields when saving a message.
shell (sh)	Launches *shell*.
size	Lists messages by size.
source *file*	Reads commands from *file*.
top	Displays the first five lines of a message.
type *list* (t)	Prints messages in *list*.
Type (T)	Prints list of files, as well as ignored header fields.
unalias	Discards previous aliases.
undelete (u)	Undeletes a message that was previously marked for deletion.
unread (U)	Marks previously read messages as being unread.
unset	Discards previous variables set with the set command.
visual (v)	Launches visual editor and edits each message in a list.
write *file* (w)	Writes the message body, without headers, to *file*.
xit (x)	Quits mail without saving changes to the mailbox.
z	Displays next window of messages.
z-	Displays previous window of messages.

Tilde Commands

These commands are used when composing messages. They must be placed at the beginning of lines.

~!*command*	Runs *command*, and then returns to the message.
~b*name(s)*	Adds *name(s)* to the Bcc field.
~c*name(s)*	Adds *name(s)* to the Cc field.
~d	Reads the dead.letter file from your home directory.
~e	Launches the text editor for further editing.

`~fmessage(s)`	Inserts *message(s)* into the message being sent.
`~Fmessage(s)`	Inserts *message(s)* into the message being sent, including headers.
`~h`	Edits the header fields.
`~mmessage(s)`	Inserts *message(s)* into the message being sent, indented by a tab.
`~Mmessage(s)`	Inserts *message(s)* into the message being sent, including headers, indented by a tab.
`~p`	Prints current message and the header fields.
`~q`	Quits current message and sends it to the dead.letter file.
`~rfilename`	Inserts *filename* into the message.
`~sstring`	Sets subject as *string*.
`~tname(s)`	Adds *name(s)* to the list of recipients.
`~v`	Starts the visual editor for editing the message (as identified by the VISUAL shell environment variable).
`~wfilename`	Writes the message to *filename*.
`~|command`	Pipes the message through the *command* (usually `fmt`).
`~:mail-command`	Executes `mail-command`.
`~~string`	Inserts *string* into message, prefaced by ~.

Options

`-b list`	Sends blind carbon copies to *list*, which is a comma-separated list of names.
`-c list`	Sends copies to users in *list*.
`-f file`	Uses mbox (or *file*, if specified) when launching mail; used as an alternative mailbox.
`-i`	Ignores interrupt signals, which is useful when you're using a Linux machine on a noisy dial-up line.
`-I`	Forces interactive mode.

-n	Doesn't read /etc/mail.rc when starting.
-N	Suppresses display of message headers when reading mail or editing a mail folder.
-s *subject*	Uses *subject* as the subject of the mail message.
-v	Works in verbose mode, in which the details of delivery are displayed.

Mail Options

You can set the following options either via the set and unset commands or in the mail.rc file.

append	Appends messages saved in mbox, rather than prepending them.
ask, asksub	Asks you for the subject of a message.
askcc	Asks you for additional Cc recipients.
askbcc	Asks you for additional Bcc recipients.
autoprint	Displays the next message after deleting the current message.
debug	Displays debugging information.
dot	Inserts a dot (.) alone on the last line of a message.
hold	Holds messages in the system mailbox.
ignore	Ignores interrupt signals; displays them as @.
ignoreeof	Ignores Ctrl-D at the end of a file.
metoo	Includes the sender as part of a group.
noheader	Suppresses display of message headers when reading mail or editing a mail folder.
nosave	Does not send deleted letter to the dead.letter file.
Replyall	Switches reply and Reply commands.
quiet	Suppresses printing the version when first invoked.
verbose	Works in verbose mode, in which the details of delivery are displayed.

Option String Values

EDITOR	Specifies editor to use with the edit command and ~e escape.
LISTER	Specifies path name of the directory lister to use in the folders command. The default is /bin/ls.
PAGER	Specifies path name of the program to use in the more command or when the crt variable is set. The default paginator is more.
SHELL	Specifies path name of the shell to use in the ! command and the ~! escape. The default system shell is used if this option is not defined.
VISUAL	Specifies path name of the text editor to use in the visual command and ~v escape.
crt	Determines how long a message must be before PAGER is used to read it. The default is the height of the terminal screen.
escape	Defines the escape character; the default is ~.
folder	Defines the directory storing folders of messages. If it begins with /, then it's considered an absolute path name; otherwise, it's considered relative to your home directory.
MBOX	Defines your mbox file; the default is mbox in your home directory.
record	Specifies path name of the file used to store outgoing mail; if not defined, outgoing mail is not stored.
indentprefix	Identifies string used for indenting message via the ~m escape, instead of tabs.
toplines	Defines the number of lines to be printed with the top command.

Examples

This displays your mail:

```
$ mail
```

This begins the process of sending electronic mail to reichard@mr.net:

```
$ mail reichard@mr.net
```

Related Commands

```
elm
fmt
pine
sendmail
```

messages **Count Messages**	**messages** *folder name*

Purpose

The messages command counts the number of messages in a *folder name*, keying off of the number of times the From field appears.

metamail **MIME-Enabled Mail**	**metamail** *option(s)*

Purpose

The metamail command works with multimedia mail messages, as defined by the Multimedia Internet Mail Extension (MIME) format. It reads a mailcap file to determine how to display nontext messages. Other mail programs that must display nontext messages also call this command.

Unless you run into unusual circumstances, you'll never use metamail directly; instead, your mail package will invoke it to display nontext messages. Because users won't use this command directly, we devote little space to it.

● CROSS-REFERENCE

We encourage you to check the online manual pages to see how to add metamail support to a mail-reading program or add lines. (Type man metamail.)

**metasend
Send MIME Mail**

metasend *option(s)*

Purpose

The metasend command sends an existing data file as a nontext multimedia mail message. You can specify a message recipient, subject, carbon-copy recipients, Multimedia Internet Mail Extension (MIME) content type, filename, and encoding on the command line; if you don't, you'll be prompted for this information after you launch the command.

Options

-b	Works in batch mode, exiting if information is missing from the command line.
-c *cc*	Sets the Cc address.
-D	Sets the Content-Description value.
-e *encoding*	Sets the encoding type: base64, quoted-printable, 7bit, or x-uue.
-E	Specifies that the file is already a MIME entity, not requiring a Content-description header.
-f *filename*	Sets the data file.
-F *from*	Sets the From address.
-i *<content-id>*	Sets the *content-id* for the MIME entity, enclosed in angle brackets.
-I *<content-id>*	Sets the *content-id* for the multipart entity created by metasend.
-m *MIME-type*	Sets the MIME content type.
-n --	Specifies that an additional file is to be included.
-o *outputfile*	Sends the output to *outputfile*.

8

-P *preamblefile*	Specifies a file to be used as the preamble of the MIME message.
-s *subject*	Sets the Subject field.
-S *splitsize*	Sets the maximum size before splitting a message into parts via splitmail.
-t *to*	Sets the To address.
-z	Deletes temporary files, even if delivery fails.

Related Commands

```
audiosend
mailto
mmencode
pine
splitmail
```

---

mimencode	**mimencode**
Enable MIME Encoding	*option(s)*

8

Purpose

The mimencode command translates to and from the Multime-dia Internet Mail Extension (MIME) standard. Because Windows 95/98/NT don't support uuencoding, MIME encoding is preferable.

Options

-b	Specifies base64 encoding (the default).
-q	Specifies quoted-printable encoding instead of base64.
-u	Decodes input, but does not encode it.
-p	Translates carriage-return/line feed sequences into newlines.
-o *filename*	Sends output to *filename*.

Related Command

```
mmencode
```

mmencode
Enable MIME Encoding

mmencode
option(s)

Purpose

The mmencode command translates to and from the Multimedia Internet Mail Extension (MIME) standard. Because Windows 95/98/NT don't support uuencoding, MIME encoding is preferable.

Options

-b	Specifies base64 encoding (the default).
-q	Specifies quoted-printable encoding instead of base64.
-u	Decodes input, but does not encodes it.
-p	Translates carriage-return/line feed sequences into newlines.
-o *filename*	Sends output to *filename*.

Related Command

mimencode

newsgroups
List Unsubscribed
Newsgroups

newsgroups *option(s)*

Purpose

The newsgroups command compares the contents of your .newsrc file (which contains a list of subscribed newsgroups) with the listing of all active newsgroups.

Options

-flag	Lists newsgroups not found in your .newsrc file.

pattern   Prints a list of unsubscribed newsgroups
                            matching *pattern*.

Related Commands
newsrc
rn

---

pine
Read Electronic Mail   **pine** *option(s) address*

Purpose

The pine command is used to read e-mail and Usenet news. It
supports Multimedia Internet Mail Extension (MIME), allowing
you to save MIME objects to files. In some cases, it can also initi-
ate the correct program for viewing the object.

Outgoing mail is usually handed off to sendmail, but it can be
posted directly via SMTP.

●─CROSS-REFERENCE

There are many command-line options; see the online manual pages for
more information. (Type man pine.)

●─TIP

Netscape Communicator includes an excellent mail program. If you're
connecting directly to a mail server and don't need any other transport
mechanisms, you should consider using Netscape, which is now open-
source software and part of every Linux distribution.

Related Commands
elm
mail
sendmail

Pnews
Post News
Articles

Pnews
Pnews Pnews *newsgroup title*
Pnews -h *headerfile*

Purpose

The Pnews command posts news articles to specific newsgroups. It's an interactive program, which means that it guides you through the process of adding an item to a newsgroup. After you enter the relevant information, the new news item is sent to the Usenet via the inews program.

The Pnews command will include a signature file, if the file is .news_sig and stored in your home directory. The inews program adds a signature via the .signature file stored in your home directory. (If both files exist, then they both will be added to a news item.)

Pnews uses the default system editor to compose messages, which is defined with the EDITOR variable. This program also interacts with the trn newsreader; you'll want to look through the online manual pages for more information.

●─TIP────────────────────────

Netscape Communicator includes an excellent newsreader. If you're connecting directly to a news server and don't need any other transport mechanisms, you should consider using Netscape, which is now open-source software and part of every Linux distribution.

Option

-h   When used with trn, Pnews inserts a previous article that is the subject of the current article.

Example

    $ Pnews

Related Commands

    inews
    Rnmail
    trn

popclient Retrieve Electronic Mail	popclient *option(s)* *host*

Purpose

The popclient command retrieves e-mail from a mail server running the Internet Post Office Protocol (POP). It supports both POP2 (as specified in RFC 937) and POP3 (RFC 1725), although most newer mail servers support POP3.

This command grabs the mail from the remote server (specified by *host*) and stores it in a mail folder on your hard disk. From there, you read it with a mail program, such as mail or elm.

●—TIP

The fetchmail command is a newer version of popclient–most Linux distributions contain one or the other.

Options

-2	Uses Post Office Protocol version 2 (POP2).
-3	Uses Post Office Protocol version 3 (POP3).
-a	Uses POP3 and retrieves old (previously retrieved) and new messages from the mail server.
-c	Writes messages to standard output instead of to disk.
-F	Uses POP3 and deletes old (previously retrieved) messages from the mail server before retrieving new messages.
-f *path name*	Sets an alternate name for the .poprc file.
-k	Keeps old messages on the mail server.
-K	Deletes messages on the mail server after retrieval.
-l *lines*	Retrieves *lines* lines of each message body and headers.
-p *string*	Passes *string* as the password when logging on to the mail server. If you don't specify a password, you'll be prompted for a password when you actually log in to the mail server.

--protocol *protocol*	Sets the protocol to use with the remote mail server. The protocol can be any of the following: POP2 (Post Office Protocol 2) POP3 (Post Office Protocol 3) APOP (POP3 with MD5 authentication) RPOP (POP3 with trusted-host-based authentication, like `rlogin` or `rsh`)
-o *folder*	Appends messages to file in *folder*.
-r *folder*	Grabs messages from *folder*, an alternative folder on the mail server.
-s	Works in silent mode.
-u *name*	Passes *name* as the user to the mail server; by default, this is your login name on your machine.
-v	Works in verbose mode, in which all messages between you and the server are displayed.

Related Command
```
elm
fetchmail
mail
```

postnews
Post News

postnews option
headerfile newsgroup(s)

Purpose

The postnews command posts a news item to a Usenet newsgroup. You can specify the newsgroup (or newsgroups) on the command line; if you don't, the postnews command will prompt you for a newsgroup. If you do specify newsgroups, you need to separate them with commas but no spaces. After you specify the newsgroup, a text editor allows you to create the posting.

At any point, you can terminate the posting by entering nonconforming input, such as a fictional newsgroup name.

Option

-h   Specifies that the header is in *headerfile*.

Related Command

inews

printmail **Print Electronic Mail**	**printmail** *option* *filename*

Purpose

The printmail command formats mail in anticipation of printing.
It copies your messages from your user mailbox or a specified filename, with each message separated by a line of dashes. It's actually a call to the readmsg command, and it's usually part of a
pipeline (like printmail | lpr).

Option

-p   Uses a form feed instead of dashes
                             to separate messages.

Related Commands

elm
readmsg

procmail **Process Mail**	**procmail** *option(s)* *argument(s)*

Purpose

The procmail command works "under the hood" to process mail,
usually through the .forward file mechanism as soon as mail
arrives. It can also be installed to work immediately through the
mail program.

The procmail command sets some environment variables to
default values, reads the mail message from standard input until

an end-of-file marker appears, separates the body from the header, and then, if no command-line arguments are present, looks for a file named $HOME/.procmailrc. This file routes the message to the correct folder.

Arguments containing = are considered to be environment-variable assignments. Any other arguments are presumed to be rcfile paths.

● **CAUTION** ──────────────────────────────────

This is a complex command that can cause some damage to mail processing if not configured properly. Check the online manual pages for more detailed information about procmail. (Type man procmail.)

Options

-a argument	Sets $1 to argument.
-d recipient	Turns on explicit delivery mode, in which delivery will be to the local user recipient. Cannot be used with -p.
-f fromwhom	Regenerates a leading From line with fromwhom as the sender (instead of -f, one could use the alternate and obsolete -r). If fromwhom consists of a single -, then procmail will update the time stamp only on the From line.
-m	Turns procmail into a general-purpose mail filter.
-o	Overrides fake From lines.
-p	Preserves the old environment.
-t	Makes procmail fail softly; if procmail cannot deliver to any destination, the mail will not bounce, but instead will return to the mail queue, with another delivery attempt made in the future.
-Y	Works with Berkeley mailbox format, ignoring Content-Length fields.

Signals

TERMINATE	Terminates prematurely and requeues the mail.
HANGUP	Terminates prematurely and bounces the mail.
INTERRUPT	Terminates prematurely and bounces the mail.
QUIT	Terminates prematurely and silently loses the mail.
ALARM	Forces a timeout.
USR1	Equivalent to VERBOSE=off.
USR2	Equivalent to VERBOSE=on.

Related Commands

```
biff
mail
sendmail
```

readmsg **Read Mail Message**	**readmsg** *option(s)* *selection folder*

Purpose

The readmsg command extracts messages from a mail folder. You'll usually do this when you're preparing mail in a text editor and want to quote a specific, existing message from your mail folder.

You use the selection argument to specify which message to grab from your mail folder. A wildcard (*) means to pull all messages, whereas a number refers to a specific message (with 0 or $ referring to the last message in the mailbox). In addition, you can pull messages that contain a specific string; these strings don't need to be enclosed in quotes. In this instance, the first message that contains the string will be returned.

● **NOTE** ─────────────────────────────

The method just described, by the way, is case-sensitive.

You can also use readmsg from within the elm newsreader rather than from within an external editor, but it works a little differently in that situation. The mailbox used for retrieving messages is the current mailbox, not your inbox; the current elm message will be pulled; and the numbering scheme is a little different.

Options

-a	Returns all messages that return the string on the command line, not just the first message.
-f *folder*	Uses *folder* instead of the incoming mailbox. This is useful when you want to search through mail you've already sent.
-h	Includes all header information, not just the default From, Date, and Subject fields.
-n	Excludes all headers from retrieved messages.
-p	Places form feeds (Ctrl-L) between messages headers.

Related Commands

```
elm
newmail
```

---

richtext	**richtext** *option(s)*
Display Rich Text	*filename*

Purpose

The richtext command displays "rich text" documents — usually mail messages — on an ASCII terminal, using termcap settings to highlight and underline text. Rich text is part of the Multimedia Internet Mail Extension (MIME) format for multimedia Internet mail — not Microsoft's Rich Text Format (RTF).

Options

-c	Displays text with no formatting.

-f	Specifies termcap escape codes for bold and italic text.
-m	Interprets < in multibyte Japanese and Korean sequences as a true less-than symbol and not as the start of a rich text command.
-n	Tells the command to perform no corrections on the raw rich text.
-o	Uses overstriking for underlining, when appropriate.
-p	Summons system PAGER from environment variables.
-s charset	Uses specified charset when processing text. Charset can be one of us-ascii (the default), iso-2022-jp, and iso-2022-kr.
-t	Overrides termcap escape codes.

Related Commands

```
mailto
metamail
termcap
```

---

rmail Read Mail	rmail *username*

Purpose

The rmail command interprets incoming mail received via the uucp command. With the advent of the Internet, this command has lessened in usage.

Related Command

```
sendmail
```

Rnmail
Respond to News
Via Mail

Rnmail
Rnmail *destination_list*
option

Purpose

The Rnmail command responds to news articles via e-mail, instead of posting the message to newsgroups. It's an interactive program, which means that it guides you through the process of sending mail, prompting you for information about the recipient of the message and more.

Rnmail includes a signature file, if the file is .news_sig and stored in your home directory. The inews program adds a signature via the .signature file stored in your home directory.

●—NOTE

If both files exist, then they both will be added to a news item.

Rnmail will use the default system editor to compose messages, which is defined with the EDITOR variable. This program also interacts with the trn newsreader.

●—CROSS-REFERENCE

You'll want to look through the online manual pages for more information about the Rnmail command. (Type man Rnmail.)

Option

-h   When used with trn, Rnmail will insert a
                            previous article that is the subject of the
                            current article.

Example

```
$ Rnmail
To:
Title/Subject:
Prepared file to include [none]:
Editor [usr/bin/vi]:
Check spelling, Send, Abort, Edit, or List?
```

8

Related Commands

```
inews
Pnews
trn
```

showaudio
Play Audio E-Mail

showaudio *filename(s)*

Purpose

The showaudio command plays an audio e-mail message created with audiocompose. It is routinely summoned by a mailcap file, generally with the metamail program. Usually, it will play the audio on your low-fi computer speaker.

Related Commands

```
audiocompose
audiosend
metamail
```

showexternal
Show External Mail

showexternal *body-file*
access-type name

Purpose

The showexternal command fetches and displays the body of a mail message that is included by reference, using the Multimedia Internet Mail Extension (MIME) type message/external-body. It's not usually used on its own, but rather is called by metamail via a mailcap entry.

Related Command

```
metamail
```

shownonascii
Show in
Non-ASCII Font

shownonascii option
charset-f
ont-name filename(s)

●—**X Window System Command** ─────────────

Purpose

The shownonascii command displays all or part of a mail message in a non-ASCII font. By default, it will open up an xterm window using the font named in the first argument, running the more command to view all the files named on the command line.

Option

-e *command*   Uses *command* instead of more to display the file.

Related Commands

mailto
metamail

showpartial
Show Partial
Format

showpartial *file ID*
partnum totalnum

Purpose

The showpartial command is used to display the body of a Multimedia Internet Mail Extension (MIME)-formatted message that is of the type message/partial. When it is called on the last piece, it will put together the pieces and call metamail to display the full message. It is intended to be called by metamail via a mailcap entry.

Related Command

metamail

| showpicture
Show Picture
in Mail | showpicture
option
filename(s) |

●—**X Window System Command** ———————————————

Purpose

The showpicture command displays an image that has been attached to a mail message via Multimedia Internet Mail Extension
(MIME). It loads the X Window System xloadimage command to
do so. It is meant to be summoned by metamail from a mailcap file.

Option

-viewer   Specifies a new image viewer.

Related Commands

metamail
xloadimage

| splitmail
Split Mail | splitmail *option(s)*
filename |

Purpose

The splitmail command takes a large mail message (stored in
filename) and splits it into Multimedia Internet Mail Extension
(MIME)-compliant partial messages, using the message/partial
MIME type.

Options

-d	Delivers the mail.
-v	Works in verbose mode.
-i	Applies similar message-ID fields.
-s	Changes default chunk size for message (default is 250,000).

Related Commands

```
mailto
metamail
```

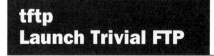

tftp
Launch Trivial FTP

tftp *host name*

Purpose

The tftp command launches the Trivial File Transfer Protocol (TFTP) program, used to upload and download files from a server.

Commands

ascii	Changes to ASCII mode.
binary	Changes to binary mode.
connect *host name*	Sets the *host name* to connect to.
get *filename*	Gets *filename* from host.
mode ascii	Changes to ASCII mode.
mode binary	Changes to binary mode.
put *filename*	Puts *filename* on remote host.
quit	Quits tftp.
status	Shows the current status.
timeout *timeout*	Sets the total transmission timeout, in seconds.
verbose	Toggles verbosity.

8

trn
Launch Threaded
Newsreader

trn *option(s)*
newsgroup(s)

Purpose

The trn command launches a newsreader that allows you to read through threaded Usenet newsgroup articles. *Threading* means that articles are interconnected in reply order. This is a complex but useful command.

● CROSS-REFERENCE

It is worth your time to read through the voluminous online manual pages for more information about the options, etc. (Type man trn.)

● TIP

Netscape Communicator includes an excellent newsreader. If you're connecting directly to a news server and don't need any other transport mechanisms, you should consider using Netscape, which is now open-source software and part of every Linux distribution.

uudecode
Decode a File

uudecode *filename*

Purpose

The uudecode command decodes a file, converting it from a format suitable for sending via electronic mail.

Related Command

uuencode

uuencode
Encode a File

uuencode *filename*

Purpose

The uuencode command encodes a file, converting it into a format suitable for sending via electronic mail.

Related Command

uudecode

| **uustat**
Return UUCP Status | **uustat** *option(s)* |

Purpose

The uustat command returns information about the UUCP
(UNIX-to-UNIX Copy Program) status.

● CROSS-REFERENCE

See the online manual pages for a list of the available options. (Type
man uustat.)

| **uux**
Execute
Command Remotely | **uux** *option(s)*
command |

Purpose

The uux command executes a command on a remote system, or
executes a command on the local system using files from remote
systems.

● CROSS-REFERENCE

See the online manual pages for a list of the available options. (Type
man uux.)

| **vrfy**
Verify E-Mail Address | **vrfy** *option(s)*
address host name |

Purpose

The vrfy command verifies the existence and accuracy of an
e-mail address. If the host is known, that information can be
added to the command line, increasing the chances that the existence and accuracy can be verified. If the host name is not specified, the information may have to go through other mail systems,
which can decrease the accuracy.

CROSS-REFERENCE

See the online manual pages for a list of the available options. (Type man vrfy.)

wnewmail **Check for Mail**	**wnewmail** *filename*

Purpose

The wnewmail daemon checks every 10 seconds to see if there is any new mail. It's similar to biff and xbiff, except with less flexibility.

Related Commands

```
biff
newmail
xbiff
```

xbiff **Check for Mail**	**xbiff** *option(s)*

X Window System Command

Purpose

The xbiff command is an X Window System version of the biff command, which notifies you when incoming mail is received.

Options

-file *filename*	Specifies the name of the mail file to be monitored. The default is /usr/spool/mail/username.
-update *seconds*	Specifies how often xbiff should check for mail, in seconds. The default is every 30 seconds.
-volume *percentage*	Specifies the loudness of the bell (system sound), as a percentage of the full audio.

-shape   Specifies whether the mailbox window
                          should be shaped.

Related Command
    biff

xmh   Handle Mail   xmh *option(s)*

● — X Window System Command ─────────────

Purpose
The xmh command is an X-based front end to the mh mail handler.
On its own, it calls the mh package.

Options

-flag   Flags you when new mail arrives.
-initial *folder*   Specifies another folder for new mail.
-path *directory*   Specifies another directory for mail folders.

Related Commands
    mail
    metamail
    mh

Programming
Commands

9

The commands described in this chapter are some of the basic programming commands that ship with most Linux implementations. The Linux operating system is actually a programmer's dream environment; these commands will get you going, but additional programming tools are covered in the online manual pages.

Many of these commands are GNU commands. Although the number of programming tools available for Linux programmers — mostly commercial products — is increasing, the backbone of all Linux programming is the GNU suite of programming tools from the Free Software Foundation.

ansi2knr Convert ANSI to K&R	ansi2knr *input_file* *output_file*

Purpose

The ansi2knr command converts a standard ANSI C file to a file that meets Kernighan & Ritchie C (K&R C programming language) specifications. Be warned that no error messages are given, so if the translation failed, you won't know.

Example

```
$ ansi2knr oldfile.c newfile.c
```

ar Create Archive Files (GNU Command)	ar *options* *membername file(s)*

9

Purpose

The ar command is used to create, modify, and extract from archive files. An *archive file* is a collection of files stored in a single file, which makes storing and managing the collection of files easier in file system and device usage. All the important file elements, including permissions, owners, time stamps, and groups, are saved in the archive.

The ar command is used most in programming situations, because it is used to create libraries that contain frequently used subroutines.

A *membername* is a file that already exists within the archive. Some of the options, particularly those that specify the order of files within the archive, rely on a *membername*.

Two arguments to the ar command are required: an option of some sort that specifies the operation, and the name of the file. This command can be confusing, because the option usually must begin with p.

Options

-a   Adds new files after a *membername*.

-b   Adds new files before a *membername*. This is the same as the -i argument.

-c   Creates a new archive.

-d   Deletes specified files. If you run this option and don't specify files, nothing will be deleted.

-f   Truncates the names of a file to a specific length.

-i   Inserts new files before a *membername*. This is the same as the -b argument.

-m   Moves files within an archive. At times, the specific order of files is important in an archive, especially when programming libraries are involved. The named files will be moved to the end of the archive.

-o   Uses original dates when extracting files. This is essential if you want to maintain the original time stamps, because ar will apply the time stamp at the time of extraction to the files.

-p   Prints the names of the files within the archive.

-q   Quick appends, which means that specified files are added to the end of the archive. This option is not countered by any other options (such as -a, -b, and -i), because all new files are automatically placed at the end of the archive. However, the archive's symbol-table index is not updated, which means that the -s argument or the ars or ranlib command must be used to update it.

-r   Replaces files within the archive. An existing file within the archive with the same name is automatically deleted.

-s   Updates the symbol-table index. This is the equivalent of the ranlib command.

-t   Lists a table with the names of files within the archive, or it can match a list of files with the names of the files within the archive.

-u   Inserts only newer files when replacing files with the -r argument.

-v   Tells ar to work in verbosc mode, listing the files within the archive that are acted upon.

-x   Extracts files from the archive.

Related Commands

ars
ranlib

as
Create Object Files
(GNU Command)

as *option(s) files*

Purpose

The GNU **as** assembler command creates object files from assembly files. Basically, it's used to assemble files created with the **gcc** C compiler before they are linked with **ld**.

You can assemble either from an existing C file or from standard input (your keyboard). If you're inputting a file via keyboard, you need to use Ctrl-D to tell **as** that input has ended.

Options

-a	Turns on assembly listings, which is output as files are assembled. However, -a can be used in conjunction with other options to form the following options:

	-ad	Omits debugging directives.
	-ah	Includes high-level source code if the source file can be found and the code was compiled with -g.
	-al	Includes assembly listing.
	-an	Omits form processing.
	-as	Includes symbol listing.
	-a*file*	Specifies listing filename.

--defsym	Defines the symbol SUM to equal VALUE (an integer SYM=VALUE constant) before a file is assembled.
-f	Assembles in fast mode, which skips preprocessing in those cases where the source is compiler output.
-I*path*	Adds *path* to the list of .include directives.

-K	Warns when difference tables are altered for l ong displacements.
-L	Keeps local symbols in symbol tables, starting with *L*.
-M	Assembles in MRI compatibility mode.
-o *objfile*	Specifies the object-file output as *objfile*.
-R	Folds data section into text section.
-v	Returns as version.
-W	Suppresses warnings.
--| *files*	Gets source files to assemble (| *files*) or assemble from standard input (--).

Related Commands

gcc
ld
nasm

bison
Generate Parser
(GNU Command)

bison *option(s)*

9

Purpose

The bison command takes the grammar specification in the file filename.y and generates an LR parser for it. The parsers consist of a set of LALR parsing tables and a driver routine written in C. Parse tables and the driver routine are usually written to the file y.tab.c.

The bison command is a GNU replacement for the yacc command, although a few differences exist between bison and yacc; for instance, generated files do not have fixed names, but instead use the prefix of the input file.

●—CROSS-REFERENCE
You'll want to check the online manual pages for more details. (Type man bison to see the bison man page.)

Options

-b *prefix*	Changes the prefix prepended to output filenames to *prefix*. The default is y.
-d	Writes a header file containing macro definitions for the token type names defined in the grammar and for the semantic value type YYSTYPE, as well as external variable declarations.
-l	Doesn't insert code into existing files.
-o *outfile*	Uses *outfile* as the parser file.
-p *prefix*	Renames the external symbols used in the parser so that they start with *prefix* instead of yy.
-t	Changes the preprocessor directives to include debugging information.
-v	Writes a human-readable description of the generated parser to y.output.

Related Command

yacc

---

cc	**cc *option filename***
C Compiler	

9

Purpose

The cc command is the standard C-compiler command. Most Linux distributions feature gcc, the GNU C Compiler, as their C-language tool of choice. (In fact, in most cases running cc will simply run the gcc command.)

●—CROSS-REFERENCE

Check the listings for gcc later in this chapter for more information about options.

Related Command

gcc

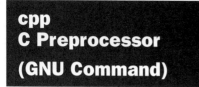

cpp
C Preprocessor
(GNU Command)

cpp option(s) inputfile outputfile

Purpose

The C preprocessor (cpp) is a macro processor that is used by the
C compiler to transform your program before actual compilation.

● **CROSS-REFERENCE**

For a more detailed explanation, see the info entry for cpp.info and
the online manual pages. (Type man cpp to see the cpp man page.)

Related Commands

gcc
imake

ctags
Create Tag File
(GNU Command)

ctags option(s)

Purpose

The ctags command creates a tag-table file in a format usable
by vi. Supported syntaxes are C, C++, Fortran, Pascal, LaTeX,
Scheme, Emacs Lisp/Common Lisp, Erlang, Prolog, and most
assembler-like syntaxes.

● **CROSS-REFERENCE**

See the online manual pages for more information. (Type man ctags.)

**etags
Create Tag File
(GNU Command)**

etags *option(s)*

Purpose

The etags command creates a tag-table file in a format usable by emacs. Supported syntaxes are C, C++, Fortran, Pascal, LaTeX, Scheme, Emacs Lisp/Common Lisp, Erlang, Prolog, and most assembler-like syntaxes.

●—CROSS-REFERENCE

See the online manual pages for more information. (Type man etags.)

**flex
Generate Scanner
Program**

flex *option(s) filename*

Purpose

The flex command generates scanner programs that recognize lexical patterns in text. This command reads the given input files, or its standard input if no filenames are given, for a description of a scanner to generate. The description is in the form of pairs of regular expressions and C code, called *rules*. The output is a C source file. This file is compiled and linked with the -lfl library to produce an executable.

●—CROSS-REFERENCE

See the online manual pages for an extensive description of the flex command. (Type man flex.)

g77Compile Fortran Program (GNU Command)   *g77 option(s) filename*

Purpose

The g77 command compiles Fortran programs.

●─CROSS-REFERENCE───────────────────

See the info listing for g77 for information on Fortran and the options for this command. (Type info g77.)

gawk GNU AWK (GNU Command)   *gawk option(s) filename*

Purpose

The gawk command is the GNU version of the AWK programming language — not necessarily a complex language, but an involved one.

●─CROSS-REFERENCE───────────────────

You'll want to check the online manual pages or perhaps even an AWK programming book for more information. (Type man gawk.)

gcc GNU C Compiler (GNU Command)   *gcc option filename*

                                                   g++ option filename

Purpose

The gcc and g++ commands are the C-language and C++-language compilers used in Linux. (Both commands also support Objective-C.) Both process input files through one or more of four stages:

preprocessing, compilation, assembly, and linking. The gcc command assumes that preprocessed (.i) files are C and assumes C-style linking, whereas g++ assumes that preprocessed (.i) files are C++ and assumes C++-style linking. Commands work with the following filename extensions. The descriptions show the actions taken on those files:

.c   C source; preprocess, compile, assemble

.C   C++ source; preprocess, compile, assemble

.cc   C++ source; preprocess, compile, assemble

.cxx   C++ source; preprocess, compile, assemble

.m   Objective-C source; preprocess, compile, assemble

.i   Preprocessed C; compile, assemble

.ii   Preprocessed C++; compile, assemble

.s   Assembler source; assemble

.S   Assembler source; preprocess, assemble

.h   Preprocessor file; not usually named on command line

Files with other suffixes are passed to the linker. Common cases include

.o   Object file

.a   Archive file

9

●─**NOTE**───────────────────────────────────

A primer on programming and the use of the C language is not presented here; entire libraries cover C programming much better than we can in this limited forum. In addition, hundreds of options are available for this command; you'll want to check the info pages for more information. (Type info gcc.)

gdb **GNU Debugger** **(GNU Command)**	**gdb *program option(s)***

Purpose

The gdb command is the debugger when creating C, C++, or Modula-2 programs. It starts your program, makes sure it stops under specified conditions, reports what caused your program to stop, and makes changes so that one error doesn't cascade into a series of errors.

It can be launched with no arguments or options, but generally you'll want to launch it with an executable program as the argument.

Commands

run [arglist]	Starts your program (with arglist, if specified).
bt	Displays the program stack.
print expr	Displays the value of an expression.
c	Continues running the program after stopping.
next	Executes the next program line after stopping, stepping over any function calls in the line.
step	Executes the next program line after stopping, stepping into any function calls in the line.
help	Displays help information.
quit	Exits gdb.

Options

-help	Lists all options.
-s file, -symbols=file	Reads symbol table from file.
-e file, -exec=file	Uses file as the executable file to execute when appropriate, and for examining pure data in conjunction with a core dump.
-se=file	Reads symbol table from file and uses it as the executable file.
-c file, -core=file	Uses file as a core dump to examine.
-x file, -command=file	Executes gdb commands from file.
-d directory, -directory=directory	Adds directory to the path to search for source files.
-nx, -n	Does not execute commands from any .gdbinit initialization file. Normally, the commands in these files are executed after all the command options and arguments have been processed.

-q, -quiet	Does not print the introductory and copyright messages.
-batch	Runs in batch mode.
-cd=*directory*	Runs gdb using *directory* as its working directory instead of the current directory.
-f, -fullname	Outputs the full file filename in a format used by emacs.
-b *bps*	Sets the line speed of any serial interface used by gdb for remote debugging.
-tty=*device*	Uses *device* for your program's standard input and output.

Related Commands

emacs
xxgdb

gprof
Produce Execution
Profile

gprof *option(s)*

Purpose

The gprof command produces an execution profile of C, Pascal, or Fortran77 programs. The effect of called routines is incorporated in the profile of each caller. The profile data is taken from the call graph profile file (gmon.out, by default), which is created by programs that are compiled with the -pg option of cc, pc, and f77. The -pg option also links in versions of the library routines that are compiled for profiling.

The gprof command reads the given object file (the default is a.out) and establishes the relation between its symbol table and the call graph profile from gmon.out. If more than one profile file is specified, the gprof output shows the sum of the profile information in the given profile files.

Options

-a	Suppresses printing of statically declared functions.

-b	Suppresses printing of descriptions of each field in the profile.
-c	Determines the static call graph of the program with a heuristic that examines the text space of the object file.
-e *name*	Suppresses the printing of the graph profile entry for routine *name* and all of its descendants (unless they have other ancestors that aren't suppressed).
-E *name*	Suppresses the printing of the graph profile entry for routine *name* (and its descendants), like -e, and also excludes the time spent in *name* (and its descendants) from the total and percentage time computations.
-f *name*	Prints the graph profile entry of only the specified routine *name* and its descendants.
-F *name*	Prints the graph profile entry of only the routine *name* and its descendants, like -f, and also uses only the times of the printed routines in total time and percentage computations.
-k *fromname toname*	Deletes arcs from routine *fromname* to routine *toname*.
-s	Produces a profile file gmon.sum that represents the sum of the profile information in all the specified profile files.
-z	Displays routines that have zero usage (as shown by call counts and accumulated time).

Related Commands

cc
monitor
profile
prof

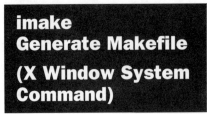

imake *option(s)*

Purpose

The imake command generates makefiles from a template, a set of cpp macro functions, and a per-directory input file called an Imakefile. This allows machine dependencies (such as compiler options, alternate command names, and special make rules) to be kept separate from the descriptions of the various items to be built.

Options

-D*define*	Sets directory-specific variables; sent to cpp.
-I*directory*	Sets the directory containing the imake template and configuration files.
-T*template*	Specifies the master template file.
-f *filename*	Sets name of the per-directory input file.
-C *filename*	Specifies the name of the .c file being constructed in the current directory.
-s *filename*	Specifies the name of the make description file to be generated, but does not invoke make.
-e	Executes the final Makefile.
-v	Prints the cpp command line used to generate the Makefile.

Related Commands

make
xmkmf

make Make Program (GNU Command)	make *option(s) target*

Purpose

The make command manages a group of files that make up a program. When there are changes to a program, such as a change in the source code, the make command can create a new program, keeping existing portions of the program while incorporating the changes. The make command determines which pieces of a program need to be recompiled and issues the commands to recompile them.

The make command is used most often with the C programming language (as well as X Window System software), but it can be used with any programming language whose compiler is run with a shell command.

The make command uses a Makefile to determine what changes are necessary and then issues the commands needed to update the files. Typically, the executable file is updated from object files, which are derived from source files.

You typically need to only run make on a command line to perform all the recompilations automatically. A README file included with the distribution will typically provide more detailed instructions.

Options

-b   Ignored; included for compatibility with non-GNU
            versions of make.

-m   Ignored; included for compatibility with non-GNU
            |versions of make.

-C *dir*   Changes to *dir* directory before doing anything.

-d	Returns debugging information in addition to the normal information.
-e	Uses environment variables over variables specified in makefiles.
-f *file*	Uses *file* as a makefile.
-i	Ignores errors arising from compilation problems.
-I *dir*	Specifies *dir* as a location to search for included makefiles.
-j *jobs*	Sets the number of *jobs* (commands) to run simultaneously.
-k	Continues as much as possible after an error.
-l *load*	Specifies that no new jobs (commands) should be started if other jobs are running and the load average is at least *load* (a floating-point number).
-n	Prints the commands as though they were executed, but does not execute them.
-o *file*	Skips remaking *file*, even if the makefile indicates that it should be remade.
-p	Prints the database generated from the makefile, and then runs the command.
-q	Works in question mode, returning an exit status that is zero if the specified targets are already up to date, and nonzero otherwise.
-r	Eliminates built-in implicit rules.
-s	Silent; doesn't print the commands as they are executed.
-S	Cancels the effect of the -k option; useful in a recursive make.
-t	Touches files instead of running their commands.
-w	Returns the working directory before and after other processing.
-W *file*	Pretends that the target *file* has been modified. Use this with the -n option to see what would happen if you actually did modify the file.

Related Commands

gcc
makedepend

makedepend Parse Makefile (X Window System Command)	makedepend *option(s)* *source file(s)*

Purpose

The makedepend command reads a source file and parses it like a C-preprocessor, processing all #include, #define, #undef, #ifdef, #ifndef, #endif, #if, and #else directives so that it can correctly tell which #include directives would be used in a compilation.

Every file that a source file includes, directly or indirectly, is a dependency. These dependencies are then written to a makefile in such a way that make will know what to recompile when a dependency has changed.

By default, makedepend sends output to makefile (if it exists) or Makefile.

Options

-a	Appends dependencies to the end of the file instead of replacing them.
-Dname=*def*	Defines name in the makedepend symbol table.
-f*makefile*	Defines an alternate filename for the makefile.
-I*includedir*	Specifies an include directory by prepending includedir directories listed in an #include directive.
-m	Issues a warning when a file is to be included more than once.
-o*objsuffix*	Specifies a *suffix* for an object file, instead of the default .o.
-p*objprefix*	Specifies a *prefix* for an object file (usually a new directory).
-s*string*	Sets a new starting string delimiter for the makefile.
-w*width*	Sets the line width. The default is 78 characters.
-v	Runs in verbose mode, where the names of files included are sent to the screen.

-Y*includedir*   Replaces the standard include directories with
includedir.

Related Commands

cc
make

---

makestrs **Make Strings** **(X Window System** **Command)**	**makestrs** *option(s)*

Purpose

The makestrs command makes string table C source files and
headers. The C source file is written to stdout.

Options

-arrayperabi   Generates a separate array for each string.

-defaultab   Generates a normal string table even if makestrs
was compiled with -DARRAYPERSTR.

-earlyR6abi   Maintains binary compatibility between X11R6
public-patch 11 (and earlier) and X11R6 public-
patch 12 (and later).

-function*abi*   Generates a functional *abi* to the string table.

-intelabi   Works with Intel platforms conforming to the
System V Application Binary Interface (SVR4).

---

msgfmt **Create Message** **Object**	**msgfmt** *option* *filename.po*

Purpose

The msgfmt command creates a message object filename.mo from
a portable message file filename.po, which remains unchanged.

Option

-v   Works in verbose mode.

Related Commands

gettext
xgettext

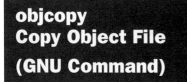

objcopy
Copy Object File
(GNU Command)

objcopy *option(s) infile*
outfile

Purpose

The objcopy command copies the contents of an object file to another object file, using the GNU BFD Library to read and write the object files. It can write the destination object file in a format different from that of the source object file.

●—CROSS-REFERENCE————————————————————

A long list of command-line options is available with this command; check the info pages on objcopy for more information. (Type info objcopy.)

p2c
Translate Pascal
to C

p2c *option(s)*
[*file*[*module*]]

Purpose

The p2c command translates Pascal programs into C. The input consists of a set of source files in any of the following Pascal dialects: H-P Pascal, Turbo/UCSD Pascal, DEC VAX Pascal, Oregon Software Pascal/2, Macintosh Programmer's Workshop Pascal, or Sun/Berkeley Pascal. In addition, Modula-2 syntax is supported.

The output is a set of .c and .h files that comprise an equivalent program in any of several dialects of C. Output code may be kept machine- and dialect-independent, or it may be targeted to a specific machine and compiler. Most reasonable Pascal programs are converted into fully functional C that compiles and runs with no further modifications, although p2c sometimes chooses to generate readable code at the expense of absolute generality.

Code generated by p2c normally does not assume characters are signed or unsigned. Also, it assumes int is the same as either short or long, but does not depend on which one. However, if int is not the same as long, it is best to use a modern C compiler that supports prototypes. Generated code does not require an ANSI-compatible compiler (unless ANSI-style code is requested), but it does use various ANSI-standard library routines.

Options

-o *cfile*	Uses *cfile* in place of file.c or module.c as the primary output file. A single dash (-o -) says to write the C code to the standard output.
-h *hfile*	Uses *hfile* in place of module.h as the output file for interface text. This only has effect if the input is an HP Pascal module or a Turbo Pascal unit.
-s *sfile*	Reads interface text from *sfile* before beginning the translation. This file typically contains one or more modules, often with interface sections omitted for speed, which the program or module being translated will use.
-p*n*	Displays progress of translation in the form of a line number/filename display. This is refreshed every *n* lines, which is 25 by default.
-c *rcfile*	Reads local configuration commands from *rcfile* instead of p2crc or .p2crc. A dash (-c -) in place of *rcfile* causes no local configuration file to be used.
-v	not read from the system configuration file --HOMEDIR--/p2crc. Because some of the parameters in this file are required, your local configuration file must include those parameters instead. This also suppresses the file named by the P2CRC environment variable.
-H *homedir*	Uses *homedir* instead of --HOMEDIR-- as the p2c home directory. The system p2crc file will be searched for in this directory.

-I*pattern*	Adds *pattern* to the ImportDir search list of places to find supported modules that are imported. The *pattern* should include a %s to represent the module name and should evaluate to a potential filename for that module's source code.
-I	Copies the system configuration file --HOMEDIR-- /p2crc to the standard output in its entirety. It should be used by itself on a command line.
-q	Works in quiet mode, suppressing status messages.
-E*n*	Aborts translation after *n* errors. The default is 0, which means unlimited errors are allowed.
-e	Echoes the Pascal source into the output file, surrounded by #ifdefs.
-a	Produces modern ANSI C. This is an override for the AnsiC parameter in the p2crc file.
-L *language*	Selects input language name, such as VAX or TURBO. This is an override for the Language parameter.
-V	Works in verbose mode, adding a .log file with further details of the translation.
-M0	Disables memory conservation.
-R	Works in regression testing mode, formatting notes and warning messages in a way that makes it easier to run diff on the output of p2c.
-d*n*	Sets the debug level to *n*.
-t	Prints debugging information at every Pascal token.
-B*n*	Enables line-breaker debugging.
-C*n*	Enables comment-placement debugging.

Perl
Perl Language

perl options programfile Purpose

Perl is the Practical Extraction and Report Language, which relies on the perl command to work with Perl code. It's an interpreted language optimized for scanning arbitrary text files, extracting information from those text files, and printing reports based on that information. It was made popular by the rise of UNIX and Linux servers on the Internet.

That is the short definition. It's also an amazingly complex and useful language, one too complex to summarize here.

● CROSS-REFERENCE

You'll want to check out the lengthy online manual pages for Perl; they cover all aspects of Perl for both the beginner and the advanced user. In addition, you might want to invest in a good Perl text.

ref
Scan for Function

ref *option(s) filename* *tag*

Purpose

The ref command displays the header of a function, checking in the tags file and then scanning the source file for the function. The information then returned is an introductory comment (if there is one), the function's declaration, and the declarations of all arguments.

Options

-c class   Specifies a *class* for the tag.
-f file   Looks for a tag (as a static function) in *file*.
-t   Outputs tag information, instead of the function header.

Related Command

ctags

rpcgen
Generate C Code

rpcgen *infile option(s)*

Purpose

The rpcgen command generates C code to implement an RPC protocol. The input to rpcgen is a language similar to C known as RPC Language (Remote Procedure Call Language).

CROSS-REFERENCE

See the online manual pages for a more detailed description. (Type man rpcgen.)

Options

-5	Generates code for the SVR4-style of RPC.
-a	Generates all files, including the sample code for client and server side.
-b	Generates code for the SunOS4.1-style of RPC (the default).
-c	Compiles into XDR routines.
-C	Generates code in ANSI C. This option also generates code that could be compiled with the C++ compiler. (Default.)
-D name	Defines a symbol *name*.
-h	Compiles into C data-definitions (a header file).
-I	Generates a service that can be started from inetd, instead of the default static service that handles transports selected with -s.
-k	Generates code in K&R C.
-K secs	Sets the default *secs* after servicing a request before exiting. To create a server that exits immediately upon servicing a request, -K 0 can be used. To create a server that never exits, the appropriate argument is -K -1.
-l	Compiles into client-side stubs.
-m	Compiles into server-side stubs, but does not generate a main routine.
-n netid	Compiles into server-side stubs for the transport specified by netid. There should be an entry for netid in the netconfig database.
-N	Uses the new style of rpcgen, allowing procedures to have multiple arguments.
-o outfile	Specifies the name of the output file.
-s nettype	Compiles into server-side stubs for all the transports belonging to the class *nettype*.

-Sc	Generates sample code to show the use of remote procedures and how to bind to the server before calling the client-side stubs generated by rpcgen.
-Ss	Generates skeleton code for the remote procedures on the server side. You need to fill in the actual code for the remote procedures.
-t	Compiles into RPC dispatch table.
-T	Generates the code to support RPC dispatch tables.

strip
Strip Symbols
(GNU Command)

strip *options filename*

Purpose

The strip command strips symbols from object files. The list of object files may include archives, but at least one object file must be given.

● CAUTION

The GNU version modifies the files named in its argument, rather than writing modified copies under different names, so be careful in your naming schemes.

Options

-F bfdname	Treats the original *objfile* as a file with the object-code format *bfdname* and rewrites it in the same format.
-g	Removes debugging symbols only.
-I bfdname	Treats the original *objfile* as a file with the object-code format *bfdname*.
-K symbolname	Copies *symbolname* from the source file.
-N symbolname	Strips *symbolname* from the source file.
-O bfdname	Replaces *objfile* with a file in the output format *bfdname*.

-R *sectionname*	Removes *sectionname* from the file. Be careful — incorrectly removing a section may make the object file unusable.
-s	Removes all symbols.
-S	Removes debugging symbols only.
--strip-unneeded	Strips all symbols that are not needed for relocation processing.
-v	Works in verbose mode, listing all the object files modified.
-x	Removes nonglobal symbols.
-X	Removes compiler-generated local symbols (usually beginning with *L* or .).

xgettext
Extract Text

xgettext *option(s)*
filename

Purpose

The xgettext command extracts strings (text) from C programs. It's used to create portable message files, which contain copies of C strings from the source code in a specified filename. The portable message file can be used as input to the msgfmt utility, which will produce a binary form of the message file used at application runtime.

Options

-a	Extract all strings.
-c*flag*	Adds comments beginning with *flag* to filename as #-delimited comments.
-d	Produces duplicates, not sorting output when writing the file and not overwriting existing output files.
-m*string*	Fills in the msgstr line with output from the xgettext command.
-n	Adds #-delimited line-number comments to the output file, indicating the line number in the source file where each extracted string is encountered.
-o*filename*	Uses *filename* as the default output file.

-p*pathname*	Sets the directory for the output files.
-x*filename*	Excludes the strings found in *filename* from the extraction process.
-P	Includes the strings in preprocessor statements.

Related Command

msgfmt

xmkmf Create Makefile (X Window System Command)	xmkmf *option(s)* *topdirectory* *currentdirectory*

Purpose

The xmkmf command creates a Makefile from an Imakefile. If your Linux system is not configured to process an Imakefile, you'll want to use a Makefile instead.

●—CROSS-REFERENCE

For the available options, see the manual online pages. (Type man xmkmf for further information.)

Related Commands

imake
make

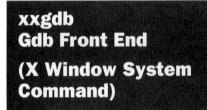

xxgdb Gdb Front End (X Window System Command)	xxgdb *option(s)*

Purpose

The xxgdb command is an X Window System front end to the gdb debugger. See the gdb command for further information.

Options

This command accepts all the gdb options, as well as the following:

-bigicon	Uses a larger icon.
-db_name	Specifies a debugger to use instead of gdb.
-db_prompt	Sets a new debugger prompt.
-i filename	Sets the initial gdb command file.
-nx	Does not execute gdb command file.

Related Command

gdb

yacc	yacc option(s) filename
Generate Parser	

Purpose

The yacc command reads the grammar specification in the file *filename* and generates an LR parser for it. The parsers consist of a set of LALR parsing tables and a driver routine written in C. Parsing tables and the driver routine are usually written to the file y.tab.c.

Options

-b prefix	Changes the prefix prepended to output filenames to *prefix*. The default is y.
-d	Writes the header file y.tab.h.
-l	Doesn't insert code into existing files.
-r	Produces separate files for code (y.code.c) and tables (y.tab.c).
-t	Changes the preprocessor directives to include debugging information.
-v	Writes a human-readable description of the generated parser to y.output.

Related Command

bison

Networking
Commands

The networking commands connect you to a remote machine (either on your own network or on the Internet) and — once connected — help you through a session. In most cases, these commands are used with TCP/IP networks (such as the Internet). However, many of these commands will also work on UUCP, AppleTalk, and other types of networks.

afpd Start AppleTalk Daemon	afpd *option(s)*

Purpose
The afpd command launches an AppleTalk Filing Protocol (AFP) interface to Linux, specifying which volumes should be made available to users. The list of the default columns is usually generated in /etc/AppleVolumes.system and one

of the following: /etc/AppleVolumes.system, $HOME/
AppleVolumes, or $HOME/.AppleVolumes.

Options

-c *maxconnections*	Specifies the maximum number of connections. The default is five.
-d	Suppresses the forking of the daemon, with a trace of all AFP commands written to standard output.
-f *volumes*	Specifies a different *volumes* file be read for a list of default volumes.
-g	Sets the name of the guest account.
-n *nbpname*	Uses *nbpname* for Name-Binding Protocol (NBP) registration.
-s *volumes*	Specifies a different *volumes* file be read.
-u	Reads the user's default volumes listing first.

Related Command

atalkd

10

atalkd
Manage
AppleTalk Network
Management

atalkd *option*

Purpose

The atalkd command manages all user-level AppleTalk network management: routing, name registration and lookup, zone lookup, and the AppleTalk Echo Protocol (AEP). Typically, this command is invoked by /etc/rc at boot time, drawing parameters from the /etc/atalkd.conf file.

Option

-f *configfile*	Uses a configuration file other than the default /etc/atalkd.conf file.

Related Command

afpd

bootpd **Launch Boot Server**	bootpd *option(s)* *config_file(s)*

Purpose

The bootpd command launches a bootstrap protocol (BOOTP) server. It's not usually run directly from a command line, but rather is called from inetd when listed in the /etc/inetd.conf file. In this manner, it's not actually launched until a boot request arrives. After that, it remains loaded until there's a span of 15 minutes without a request. A bootp configuration file (bootptab) stores name and address information needed for bootp clients to start.

This command can be invoked from the shell. A good time to start bootpd manually is when there's a lot of traffic and you don't want users to wait for the server to load. If you know a lot of bootp requests are waiting, this can get people connected faster.

Options

-c *chdir-path*	Sets the current directory used by bootpd while checking the existence and size of client boot files.
-d *debug_level*	Sets the *debug_level* variable.
-i	Forces inetd mode, in which bootpd terminates if there's no request over the course of 15 minutes. This is considered an obsolete option, but it's retained for compatibility with older versions.
-s	Forces standalone mode, in which bootpd remains in memory no matter what. This is considered an obsolete option, but it's retained for compatibility with older versions.
-t *timeout*	Specifies the time (in minutes) that bootpd will wait for a request before exiting. A value of 0 means that bootpd won't exit.

10

Configuration Files

bootptab — Specifies the name of the configuration file containing known clients and client options.

dumpfile — Specifies the name of the file into which bootpd dumps its internal database when it receives a SIGURS1 signal.

Related Commands

bootptest
inetd

---

bootptest **Test Boot Server**	**bootptest** *option(s)* *server_name*

Purpose

The bootptest command tests a BOOTP server (specified as *server_name*) by sending requests every second until a response is received or ten requests have gone unanswered.

Options

-f *bootfile* — Uses *bootfile* in the boot-file field of the request.

-h — Uses a hardware address to identify the client.

-m *magic_number* — Initializes the first word of the vendor-options field with *magic_number*.

Related Command

bootpd

dnsdomainname Display Domain Name	dnsdomainname *options* *host name*

Purpose

The dnsdomainname command returns information about the current host name; a privileged user can use the command to set a new host name.

Options

-f	Prints the full domain name.
-s	Prints the short domain name.
-F *file*	Checks *file* for the host name.

dnsquery Display DNS Information	dnsquery *option(s)*

Purpose

The dnsquery command queries name servers via Berkeley Internet Name Domain (BIND) resolver library calls.

Options

-n *name server*	Specifies the *name server,* either by IP addresses or domain name.
-t *type*	Sets the *type* of resource record of interest, to one of the following:

A	Address
NS	Name server
CNAME	Canonical name
PTR	Domain-name pointer
SOA	Start of authority
WKS	Well-known service

HINFO	Host information
MINFO	Mailbox information
MX	Mail exchange
RP	Responsible person
MG	Mail group member
AFSDB	DCE or AFS server
ANY	Wildcard

-c class   Sets the *class* of resource records of interest, to one of the following:

IN	Internet
HS	Hesiod
CHAOS	Chaos
ANY	Wildcard

-p num   Specifies the period to wait before timing out.

-r num   Sets the number of times to retry if the name server doesn't respond.

-s   Uses a stream rather than a packet.

faucet
Server-Client
Connection

10

faucet *option(s) port*

Purpose

The faucet command is a fixture for a Berkeley Software Distribution (BSD) network pipe, providing the functionality of pipes over the network. It behaves as the server end of a server-client connection and works well with the hose command (described later in the chapter), especially when you don't have easy access to the destination account (such as a root account, in which .rhosts are a bad idea). Basically, faucet creates a BSD socket, binds it to the port specified on the command line, and listens for connections. Every time faucet gets a connection, it runs *command* and its *args*.

● **CAUTION**

The faucet command is not considered to be a very secure method of networking. Use with caution.

This command has many more options available. The ones that follow are the most frequently used.

● **CROSS-REFERENCE**

Check the online manual pages for a full listing of the other options. (Type man faucet.)

Options

-localhost	Specifies that the listening socket should be bound to a specific Internet address on the local host.
-daemon	Specifies that faucet should disassociate from the controlling terminal after it has started listening on the socket, using the setsid( ) system call.
-shutdown	Turns the bidirectional socket into a unidirectional socket.
-serial	Tells faucet to wait for one child to finish before accepting any more connections.
-pidfile *filename*	Writes its process ID into *filename*.

Related Command

hose

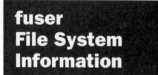

fuser
File System
Information

fuser *option(s)*
filename(s)

Purpose

The fuser command lists the process IDs of a particular file or file system. Information returned includes the following:

c   Current directory

e	Executable file
f	Open file
m	Mapped file or shared library
r	Root directory

Options

–	Resets options to defaults.
-signal	Sends a *signal* to a process. Use -1 to see a list of the signal names.
-a	Shows all files, not just the ones being accessed.
-k	Kills all the processes accessing the file.
-l	Returns a list of the signal names.
-m	Returns information about a mounted file system.
-s	Runs in silent mode.
-u	Returns names of the users of the processes.
-v	Works in verbose mode, returning process ID, username, command name, and access fields.

10 | **getpeername** **Get Socket Information** | getpeername *option(s)* |

Purpose

The getpeername command returns information about a socket connection.

Options

fd	Specifies file descriptors.
-verbose	Returns more detailed information.

hose
Server-Client
Connection

hose *option(s)*

Purpose

The hose command is a fixture for a BSD network pipe, providing the functionality of pipes over the network. It behaves as the client end of a server-client connection and works well with the faucet command (described earlier in the chapter), especially when you don't have easy access to the destination account (such as a root account, in which .rhosts are a bad idea). Basically, hose creates a BSD socket, binds it to the port specified on the command line, and listens for connections. Every time hose gets a connection, it runs *command* and its *args*.

> ●─**CAUTION**─────────────────────────────────
>
> The faucet command is not considered to be a very secure method of networking. Use with caution.

This command has many more options available. The ones that follow are the most frequently used.

> ●─**CROSS-REFERENCE**──────────────────────────
>
> Check the online manual pages for a full listing of the other options.
> (Type man faucet.)

10

Options

-delay *n*	Specifies how many *n* seconds to wait between tries.
-retry *n*	Specifies that connections should be retried *n* times.
-shutdown r	Makes it a read-only socket.
-shutdown w	Makes it a write-only socket.
-unix	Specifies that port is not an Internet port number or service name, but rather a filename for a UNIX domain socket.

Related Command

faucet

| host
Host Information | *host option(s)*
host name server |

Purpose

The host command prints information about a specified host name or server using DNS. You can also specify IP addresses, which will then be converted to host names through DNS.

Options

-a class.	Looks for ANY type of resource record
-A	Looks up the IP address for a host name and then does a reverse lookup to see if they match. Also looks up the host name of an address and then does a reverse lookup to see if they match. Also checks IP addresses for all host names in a given zone. Returns no information if everything matches.
-c *class*	Looks for a specified resource record *class* (ANY, CH, CHAOS, CS, CSNET, HS, HES-IOD, IN, INTERNET, or *). The default is IN.
-C	Lists all machines in a zone, determining if the zone's servers are authoritative.
-d	Works in debugging mode.
-dd	Works in debugging mode, but with more detail than -d.
-D	Returns the number of unique hosts in a zone, as well as the names of hosts with more than one address per name.
-e	Suppresses information about hosts outside of a specific zone.
-E	Returns the number of unique hosts in a zone, as well as the names of extra-zone hosts.

10

-f *file*	Sends output to *file* as well as standard output.
-F *file*	Sends output to *file*, with extra resource data sent to standard output.
-G *zone*	Returns the number of unique hosts in a zone and the names of gateway hosts.
-H *zone*	Returns the number of unique hosts in a zone.
-i	Returns information about an IP address: host name and class (always PTR).
-I *chars*	Ignores warnings about host names with illegal characters (specified by *chars*) in their names.
-l *zone*	Returns information about all the hosts in *zone*.
-L *level*	Specifies the level to search to when using the -l option.
-m	Prints MB, MG, and MR records; expands MR and MG records to MB records.
-o	Suppresses sending data to standard output.
-p *server*	Returns information about a primary server in a specific zone. Designed for use with the -l option.
-P *servers*	Returns information about preferred hosts; *servers* is a comma-delimited list. Used with the -l option.
-q	Suppresses warnings in silent mode, but not error messages.
-r	Requests cached information from server, not new queried information.
-R	Searches components of the local command when nonfully qualified names are found.
-S	Returns all hosts, but not subzones, to standard output, including the host class and IP addresses. Used with the -l option.

10

-t type	Requests information about *type* entries in the resource record; *type* is A, ANY, NS, PTR, or *.
-T	Prints time-to-live information for cached data.
-u	Uses TCP instead of UDP.
-v	Works in verbose mode.
-vv	Works in verbose mode, including the defaults on host.
-w	Works persistently until host returns information.
-x	Queries multiple hosts and zones; can also be used to query multiple servers with -X.
-X	Queries multiple servers as well as multiple hosts and zones.
-Z	Includes trailing dots in resource records, as well as time-to-live data and the class name.

Related Command

```
hostname
```

hostname Host Name Information	hostname *options* *host name*

10

Purpose

The hostname command returns information about the current host name. A privileged user can use the command to set a new host name.

Options

-d	Prints Domain Name System (DNS) domain name.
-f	Prints the full domain name.
-s	Prints the short domain name.

-F *file*   Checks file for the host name.

netstat *options*

Purpose

The netstat command displays network connections, routing tables, interface statistics, masquerade connections, and netlink messages. With no options, the netstat command lists all open sockets.

●—NOTE

This command has the potential of returning a voluminous amount of data. Check the online manual pages for a listing of all the data types. (Type man netstat.)

Options

-A, --af *family*	Sets the format for the address families. The *family* variable is a comma-separated list of address-family keywords: inet, unix, ipx, ax25, netrom, and ddp.
-c, --continuous-r,	Prints the selected table every second.
--route	Returns the kernel routing tables.
-i, -- interface *iface*	Returns all networking interfaces; if *iface* is listed, then it returns information about the specific interface.
-M, --masquerade	Returns a list of all masquerade sessions. Combine this with the –e option to return expanded information.
-N, --netlink	Returns netlink information.
--v, --verbose	Returns information in verbose mode.
-n, --numeric	Returns numerical addresses instead of symbolic host, port, or usernames.

10

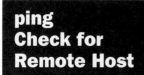

**ping
Check for
Remote Host**

ping *hostname*

Purpose

The ping command sends ICMP ECHO_REQUEST packets to network hosts to determine network performance. Basically, ping is used to see if another computer can be reached on the network.

Options

-c *count*	Stops after sending (and receiving) *count* ECHO_RESPONSE packets.
-d	Sets the SO_DEBUG option on the socket being used.
-f	Outputs packets as fast as they come back, or 100 times per second, whichever is more.
-i *wait*	Waits *wait* seconds between sending packets.
-l *preload*	Sends *preload* many packets as fast as possible before falling into its normal mode of behavior.
-n	Works in numeric mode.
-p *pattern*	Specifies "pad" bytes to fill out the packet you send.
-q	Works in quiet mode; nothing is displayed except the summary lines at startup time and when finished.
-r	Bypasses the normal routing tables and sends directly to a host on an attached network.
-R	Includes the RECORD_ROUTE option in the ECHO_REQUEST packet and displays the route buffer on returned packets.
-s *packetsize*	Specifies the number of data bytes to be sent. The default is 56.
-v	Prints verbose output.

10

rcp
Copy Remotely

rcp option(s)
file1 file2

Purpose

The rcp command copies files between machines. These can be machines on your local network or on the Internet. (Often, network administrators disable rcp and other "r" commands.)

Options

-k *realm*	Obtains tickets for the remote host in *realm* instead of in the remote host's realm.
-p	Preserves modification times.
-r	Copies directories recursively.
-x	Encrypts files with DES encryption.

Related Commands

    rlogin
    rsh

rlogin
Login Remotely

rlogin option(s)
host name

10

Purpose

The rlogin command opens a remote session on a specified host name. It uses Kerberos authorization initially, but if the remote host doesn't support Kerberos, then the standard Berkeley rhosts authorization mechanism is used.

● CROSS-REFERENCE

See the online manual pages for more detailed information on Kerberos authentication. (Type man rlogin.)

Options

-8	Allows an 8-bit input data path at all times; otherwise, parity bits are stripped except when the remote side's stop-and-start characters are other than ^S/^Q.
-d	Turns on socket debugging on the TCP sockets used for communication with the remote host.
-e	Defines the escape character, replacing the default tilde (~) character.
-E	Prevents any character from being recognized as an escape character.
-K	Turns off Kerberos authentication.
-k *realm*	Obtains tickets for the remote host in *realm* instead of in the remote host's realm, as determined by *krb_realmofhost*.
-L	Runs session in litout mode.
-x	Turns on DES encryption.

Related Commands

```
rcp
rsh
```

10

rsh	**rsh** *option(s)*
Start Remote Shell	*host name command*

Purpose

The rsh command runs a command on a remote host name. It copies its standard input to the remote command, the standard output of the remote command to its standard output, and the standard error of the remote command to its standard error. Interrupt, quit, and terminate signals are propagated to the remote command; rsh normally terminates when the remote command does.

Options

-K	Turns off Kerberos authentication.
-d	Turns on socket debugging.
-k *realm*	Obtains tickets for the remote host in *realm* instead of in the remote host's realm, as determined by *krb_realmofhost*.
-l *username*	Specifies a remote *username*.
-n	Redirects input from the special device /dev/null.
-x	Turns on DES encryption.

Related Commands

```
rcp
rsh
rlogin
```

---

rstart
Start Remotely
(X Window System Command)

rstart *option(s)*
host name command
args

Purpose

The rstart command is actually a sample implementation of a Remote Start client. It uses rsh as its underlying remote execution mechanism.

Options

-c*context*	Specifies *context* for the command, which is a general environment. The default is X.
-g	Interprets the command on the command line as a generic command, as defined in the protocol document.
-l *username*	Tells rsh that the command be run as the specified *username*.

-v   Runs in verbose mode, discarding output
                            from the remote host name's rstart
                            helper and disconnecting from the rsh
                            connection.

Related Commands
rsh
rstartd

rusers Produce User Information	rusers *option(s)* *host name*

Purpose
The rusers command produces information about the users
logged in on a specific host (or hosts) or all machines on the
local network.

Options

-a   Lists all machines, even if no one is cur-
                            rently logged in on them.
-l   Returns listings in long format: username,
                            host name, tty that the user is logged in to,
                            date and time the user logged in, amount
                            of time since the user typed on the key-
                            board, and remote host they logged in from
                            (if applicable).

Related Commands
rwho
users
who

rwall Send System Message	rwall *host name* *filename*

Purpose

The rwall command sends a message to all the users logged in on a specified host name. The message can be sent via a specified filename, or else it can be typed directly and terminated with EOF (Ctrl+D).

rwho Check Who Is Logged In	rwho *option*

Purpose

The rwho command shows who is logged in on local machines. The output is similar to that of the who command, except that the information covers everyone on the local network. If a machine does not report back to rwho in 11 minutes, then the machine is assumed to be down. Idle time for users that is under one hour is also reported.

Option

-a   Reports all users, even those who have not
                      typed at their machines in the last hour.

Related Command

    rusers

10

sliplogin
Log in via SLIP

sliplogin *loginname*

Purpose

The `sliplogin` command allows you to log in to an Internet system using a Serial Line Internet Protocol (SLIP) connection. It takes information from the /etc/slip.hosts file (matching the *loginname*) and then initiates a connection. The /etc/slip.hosts file must be configured by a root user.

sockdown
Manage System
Shutdown
(GNU Command)

sockdown *option(s)*

Purpose

The `sockdown` command performs a shutdown system call on one of its file descriptors specified by the `fd` command. The possible values to use with `sockdown` are as follows:

0	Converts to write-only file descriptor.
writeonly	Symbolic for 0.
1	Converts to read-only file descriptor.
readonly	Symbolic for 1.
2	Completes shutdown — no reads or writes allowed in the future.
totally	Symbolic for 2.

10

talk
Talk with Other Users

talk *username* [*tty*]

Purpose

The talk command allows you to chat interactively with another user currently logged in on the system. When both sides are running the talk command, the screen splits, with one user's typing appearing in one half of the screen, and the other user's typing appearing in the other half of the screen.

The *username* can be someone on your own system. If you want to chat with a user on another system, then you must specify the username as user@host. If a user has more than one terminal going, you can specify a terminal with tty. To quit talk, type Ctrl-D.

Related Commands

```
write
ytalk
```

telnet
Connect to
Remote Host

telnet *option(s)*
host name

Purpose

The telnet command launches a connection to a remote host using the Telnet protocol. From there, you can use the remote host as if it were your own machine.

Options

-a	Attempts automatic login.
-d	Turns on debugging mode.
-e *escapechar*	Sets the *escapechar*.
-l *user*	Sends *user* as the variable USER to the remote system; used with -a.
-n *tracefile*	Records trace information in *tracefile*.

uucp **Copy Files** **to Other** **Computers**	*uucp option(s)* *sourcefile destinationfile* *uucp option(s) sourcefile* *destinationdirectory*

Purpose

The uucp command copies files between systems.

●—CROSS-REFERENCE

See the online manual pages for a list of the available options. (Type man uucp.)

write **Write Network** **Messages**	**write** *user*

Purpose

The write command sends a message to another user, who can choose whether or not to carry on a conversation.

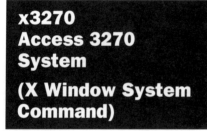

x3270 **Access 3270** **System** **(X Window System** **Command)**	*x3270 option(s)* *host name*

Purpose

The x3270 command opens a Telnet connection to an IBM host in an X window. Numerous options are available, most of which are not of general interest.

● CROSS-REFERENCE

Check out the online manual pages for a full listing of the available options. (Type man x3270.)

Related Command

telnet

ytalk Chat on the Network	ytalk *option(s)* *username*

Purpose

The ytalk command is a multiuser chat program. It can also be used to chat with talk users.

Options

-x   Disables the X Window System interface.

-s   Starts the ytalk window in a shell.

Related Command

talk

10

Mtools Commands

The Mtools series of commands work with MS-DOS files and directories on floppy disks. This allows you to use Linux with MS-DOS-formatted diskettes on DOS and Windows 95/98/NT systems.

mattrib Change File Attributes	mattrib *option(s)* *msdosfile(s)*

Purpose

The mattrib command changes the file attributes of an MS-DOS file stored on a floppy drive. Adding attribute flags is done with +, and removing attribute flags is done with -.

Attributes

a   Archive bit.

h   Hidden bit.

r   Read-only bit.

s   System bit.

mbadblocks Identify Bad Blocks	mbadblocks *drive*

Purpose

The mbadblocks command scans a specified drive (an MS-DOS floppy) for bad blocks. It marks the bad blocks as being unread.

mcd Change Directory	mcd *directory*

Purpose

The mcd command changes the current directory on an MS-DOS floppy. With no directory specified, it returns the current device and directory.

Related Command

mdir

mcopy
Copy File

mcopy *option(s)*
sourcefile targetfile

mcopy *option(s)*
sourcefile(s)
targetdirectory

Purpose

The mcopy command copies MS-DOS files to and from a Linux system, usually using a floppy drive. It can be used to copy a file to a target file, or it can be used to copy multiple files to a specified directory.

●—TIP

When using an MS-DOS floppy, you need to add **A:** to the file or directory names.

Options

t   Performs a text file transfer, translating carriage returns/line feeds to just line feeds.

m   Preserves the file modification time.

n   Works with no warning if you are overwriting an existing file.

v   Works in verbose mode.

Related Commands

    mread
    mwrite

mdel
Delete File

mdel *option msdosfile*

Purpose

The mdel command deletes an MS-DOS file, usually on a floppy drive.

Option

-v   Works in verbose mode, where the names of files are printed
to the screen as they are being deleted.

mformat Format Floppy	mformat *option(s) drive*

Purpose

The mformat command adds an MS-DOS file system to a low-level
Linux-formatted diskette. This formatting includes a boot sector,
FAT, and root directory.

Options

1   Overrides the use of a 2m format, even if the current
geometry of the disk is a 2m geometry.

2   Works in 2m format — the number of sectors on track 0,
head 0.

h   Specifies the number of heads (sides).

H   Specifies the number of hidden sectors.

l   Sets an optional volume label.

M   Sets the software sector size.

n   Sets the serial number.

t   Specifies the number of tracks (not cylinders).

s   Specifies the number of sectors per track.

S   Specifies the sizecode.

X   Formats the disk as an Xdf disk, used by OS/2.

Related Command

mlabel

mrd **Remove** **Directory Tree**	mrd *option* *msdosdirectory*

Purpose

The mrd command removes an MS-DOS directory tree, as well as any files and subdirectories within it. This occurs on an MS-DOS file system on a floppy drive.

Option

-v   Works in verbose mode, listing every file and directory as it is deleted.

mdir **List Directory** **Contents**	mdir *option(s)* *msdosdirectory*

Purpose

The mdir command displays the contents of an MS-DOS directory, usually on a floppy drive.

Options

a   Lists hidden files.

w   Prints in wide output, without displaying the file size or creation date.

mlabel **Create** **Volume Label**	mlabel *option(s) drive* *new_label*

Purpose

The mlabel command creates an MS-DOS volume label on a floppy drive. With no options, it displays the current label. If the c or s option is not set, you are prompted for a new label; at this time, if you don't enter a new label and press Enter, the existing label is deleted.

Options

c Clears an existing label, without prompting the user.

s Shows an existing label, without prompting the user.

Related Command

mformat

---

mmd **Create** **Subdirectory**	**mmd** *option directory*

Purpose

The mmd command creates an MS-DOS subdirectory on a floppy drive. An error occurs if the directory already exists.

Option

v Works in verbose mode, returning the names of the directories as they are created.

Related Command

mrd

---

mmount **Mount** **MS-DOS Disk**	**mmount** *drive* *mountargs*

Purpose

The mmount command mounts an MS-DOS disk. It reads the boot sector of an MS-DOS disk, configures the drive geometry, and mounts it, passing *mountargs* to the mount command.

Related Command

mount

---

mmove **Move/Rename** **File or Directory**	mmove *option sourcefile* *targetfile* mmove *option* *sourcefile(s)* *targetdirectory*

Purpose

The mmove command moves or renames an existing MS-DOS file or subdirectory.

Option

v   Works in verbose mode, displaying the new filename if the new name is invalid.

Related Command

mren

---

mrd **Remove Directory**	mrd *option* *msdosdirectory*

Purpose

The mrd command removes an MS-DOS directory from a floppy disk.

Option

v   Works in verbose mode, displaying the directory name as it is removed.

Related Commands

mdeltree
mmd

mread **Copy Fil**	**mread** *option(s)* *msdosfile unixfile*

Purpose

The mread command copies an MS-DOS file to a Linux system. This is an obsolete command, but some older scripts may support it. The preferred command is mcopy.

Related Commands

> ⸜ mcopy
mtype

mren **Rename File**	**mren** *option sourcefile* *targetfile*

Purpose

The mren command renames an MS-DOS file on a floppy drive.

Option

v   Works in verbose mode, displaying the new filename if the new name is invalid.

Related Command

> mmove

mtest **Configure Utilities**	**mtest**

Purpose

The mtest command reads the Mtools configuration files and prints the cumulative configuration to standard output, which can then be used as configuration files. You can use this to convert old configuration files to new configuration files.

mtype
Display File

mtype *option(s)*
msdosfile

Purpose

The mtype command displays an MS-DOS file.

Options

s   Strips the high bit from the displayed file.

t   Assumes that the file is a text file.

Related Commands

mcd

mread

mwrite
Copy File

mwrite *unixfile dosfile*

Purpose

The mwrite command copies a Linux file to an MS-DOS file system on a floppy disk. This command is considered to be obsolete and exists only to provide backward-compatibility with older shell scripts. Use the mcopy command instead.

Related Command

mcopy

Interacting via Linux Shells

Our review of Linux commands ends with one chapter on Linux shells. This material is vitally important for all Linux users. It demonstrates how you interact with the Linux operating system, and vice versa. A *shell* is a command-line method for interacting with you. With a shell, you type commands and options to run programs.

Chapter 12   Linux Shells

Linux Shells

You can't run Linux without running a *shell*, a tool that interacts with you and provides a way to directly communicate with the core of the operating system. Often, what you assume is being done by the operating system is actually being done by the shell: It accepts your commands, interprets them, and passes them along to the core operating system. It provides its own set of commands (some of which were covered in Chapter 5 as general-purpose commands; it's really a distinction without difference) and it provides its own scripting mechanisms.

Shell Types

Most Linux distributions include at least six or seven shells, but people usually stick with the default Bourne Again Shell (bash) from the Free Software Foundation, a clone of the popular Bourne shell found on most UNIX systems. In addition, many users switch to the C shell, csh, or a different version of the C shell, tcsh. Other shells include sh (Bourne Shell), ksh (Korn shell), and zsh (Z shell).

When you install your Linux distribution, you're typically asked which shells you want installed on your system. A slew of Linux shells are available, including ash and zsh. To see which shells are installed on your system, use the following command line:

```
$ chsh -l
/bin/sh
/bin/bash
/bin/csh
/bin/tcsh
...
```

To change your login shell, use one of the following command lines. The first example permanently changes your login shell while the second example changes it for the current login session only:

```
$ chsh -s /bin/csh
```

or

```
$ exec /bin/csh
```

We're not going to spend a lot of time on shells; you can find more than enough online documentation for them, and more than enough books on the market about their usage. Instead, we'll spend some time covering shell variables.

● **CROSS-REFERENCE**

See the online documentation for more information about Linux shells. (Type man bash, for example.) Also, the *Red Hat Linux Bible* (IDG Books Worldwide) contains excellent tutorials on using Linux shells.

Shell Variables

Shell environment variables provide a way of storing pieces of information that can be used by shell scripts; commands; the shell itself; or by you, as you type a command. For example, there are variables that store the name of your mailbox (MAIL variable) and the location of directories that are searched for commands (PATH variable).

The shell sets many variables. You can also set variables yourself or use them in shell scripts. You can view the contents of any shell environment variable with the use of the echo command and by preceding the variable with a dollar sign. For example, you could type the following to see what your current path is:

```
$ echo $PATH
```

Table 12-1 lists and explains the functions of the various shell environment variables.

Table 12-1 *The Shell Variables*

Variable	Explanation
IFS	The internal field separator that is used for word splitting after expansion and to split lines into words with the read built-in command. The default value is space-tab-newline.
PATH	The search path for commands. It is a colon-separated list of directories in which the shell looks for commands. The default path is system-dependent and is set by the administrator who installs bash.
HOME	The home directory of the current user; the default argument for the cd command.
CDPATH	The search path for the cd command. This is a colon-separated list of directories in which the shell looks for destination directories specified by the cd command.
ENV	If this parameter is set when bash is executing a shell script, its value is interpreted as a filename containing commands to initialize the shell, as in .bashrc. The value of ENV is subjected to parameter expansion, command substitution, and arithmetic expansion before being interpreted as a path name. PATH is not used to search for the resultant path name.
MAIL	If this parameter is set to a filename, and the MAILPATH variable is not set, bash informs the user of the arrival of mail in the specified file.
MAILCHECK	Specifies how often (in seconds) bash checks for mail. The default is 60 seconds. When it is time to check for mail, the shell does so before prompting. If this variable is not set, the shell disables mail checking.
MAILPATH	A colon-separated list of path names to be checked for mail. The message to be printed may be specified by separating the path name from the message with ?.

MAIL_WARNING	If set, and a file that bash is checking for mail has been accessed since the last time it was checked, the message "The mail in mailfile has been read" is displayed.
PS1	Sets the primary prompt. The default value is bash\$.
PS2	Sets the secondary prompt, used by many applications to provide input. The default value is >.
PS3	Sets the prompt for the select command.
PS4	Sets the value of the character used before commands in an execution trace. The default is +.
HISTSIZE	Sets the number of commands to remember in the command history. The default is 500.
HISTFILE	Sets the name of the file in which the command history is saved. The default is ~/.bash_history.
HISTFILESIZE	Sets the maximum number of lines in the history file. The default value is 500.
IGNOREEOF	Controls the action of the shell on receipt of an EOF character as the sole input. If set, the value is the number of consecutive EOF characters typed as the first characters on an input line before bash exits. If the variable exists but does not have a numeric value or has no value, the default value is 10. If it does not exist, EOF signifies the end of input to the shell. This is only in effect for interactive shells.
TMOUT	If set to a value greater than zero, the value is interpreted as the number of seconds to wait for input after issuing the primary prompt. bash terminates after waiting for that number of seconds if input does not arrive.
FIGNORE	A colon-separated list of suffixes to ignore when performing filename completion. A filename whose suffix matches one of the entries in FIGNORE is excluded from the list of matched filenames. A sample value is .o:~.

in plain english in p
sh in plain english in
glish in plain english
in plain english in p
sh in plain english in
glish in plain english
in plain english in p
glish in plain english
in plain english in p
sh in plain english in
glish in plain english
in plain english in p
sh in plain english in
glish in plain english
in plain english in p
lish in plain english
in plain english in p
sh in plain english in
glish in plain english
in plain english in p
sh in plain english in
lish in plain english
in plain english in p
glish in plain english

Index

Continued

Continued

Continued

Notes

Notes

Notes

my2cents.idgbooks.com